The Book of Howth:
The Elizabethan re-conquest of Ireland
and the Old English

The Book of Howth:

The Elizabethan re-conquest of Ireland
and the Old English

Valerie McGowan-Doyle

CORK UNIVERSITY PRESS

First published in 2011 by
Cork University Press
Youngline Industrial Estate
Pouladuff Road, Togher
Cork
Ireland

British Library Cataloguing in Publication Data
A CIP catalogue record for this book is available from the British Library
A CIP record for this publication is available from the Library of Congress

ISBN-978-185918-468-4
Typeset by Tower Books, Ballincollig, Co. Cork
Printed by Gutenberg, Malta

www.corkuniversitypress.com

Contents

In memory of
John McGowan, Barry McGill
and Eugene Smith

Acknowledgements

Thanks go first and foremost to Hiram Morgan, under whose direction this book began as a doctoral thesis. His patience, assistance and generosity far surpassed the obligations of a thesis supervisor, and his generosity and support since that time have been immeasurable. Particular thanks are also due to a number of readers who painstakingly read and commented on this work at various stages including Brendan Bradshaw, David Edwards, Thomas Herron, Brendan Kane and Colm Lennon. Vincent Carey and Maryclaire Moroney earn an especially warm thank-you for their gracious assistance and much needed encouragement through many difficulties. Ruth Canning and Gerald Power also merit particular mention. I have both thoroughly enjoyed and learned from our shared work and many discussions on the Old English. I owe a further debt of gratitude to the two anonymous readers for Cork University Press whose thoughtful comments are responsible for many of the completed work's refinements. Acknowledgement is also due to John Barry of University College Cork for his assistance with Latin translations, as well as to Julian Gaisford-St Lawrence who provided me with a privately compiled St Lawrence family history and a personal tour of Howth Castle. As always, any errors that remain are my own. Much of the initial research undertaken for this project was made possible by an Oberlin College alumni research grant. A short-term fellowship at the Folger Shakespeare Library permitted me to complete research beyond the thesis stage that substantially enhanced my study of Howth's sources. As always, no work is possible without the assistance of many librarians and archivists, here in particular the staff of the Manuscript Room at the British Library, the National Library of Ireland, Lambeth Palace Library and the Cleveland Public Library. Special thanks go to Alan Baker and LouAnn White for their invaluable interlibrary loan assistance. Gratitude goes finally, but certainly not least, to my family, Patrick, Maebh, and Mary Clare, without whose support and sacrifice this work could never have been begun, sustained or completed.

Note on Conventions

All dates are given Old Style with the year taken to begin on 1 January.

Quotes from sixteenth-century sources have been silently modernised.

The terms Old English and New English are used throughout to distinguish between the established colonial class, principally descendants of the Anglo-Norman conquest as well as those who continued to arrive over the medieval period, and those who arrived as officials, soldiers and planters in the Tudor period, particularly from the 1550s on. Contemporaries and historians have referred to the original colonial community variously as Anglo-Hibernici, English 'of that country birth', English of Ireland, English of Irish birth, English-Irish or, though less favoured, Anglo-Irish. The label Old English was coined in 1596 by Edmund Spenser and did not come into regular use until the seventeenth century, but has been adopted for use here as it most closely reflects the routine use of the terms 'old' and 'new' to distinguish between the two colonial groups in *The Book of Howth*.

Introduction

In the midst of the early parliamentary sessions of 1569–71 Christopher St Lawrence, 7th Baron of Howth, began to compile material on the history and state of conquest in Ireland. His compilation ultimately became a ten-year-long project as Howth continued to add entries to it over the decade of the 1570s. The product of his work, known as *The Book of Howth* since at least the 1590s when it was referred to as such by Meredith Hanmer, was sought out in the decades following its completion by influential figures such as Sir John Davies, William Camden and Sir James Ware. Since the seventeenth century, however, it has lain virtually dormant, referred to only intermittently for the odd quotation, its references to events such as the Battle of Knockdoe or St Lawrence family history. Howth's manuscript was saved from further obscurity or even complete loss by virtue of its preservation among the papers of Sir George Carew at Lambeth Palace Library, but its publication as calendared along with Carew's other papers in 1871 by J.S. Brewer and William Bullen did little to advance the study of Howth's collection.[1] This edition may even have deterred consideration of the manuscript as a document of value to the history of early modern Ireland, for the editors' commentary and transcription imposed on the collection the impression that it represented little more than the sum of inchoate and random collection activity of indeterminate date and authorship. Though certainly unpolished, as even a cursory glance at the manuscript reveals, this was the work of the 7th Baron of Howth, and it was erratic neither in its conception nor its execution: it represents a compilation purposefully undertaken in direct response to the deteriorating position of the Old English community to which Howth belonged. It reflects furthermore Howth's belief that Sir Henry Sidney's policies threatened rather than advanced English conquest in Ireland.

A comprehensive assessment of sixteenth-century Irish history, dominated by intensified conquest, is incomplete and essentially impossible without consideration of the activities and experiences of the Old English, for they were subject to the forces and effects of conquest no less than the Irish, or even New English, communities. Though the Old English were in part responsible for the initiation of reform, they relatively quickly lost control of its progress as their influence was eclipsed by newly arriving English-born administrators. By the early Elizabethan period many of the Old English had already begun to face unforeseen consequences as the security of their political and military status and influence, their social and economic stability, and their religious preference were threatened, and their cultural identity under scrutiny. Recent studies by Ciaran Brady, Nicholas Canny, Vincent Carey, David Edwards and Colm Lennon, among others, have demonstrated the emergence of these challenges as a result of intensified conquest and the divergent responses of various individuals and groups within the Old English community to them.[2] It is precisely this context on which Howth's manuscript has bearing, for it is one of the few written records to provide a personal and immediate oppositional response to a critical phase in those developments. The significance of Howth's collection is heightened by the fact that it is not a static document grounded in one moment or event: as Howth collected over the course of the 1570s his manuscript reflected the evolution of both intensified conquest in this period and his own response to it. The particular nature of the manuscript's collected form seems at first to defy elucidation; however, persistence and attention to its detail are rewarded by a wealth of information.

The following chapters undertake for the first time a sustained analysis of both Howth's life and his manuscript. Chapter One provides an overview of the contexts within which Howth worked. It focuses on the two developments out of whose intersection his compilation was born: the increasing pressures placed on the Old English by the arrival of the New English, and the construction of histories as a colonial tool. Over the Elizabethan period, competing historical presentations of the conquest became another arena in which Old English and New English writers lobbied on behalf of their respective positions. Howth's compilation depended on texts that preceded him, and his own work would quickly become a source to which others turned.

As an individual Howth has received very little historical consideration, usually accorded only passing mention for his role in the cess controversy of 1577–8 and for the domestic abuse case against him in 1579. Chapter Two therefore outlines Howth's position in Elizabethan Ireland by providing brief family background and a more comprehensive illustration of his political position as it developed from one of co-operation with the Dublin administration in the early 1560s to one of opposition to Sidney's administrations. Detailed attention to Howth's role in the cess controversy also serves to bring to light far greater information about this episode than has been considered heretofore. This chapter then addresses Howth's trial and imprisonment for domestic abuse in 1579 at some length, for this case is relevant not only to Howth's own position in Elizabethan Ireland but to the larger role that cultural imperialism played in the deterioration of the Old English community. It concludes by outlining Howth's subsequent though ultimately tenuous reconciliation with the Dublin authorities.

Chapter Three begins with a detailed analysis of his compilation's structural elements, its construction, organisation, and contributing scribal hands. This reveals many previously unrecognised elements that are essential to the work's assessment, such as the authorial role Howth played in its creation, the purposefulness with which he compiled, the organisational strategies employed as entries were collected, and his use of scribal assistants. Collectively, these elements reveal that we can securely dismiss former perceptions of The Book of Howth as an uncertain collection and read the manuscript instead as a reflection of Howth's perspective. Analysis of the manuscript's construction furthermore permits determination of its period of creation, another element essential to a consideration of the work's contents and what they convey of Howth's position and perspective. Building on the manuscript's structural analysis, this chapter next considers in detail the contents of Howth's compilation. Systematic attention to Howth's entries again reveals a number of previously unrecognised elements that prove themselves fundamental to the work's overall assessment. Many of the entries represent composition original to Howth; others, however, draw heavily on a number of available sources in manuscript and print, some of which are identified here for the first time, such as Pembridge's Annals. While identification of Howth's sources sheds light on the circulation of materials in the Pale and hence the intellectual milieu in which he worked, here it is essential to analysis of Howth's manuscript for two reasons: firstly, because it permits the isolation of passages of original composition from copied passages, and secondly because once Howth's sources are identified his versions can be carefully compared with them. Such comparison reveals that Howth often modified or excerpted works as he copied from them, and delineation of the manner in which he did so indicates the collection's rhetorical purpose. Cataloguing Howth's entries also permits identification of the subjects in which he was interested and is again central to a determination of the collection's rationale, for it reveals the remarkable consistency of Howth's concerns as he returned time and again to examine themes such as misgovernment or the displacement of an established colonial community.

Chapter Four synthesises the structural and content analysis of Chapter Three to examine at greater length the principal subjects that concerned Howth. Here we can see, based on the dating of various passages made possible by Chapter Three's structural analysis, that Howth was responding to specific events and that his passages can be placed within quite specific historical contexts, an exercise that illuminates both his collection and events of the period. This chapter also demonstrates that Howth's manuscript reflects his evolving opposition to government policies and the motivation for that opposition, information that augments what can be determined of his political position from extant documentation such as the *State Papers Ireland*. The rationale Howth's work provides for his oppositional stance is applicable beyond merely the analysis of his manuscript. It furthers assessments of events such as the parliamentary opposition of 1569–71 and the cess controversy of 1577–8 as well as larger patterns such as Old English displacement.

Chapter Five reviews the circulation, transmission, and uses of Howth's work. Though the collection has come to be regarded with some scepticism and languished largely underutilised by recent historians, there was a vibrant traffic in its use in the decades following its completion. The study of a number of formerly misidentified manuscript fragments in Lambeth Palace Library and Trinity College, Dublin shows that these are copies of Howth's work, revealing that it was in circulation soon after its completion. The relatively frequent reference made to Howth's work in the late sixteenth and seventeenth centuries indicates that collectors, administrators and historians were aware of Howth's work and actively sought it out as a source of information. Its early use, however, neither incorporated nor generated sustained consideration, and by the eighteenth century Howth's collection had fallen into disuse. In spite of J.H. Round's suggestion in the later nineteenth century that it warranted study, The Book of Howth has not ever been thoroughly assessed; thus its purpose has gone virtually unrecognised and its value therefore underappreciated.

Finally, the conclusion returns largely to Chapter Two's biographical information and Chapter Four's analysis of Howth's compilation to integrate what can now be understood more clearly of his position in

Elizabethan Ireland and its relevance to the larger historical patterns of the sixteenth century, primarily Old English displacement. Howth identified his community as one in the throes of displacement effected by inefficacious policies of intensified conquest. His delineation of its causes – the loss of Old English ability to influence and control political, economic, social and military systems – contributes to considerations of the implementation of early imperialism within the context of centralised institutions of power. It also both illuminates and is enhanced by studies of the transformative factors affecting aristocracies across Europe in the sixteenth century, as well as contributing to debates among historians concerning a pivotal period of English control in Ireland.

1. Contexts:
Tudor conquest, the Old English and historical writing

The Tudor period saw Ireland transformed. At the outset Ireland was a lordship, governed by the powerful 8th Earl of Kildare in control of a network of resources and allies straddling the colonial and Gaelic worlds. By its end, Hugh O'Neill's submission in 1603 within days of Elizabeth's death brought the Nine Years War to a close, opening Ireland to the extension of British control across the entire island. The Tudor drive for security, centralisation and defence, a function of its domestic and foreign affairs, pulled Ireland increasingly into England's orbit, initially in alternating stages of reform and conquest. Over Elizabeth's reign more radical and aggressive strategies effected the final transformation.[1] The magnitude of these developments on the Gaelic world was substantial, but they also proved consequential for the traditional colonial class, the Old English, whose position of influence was jeopardised by the formation of a new colonial class, the New English.

Ciaran Brady noted some time ago that the 'alienation of the community of the Pale from the royal administration in Dublin during the latter half of the sixteenth century remains one of the least explained developments in Tudor Ireland'.[2] If still insufficiently understood, the key stages by which it progressed can be identified easily enough. Conflict between the Old English and the Dublin administration became apparent in the wake of early reforms under Thomas Cromwell, as Brendan Bradshaw has emphasised, when resistance arose as a result of the influx of soldiers and the establishment of permanent garrisons in the aftermath of the Kildare Rebellion, and developed into a clearly identifiable oppositional movement in the parliament of 1536–7.[3] Soon thereafter their traditional military and conciliar positions were revived briefly under St Leger's tenure as lord deputy.[4] That development was reversed under the Earl of Sussex as viceroy when the Old English began to lose appointments given instead to a circle surrounding Sussex, several of whom would receive

1

increasingly influential positions, including his brother Henry, given command of the garrisons at Laois and Offaly, and his brother-in-law William Fitzwilliam, given charge of the garrison at Athlone, who was later to become vice-treasurer and later still, lord deputy; Sidney, also a brother-in-law, became vice-treasurer, and, like Fitzwilliam, also later lord deputy, and George Stanley was made marshal of the army.[5] Compounding this loss of office, rather than acquiring land confiscated for the creation of the Laois–Offaly plantation as expected, only fifteen of the eighty-eight men granted land were Palesmen, much of it going instead to those in the military.[6]

The Elizabethan era saw the Old English facing greater challenges. This period has been singled out in particular by Ciaran Brady, Nicholas Canny and Jon Crawford as one during which key developments took place in the office of viceroy, the Irish privy council, and methods of conquest such as plantation and provincial presidencies, an office monopolised by the New English.[7] Commensurate with these developments which affected them detrimentally, Old English opposition crystallised and intensified. Tensions rose early in Elizabeth's reign as influential figures such as George Dowdall, Archbishop of Armagh, and legal students in London lodged grievances against Sussex's implementation of the cess in 1562.[8] Many of the Old English anticipated the rectification of these difficulties when Sidney arrived for his first term as lord deputy in 1565. However, opposition soon resurfaced, first in the early parliamentary sessions of 1569 and followed quickly by the Butler Revolt and first Desmond Rebellion (1569–73). Conflict over Sidney's implementation of the cess (1577–8) during his second term as lord deputy further aggravated tension between the Old English and the Dublin administration, resulting in two terms of imprisonment in 1577 and 1578 for members of the opposition.[9] The relationship between the viceroy and members of the Old English community deteriorated yet further in the early 1580s with the Baltinglass Rebellion and Nugent Conspiracy, and parliamentary opposition arose once more in 1585–6 under Sir John Perrot as lord deputy.[10] The Munster plantation, created by massive land confiscations in the aftermath of the second Desmond Rebellion (1579–83), led to years of legal suits concerning land illicitly redistributed, while New English such as Sir Walter Raleigh and Edmund Spenser profited substantially from territory granted to them. By the 1590s Counter-Recusancy had attracted many Old English, and New English authorities feared this attachment would bring Hugh O'Neill far greater support from that community than he ultimately secured.

Though frequently categorised as homogeneous by New English observers, Old English families and individuals responded in vastly different ways to the ramifications of intensified Tudor conquest. Some, such as Lucas Dillon, accommodated themselves comfortably, while the barons of Howth and Delvin, along with others, attempted to counter policies through recourse to legal measures. A few, such as Richard Stanihurst, felt compelled to leave. Most remained in Ireland, however, and – though far less conciliatory than Dillon – sought to regain influence, as the Barnewall family and barons of Howth would do.[11] Many of those who remained, as Colm Lennon has demonstrated in numerous works, began to participate more openly in Counter-Reformation Catholicism, sending their sons to schools on the continent as opposed to Oxford, Cambridge or the Inns of Court, as their families had traditionally done.[12] Yet others, like Baltinglass, moved beyond legally staged resistance to open rebellion, grounding their opposition in religion, as did many other members of the nobility across Europe in the sixteenth century.[13] As Old English opposition evolved, intensified, fragmented and placed itself within wider European religious and political contexts, it not only acquired greater diversity and complexity, it became a factor as central to the implementation of conquest as the Irish. Understanding the motivation, development and ramifications of this opposition is vital, of course, in elucidating the process of Old English alienation, but ultimately vital also, and more substantially, to the history of the Tudor re-conquest of Ireland.

The effects of reformed religion, government and conquest on peers such as Kildare and Ormond, who by virtue of their position have left a more extensive historical record, can be tracked more closely.[14] However, relatively few written works remain that originated from within either the Old English aristocracy or the larger Old English community on which to base a detailed and comprehensive assessment of the impact on them of Elizabethan reform, and why it consequently generated such a variety of responses.[15] *The Book of Howth*, compiled within the critical gestational period of intensified conquest and Old English opposition, is a unique and significant contribution to our understanding of Old English opposition. It offers a rare extended commentary on both the specific policies and larger patterns of conquest as well as providing a reflection of their effect on his community. Howth's choice of historical compilation as the vehicle through which to present his position is a reflection of the developing intersection of Tudor conquest, the challenges it presented to the Old English and the manner in which history had been adapted to the needs of conquest, providing its explanation and its validation. The relationship between these three developments would play an important corollary role in the Tudor conquest of Ireland, since the adoption of historical narrative as a colonial tool could be used to denigrate and therefore justify the displacement of the Old English, as well as the Gaelic Irish.

Interest in histories and the production of them underwent a revolution in Tudor England, facilitated in no small part by print. Individuals continued to maintain commonplace books and manuscripts were sought out, created and maintained alongside print, but the chronicle form was ultimately abandoned in favour of narratives and increasingly critical inquiry and use of sources.[16] From Edward Hall, John Leland and John Stow, to *Holinshed's Chronicles* and William Camden, the 'authorial voice' no less than its subject acquired a new visibility and authority.[17] How the past was understood, and perhaps more importantly, contested and utilised has been a subject of considerable study as England defined itself and its place on the world stage.[18] As the century progressed, attention to history flourished, generating new genres and influencing still others, including antiquarian works, almanacs, plays and civic pageantry.[19] Nonetheless, as Paulina Kewes has noted, instruction remained history's core purpose.[20] This function was made more potent when coupled with the power of the historian who, unlike the chronicler, processed cause and effect.[21] Ideological conflict, particularly in the arena of confessionalism, fuelled the production of histories and counter-histories as Felicity Heal's study of Catholic responses to the 'Protestant determination to appropriate the past' demonstrates.[22] Contested representations of the past would also fuel the construction of histories in Ireland, not immediately as a function of confessional conflict but as a function of intensifying Tudor conquest and the competition it generated between the Old and emerging New English communities.

Controlling the construction of Ireland's history was as central to the Tudor re-conquest as control of its legal, political, military, economic and social systems. The Tudor concern to establish England's right to Ireland, for example, saw the revival of numerous classical and medieval histories, including Arthurian legend, as proof of Ireland's long-standing submission to England in the wake of the Reformation when *Laudabiliter*, with its assertion of papal authority, could no longer be invoked (by which the English Pope Adrian IV authorised an English conquest of Ireland under Henry II, r.1154–89).[23] Similarly, and perhaps more familiarly, Giraldus Cambrensis's denigration of Ireland's Gaelic population was frequently cited by writers who advocated conquest as opposed to the reformation of a population deemed inferior and uncivilised.[24] The increasing turn to history as a colonial tool in the Elizabethan period is in direct correlation to the intensification of conquest in this period.[25] It surfaced not only in texts expressly labelled history, such as those composed by Edmund Campion, Richard Stanihurst or Meredith Hanmer, but also appeared in a variety of locations including reform proposals and parliamentary legislation. History was imperative, as William Herbert explained in *Croftus Sive de Hibernia Liber* 'because once we have examined these matters properly, we shall easily discover the founts and origins of almost all those evils which, to a greater or lesser degree, have harassed Ireland for so many centuries'.[26]

The application of history to Tudor conquest evolved, as the following selection of texts demonstrates, for the recourse to history was actually a tool first used by the Old English early in the Tudor period and meant to advance their standing, but one which was turned on them later in the sixteenth century as the New English successfully wrested control of the conquest away from them. It began with two texts composed by members of the Old English during the reign of Henry VIII: William Darcy's 'Articles Presented to the King's Council in England' and Patrick Finglas's 'Breviate of the Getting of Ireland and the Decay of the Same'.[27] These two texts set the stage for the relationship between historical discourse and conquest as it was to evolve over the remainder of the century. Darcy's text, although composed principally in complaint against the 9th Earl of Kildare, identified a number of practices that compromised the security of English rule in Ireland, not least of which was negligent, non-resident landlords, and traced these practices to the fourteenth century in support of his purpose.[28] Finglas's lengthier treatise was concerned primarily with reform proposals, but this constituted only the final two-thirds of the text. The opening third was devoted to addressing the history of problems in Ireland, which he traced in greater detail than Darcy as well as further back to the twelfth century. Finglas pinpointed the causes of deteriorating English control, as his title suggested he would, and he also pinpointed more precisely the moment in time when they occurred. Both Ulster and Munster, he argued, had been secure for 160 years following the Anglo-Norman conquest, or until the reign of Edward III.[29]

Darcy and Finglas not only initiated what would become a pattern of predicating reform on a presentation of the past, the specific content of Finglas's history in particular would be revived in later texts that accompanied intensified conquest. Finglas's 'Breviate', for example, resurfaced when a copy of it was taken to London in late 1533 by his son in the midst of Thomas Cromwell's plans to reform the Irish lordship.[30] A number of the proposals from the 'Breviate' then appeared in Cromwell's Ordinances for Ireland the following year.[31] Finglas, as well as Darcy, had called for increased crown oversight. However, the impediments to English control they outlined emphasised not the Gaelic Irish but rather practices within the colonial community such as coign and livery and, more substantially, the prevalence of Gaelicisation. It was this depiction of problems within the traditional colonial community that was seized upon, rather than English negligence, when Finglas's 'Breviate' was revived yet again in 1569 for inclusion in the 1569 Act for the Attainder of Shane O'Neill.

O'Neill's attainder presented the necessity of transferring colonial authority from the Old English to the New English by grounding it in a historical presentation of the conquest's past failures.[32] By far the longest of any of the attainders passed in Ireland in the sixteenth century, the language attainting O'Neill comprised only the closing twelve lines of a preamble that stretched to thirteen pages in print. The remainder of the preamble attended instead to history. It contains in fact three distinct histories: the first a history of O'Neill's treasonous behaviour, the second a history of England's six-fold right to Ireland and the third a history demonstrating Elizabeth's title to Ulster taken from Finglas's 'Breviate'.

In laying out these histories the attainder devotes as much attention to Henry Sidney, then lord deputy, as it does to O'Neill. Sidney is hailed as the individual responsible for eradicating the threat Shane O'Neill had posed, but more substantially he is hailed as the individual who – poised at this pivotal moment in time – is responsible for rectifying failed conquest and leading Ireland into a future of completed conquest. The question of time and eras is essential to the attainder's use of history to address the question of failed conquest and its successful completion. It is here that we see a justification for Old English colonial displacement, for the attainder's repeated references to conquest now completed after '404 years' implied that the previous four centuries, when the conquest had been left in the hands of the Old English, had been a failure. History and the text of Finglas had both been used here, but to different ends. Failed conquest was no longer the result of English negligence: it was the fault of the Old English who could no longer be entrusted with its management if Sidney was to move the conquest to completion.

History acquired a new importance in the years immediately following its use in O'Neill's attainder. Howth would begin to compile his own counter-history, Edmund Campion composed his *Two Books of the Histories of Ireland* (completed in 1571), and even Rowland White, concerned primarily with reform measures, came to see that history could not be avoided. When White composed 'A Discourse Touching Ireland' prior to the passage of O'Neill's attainder, for example, he stated specifically that he saw no need to 'meddle' in history because 'it toucheth not much in my mind the reformation of the realm to discourse in the circumstance of the same'.[33] However, by the time he composed 'The Disorders of the Irishry' in 1571, White had changed his mind. In that text his proposals for reform were solidly grounded in an address of the past.[34] In the interim between White's two texts, history – and its relationship to colonial identity and successful conquest – had become critical to the rapidly developing competition for power between the Old English and New English.

Campion used his history of Ireland to ameliorate emerging discord between the Old and New English, as Lennon has argued, but he also drew attention to the 'degeneration', or Gaelicisation of the Old English.[35] His second chapter was devoted in its entirety to a list of Old English families whose identities were categorised under labels such as 'waxing Irish', 'mere Irish', 'very Irish' and 'very wild Irish'.[36] It was a list Campion noted he acquired from Sidney, described by Campion at the text's end as 'skilful in antiquities'.[37]

Historical writing in Ireland and England would be intertwined materially in *Holinshed's Chronicles*. This text offers a fundamental contribution to our appreciation of identity formation as competition grew between the Old and New English.[38] The section on Ireland composed by Richard Stanihurst for the 1577 edition provided a defence of the Old English.[39] A very different perspective was provided, however, as John Hooker expanded upon this section for the 1587 edition. Hooker had long since acquired the enmity of the Old English. He arrived first in Ireland in 1569 when he served as solicitor for Sir Peter Carew in a contentious legal dispute that resulted in Carew's successful acquisition of land held by Old English families.[40] Hooker then acquired a seat in the 1569–71 parliament where he was responsible for antagonising Old English members in vitriolic speeches condemning their opposition to Sidney's legislation. Importantly, *Holinshed's Chronicles* not only brought colonial identity formation and competition within historical discourse into print, it did so for a reading audience in England.

The New English drive against the Old English that picked up again when Sidney returned for a second term as lord deputy in the later 1570s spawned renewed conflict that played out again both in politics and in the use of history. One of the places in which this can be seen is in the cess controversy of 1577–8 when leading members of the Old English nobility and gentry sought to overturn Sidney's economic policies by sending legal representatives to present their case at court. The conflict between Sidney and the cess opposition raged for nearly two years, during which time the cess opponents, including Howth, one of the movement's leaders, were incarcerated twice in Dublin Castle.[41] Mandated by Elizabeth to resolve the situation, Sidney sent the chancellor, William Gerrard, to court laden with legal and financial documents in defence of his position. Gerrard did more than merely present documents to the privy council. His 160-folio package of material was prefaced with a historical analysis of the Old English that integrated their responsibility for failed conquest as identified in Shane O'Neill's attainder with a discussion of their degeneration that picked up Campion's themes and expanded upon them with the detail of Finglas. It was the Old English adoption of Gaelic dress and language, their intermarriage and fosterage with the Irish, and their abandonment of English law in favour of Brehon law that, Gerrard argued, bred their own decline and failed conquest, and, therefore, the need for policies such as Sidney's. Moreover, like Finglas, Gerrard also traced these problems to the period of Edward III (r.1327–77), the historical moment by which, in his analysis, the Old English had become the impediment to completed conquest they had been ever since.[42] This opening commentary so thoroughly discredited the Old English that by the time Gerrard finally reached his presentation's purpose, the cess controversy, the rhetoric of the preface implied there was really little need to entertain the legitimacy of Old English opposition.

If the Old English were discredited by denigration in Gerrard's text, they were reduced, as Maryclaire Moroney notes, to little more than a 'shadowy presence' in another text written in support of Sidney soon after Gerrard's that also relied on history: John Derricke's *Image of Irelande*.[43] Written in 1578 but not published until 1581, this text prefaced its central discussion with a history of select English rulers: Arthur, Henry II, Edward III, Henry VIII and Elizabeth. Although Derricke discussed these rulers within the context of Reformation history, readers familiar with the history of conquest also would have recognised, without being reminded of, the critical importance of Henry II, Henry VIII and Elizabeth to its pivotal stages. A reader familiar with the state of the relationship between historical discourse and conquest at that point would also have understood the significance of Arthur and Edward III. Arthurian legend, as already noted, had come to replace *Laudabiliter.* Edward III might at first appear anomalous on this list, but as several of the histories discussed here have shown, he too had become central to New English histories of Ireland, for under his reign the Statutes of Kilkenny were passed in 1366. This legislation sought to control what had by then already been identified as the problem of the colonial community's adoption of Irish custom. Whereas Derricke's attention to Arthur, Henry II, Henry VIII and Elizabeth silently referenced conquest over the Irish, the reference to Edward III silently alluded to the perceived 'problem' of the Old English. This understood reference to Old English Gaelicisation as the cause of failed conquest and the 'gratifying reassurance of English . . . cultural authority' that Moroney notes the text offers implied the need for more aggressive measures against the Old English.[44]

The importance of history to Old English identity and their competition with the New English for control of the conquest continued throughout the remainder of the Elizabethan period. The Old English were no longer a shadowy impediment but, according to Edmund Spenser in *A View of the Present State of Ireland* (1596), where he describes them as 'more stubborn and disobedient to law and government than the Irish, and more malicious against the English'.[45] A 'useable past' had been created that, in addition to justifying the use of violent means against the Irish, also justified Old English displacement, both integral to New English dominance. Tracking the manner in which history was used to achieve this provides additional context for documents such as the Attainder of Shane O'Neill, texts such as Derricke's *Image of Irelande* and, central to this study, *The Book of Howth.* Howth's work offers a new and vital link in understanding the role that historical presentation played at a pivotal moment in Tudor conquest. Its value is all the greater as a rare example, along with Stanihurst, of extended historical discussion emanating from within the Old English community. Its presentation of the history and state of conquest in defence of the Old English offers as well a new and vital source through which to understand their history. Once completed, Howth's compilation would become part of the corpus of texts to which later writers turned, a subject taken up in Chapter Five.

2. Christopher St Lawrence, 7th Baron of Howth
(c.1510–89)

The life of the 7th Baron of Howth spanned much of the sixteenth century, coinciding with many of the pivotal events that would transform English control in Ireland, and ultimately the position of the Old English: the transition from lordship to kingdom, the effects of the Reformation and Counter-Reformation, the shift from policies of conciliation to policies of conquest, the incursion of New English colonists and careerists, the advent of plantations and provincial presidencies, recurring rebellion, and increased English fears of foreign assistance to rebels or invasion. The effect of these events on some families unfolded over several generations. However, because of the particular span of Howth's life, the impact of this succession of transformative events was felt when he was an adult. His experience is, therefore, a poignant example of the manner in which intensified conquest imposed what could seem rapid and, to Howth, destabilising change.

Howth began his tenure as baron at the age of forty, working co-operatively with the Earl of Sussex, then lord lieutenant, even as other members of the Old English community began to emerge in opposition to him in the early 1560s. By the mid 1570s, when Sidney returned for what would be his final term as lord deputy, Howth had not only joined the opposition, he had taken a leading role in it. Determining precisely what led Howth to change his position, as opposed to recognising merely that he did so, is imperative in understanding why he came to oppose rather than support measures designed to advance conquest. To date little attention has been given to Howth beyond passing mention of his role in the cess controversy of 1577–8 and the sensationalised domestic abuse case against him in 1579. Together these cases create an impression of Howth as obstreperous and destructive to the platforms of conquest. As irascible as Howth may well have been, this isolated period of intensive political and legal difficulty in his life has been permitted to subvert the value Howth's experience offers by directing attention to his expression of opposition rather than to an examination of its causes. The events of Howth's life as represented in the archival record reveal the impact of intensified conquest on him and his response. Why he responded as he did is revealed in his manuscript.

Family and Economic Background

The context of change wrought by intensified conquest within which Howth was by necessity forced to conduct himself was grounded in events of the later medieval period that affected the St Lawrence family as it did others. The family's sense of status as members of the established colonial elite was founded on their claimed ancestral heritage as members of John de Courcy's conquering Anglo-Norman entourage. It was sustained by the economic and political advantages afforded them by the geographic location of their core landholdings close to the centre of English administration in Dublin. The family's real rise in prominence began in the fifteenth century. To preserve their newly acquired position, however, the lords of Howth were quickly forced to accommodate Kildare ascendancy and, later, the ramifications of its decline. Before addressing the specifics of Howth's experience, a brief history of his family's position helps to clarify the forces of change that confronted Howth.

The geographic location of the St Lawrence family seat at Howth Castle with its surrounding lands, including the port, granted them economic and political advantages. Well inside the Pale, eight miles north of Dublin, they were not subject by proximity or for political preservation to the more intensive processes of Gaelicisation, unlike Old English families such as the Nugents or Fitzgeralds who held march lands.[1] Nonetheless, as the Pale was inhabited by many Irish-speakers and subject at the least to this aspect of Gaelicisation, it is unlikely that the St Lawrence family was unfamiliar with the Gaelic language or various aspects of Gaelic culture, particularly given the inclusion of Irish history and tales in *The Book of Howth*, though there is no evidence that they engaged in fosterage or intermarriage as did other colonial families.[2] Interaction between the colonial and Gaelic communities was often less peaceful, however, and the Pale was frequently subject to raids, as were other areas of English settlement. Defending the Pale from such attacks would, in fact, provide successive generations of the St Lawrence family with the opportunity to demonstrate their loyalty, status and identity.

The family conducted themselves as participants in a Pale society reflective of English culture and sought to present themselves as such in other ways as well. The 7th Baron, in fact, made renovations to Howth Castle and its grounds that clearly attempted an appearance for his primary residence reflective of the Elizabethan aristocracy.[3] The St Lawrence family was firmly grounded within Pale society through a pattern of intermarriage common to much of the Old English aristocracy and gentry in areas of English settlement, reinforcing their place within established political and social networks.[4] Marriages were commonly arranged with families such as the Plunkets, Berminghams and Barnewalls, though on occasion also with the Nugents and Fitzgeralds. Another pattern common to Pale gentry was the education of their sons in England, often in Oxford but more frequently at the Inns of Court, a pattern to which three of the 4th Baron of Howth's sons would adhere by attending Lincoln's Inn.

This geographic and social position affected the Howths' economic standing as well. Their properties in counties Dublin and Meath were in areas of long-standing agricultural productivity, affording them moderate income and the privileges – and responsibilities – of the landed aristocracy.[5] Their worth by the Tudor period was approximately £130, though this is probably an underestimate.[6] Without sufficient income or opportunity to increase drastically their holdings – and there is no evidence that they acquired land in the wake of the dissolution of the monasteries – their moderate ancestral holdings surrounding Howth by the tenure of the 4th Baron (1526–42) were augmented by propitious marriages.[7] By the Elizabethan period the family held over 4,000 acres (see Appendix A).[8]

Their geographic location proved just as significant in providing the asset of a well-placed harbour. Howth harbour had been a favoured site for shipping since the medieval period. Deemed slightly safer than Dublin, though it also held dangers, Howth was better able to accommodate larger ships that could not dock in the increasingly silted-up anchorage at Dublin.[9] Along with other ports throughout the medieval period, its traffic necessitated the regular increase of customs officials posted to monitor activity there.[10] This was due in part to the requirement that ships dock first at Howth before sailing on to Drogheda, for the collection of customs as well as to take on local pilots to steer them safely to Drogheda.[11] By the late sixteenth century Drogheda had emerged as the pre-eminent point of trade, which meant an increase in the traffic at Howth as well.[12] A harbour meant also the growth of industries serving the shipping trade, and Howth supported a community of shipbuilders by at latest the fourteenth century.[13] In addition to the harbour's servicing of the shipping industry, its lucrative fishing industry (primarily herring, but also cod), to which the family held first right to all catches, benefited the St Lawrences.[14]

Access to this strategic harbour, which served passengers as well as the shipping industry, further augmented the family's political prestige. Viceroys and other English officials frequently landed in and departed from Howth. On these occasions, Howth Castle and its lord served as host, affording the barons a unique and prized intimacy with various lord deputies and officials unavailable to other members of the Old English aristocracy, for as officials passed through Howth they frequently spent their post-arrival or pre-departure night at Howth Castle, as did Richard, Duke of York, in 1449, Edward Poynings in 1494, and Lord Grey in 1580.[15]

The St Lawrence family had maintained a moderate but firm footing in Ireland subsequent to their arrival early in the Anglo-Norman period under the patronage of John de Courcy, but it was their support of the Yorkist faction in Ireland that prompted a significant rise in the family's prominence. This rise came, in fact, with the Duke of York's very arrival in Ireland when he landed first at Howth. York succeeded in creating a loyal faction in Ireland backed by Kildare and Desmond, a faction so loyal that the Irish parliament passed legislation contesting the validity of York's attainder in England following his defeat by the Lancastrians.[16] The 1st Baron of Howth was among those who supported York, for which he was well recompensed. He was knighted and sat on the Irish council, a position that successive barons of Howth would struggle, not always successfully, to retain. Other rewards came in the grant of lands in counties Dublin and Meath and the town of Drogheda, as well as appointments for his sons: William was appointed Admiral of Ireland; Almeric was appointed Clerk of the Rolls, and Walter became Baron of the Exchequer.[17]

The family continued to fare well under Robert, who succeeded as 2nd Baron in 1463. Appointed Chancellor of the Exchequer, the 2nd Baron was also one of the founding members of the Knights of St George, created by parliament in 1474 as a military fraternity under the direction of Kildare charged with the preservation of order within the Pale and its defence against Irish raids.[18] His sons also received appointment. Robert became Summoner of the Exchequer while Thomas began what would become a lifetime of service to the Dublin administration stretching into the mid sixteenth century, filling the offices of Attorney General, Second Justice of the King's Bench, sitting on the Irish council and on the commission to survey lands following the dissolution of the monasteries.[19] Other members of the family, however, found it more difficult thereafter to achieve and maintain political influence.

This process began almost as soon as the 2nd Baron began to achieve greater prominence. As noted above, he had already established himself within the security of a Yorkist alliance that initially incorporated a Kildare alliance as well. However, the expansion of Kildare power in the late 1470s and 1480s challenged the 2nd Baron's position, a challenge that became apparent as he attempted to take up his post as chancellor under appointment from Edward IV.[20] While awaiting the necessary reappointments due to the rapid succession of Edward IV and Edward V followed by Richard III, Howth's procurement of the office was delayed, and Kildare, then deputy-lieutenant, appointed his brother Thomas to the office. Once Richard III's official appointment of Howth took place, Kildare refused to displace his brother, initially provoking a stern letter from Richard regarding royal prerogative. When Richard relented, Fitzgerald remained as chancellor and Howth lost the appointment.[21]

The St Lawrence family was soon forced to reposition itself within the complexities of growing Kildare power. When loyalty to the Kildare faction conflicted with crown control, Howth lords would abandon their alliance. Such was the case when the 3rd Baron, Nicholas, was confronted with the Lambert Simnel affair at the outset of his tenure. Flouting Kildare advocacy of Simnel, the 3rd Baron took a minority position by opposing the Irish lords' acceptance of the pretender and their crowning of him as Edward VI. *The Book of Howth* reports that it was in fact the 3rd Baron who informed Henry VII of this threat.[22] Whether this defection was due to his father's recent displacement by Kildare, or due to his father's tenet of steady loyalty to the crown at all costs (which may have accounted for his acquiescence in the loss of the chancellorship), or a combination of the two, is subject to conjecture. Once this crisis had passed without detriment to Kildare's power, however, Nicholas reasserted his allegiance to Kildare, fighting under him at the Battle of Knockdoe. Nicholas would find it difficult to maintain Kildare alliances and the confidence of crown administrators, and his reinstatement as a Kildare ally would soon test his relationship with crown authorities.[23] Upon Surrey's arrival as lord deputy in 1520, members of the Irish council succeeded in procuring the 3rd Baron's temporary dismissal, citing his factional attachment to Kildare.[24]

The tenure of the 4th, 5th and 6th barons saw a decline in the family's political influence. They were able to preserve, if only nominally by virtue of their aristocratic status, their position in local military and judicial administration through commissions as justices and keepers of the peace, commissions for gaol delivery and commissions to muster general hostings or attend the lord deputy on journeys.[25] By the advent of Elizabeth's reign, this position, tenuous as it may have been, when coupled with the timely occasion of Sussex's objective of reducing Shane O'Neill, provided the 7th Baron with the opportunity to reassert the family's position.

Christopher St Lawrence, 7th Baron of Howth, *c.*1510–89

Howth, third son of the 4th Baron, succeeded to his title as 7th Baron as he was nearing fifty years of age following the deaths of his two elder brothers, Edward, the 5th Baron, in 1549, and Richard, the 6th Baron, in 1558, both without heirs.[26] Upon inheriting the title Howth began immediately to reverse his elder brothers' declining roles. He initially attained some influence under Sussex, later to be lost under Sidney, a situation to which Howth responded in part by joining the opposition in the cess controversy of 1577–8. Howth's position was further threatened by the domestic abuse case against him in the following year. Not only did Howth survive this episode relatively unscathed, he was promoted in its aftermath. However, when Sir John Perrot as lord deputy attempted to revive the issues of the cess and the suspension of Poynings's Law, Howth once again took a leading oppositional stance.

The earliest extant records for Howth concern his admission to Lincoln's Inn in December 1544, the institution to which many Old English aristocratic families sent their sons, including the Barnewalls, Nugents, Talbots and Prestons; he remained there for ten years.[27] His extended attendance was not uncommon, but rather reflected participation in elite Old English society as well as elite English society. Howth, though, was nearing his mid thirties when he entered. His brothers had both entered at later ages as well, Edward in 1540 at the age of thirty-two and Richard in 1541 at the same age. That the 4th Baron decided to send his sons to the Inns of Court at a seemingly late date bears closer examination within the political environment of the time.

The period of the St Lawrences' late attendance in the opening years of the 1540s follows the period of reform government under Cromwell's direction and Ireland's restructured constitutional status.[28]

Cromwell's integrationist policies that sought to replace authority in Dublin with more direct control from London catalysed resistance within the colonial community, most immediately in the Kildare Rebellion but also as a result of the establishment of garrisons, as Bradshaw and Canny have both noted.[29] The Old English aristocracy fared poorly under Grey's deputyship, and early fears of administrative displacement were compounded by the 1541 constitutional and religious reforms that failed to deliver the rewards many of the Old English expected.[30] Thus, either the 4th Baron newly appreciated the need to position his sons for office in the face of English administrative incursions, or alternatively, as the influence of the Old English was reinstated relatively quickly under St Leger's administration commencing in 1540, the 4th Baron may have seen the efficacy of positioning his sons to take advantage of revived opportunities.[31]

Whichever was the case, the Inns of Court would prove central to the position of the Old English community, providing these students with the legal education on which their later opposition to the cess would be grounded. It was, in fact, from this community of legal students that more intensive opposition to governmental measures in Ireland would emerge under Sussex in the early 1560s. Importantly, the subject of royal prerogative – which would become an issue of critical concern during the cess controversy of 1577–8 – was of particular interest at the Inns of Court during Howth's residence and one to which Howth seems to have paid attention. William Staunford had completed a treatise on the royal prerogative in 1549, following which he presented a series of lectures on it in 1551.[32] Staunford was one of the authorities to whom Howth referred as he later defended his position on the cess controversy in his compilation, as were John Fortescue and Henry of Bracton, both of whom had served as sources for Staunford's treatise and lectures.[33] Students at the Inns of Court were furthermore instructed in their duty to uphold the law even when it went against the monarch's will, a position again central to the later cess opposition.[34] Howth's formal education in London thus exposed him to two factors that would converge to influence his sense of political legitimacy: law as an institution obligated to preserve constitutional right, and affirmation of his status as a member of the nobility.

Just as importantly, Howth's time at the Inns of Court also exposed him to the way in which the students and fellows 'of Ireland' were perceived by those in England, and he may have become sensitive, if he had not been before, to issues of cultural identity that would affect the colonial relationship between the New and Old English.[35] Inns of Court records in fact contribute to considerations of emerging Old English identity as they reveal the manner in which individuals from that community were regarded. These records make no distinction between those 'of Ireland' of Irish or English descent; Irish birth was enough to dictate the status 'Irish' though clearly the individuals referenced were Old English.[36] As early as 1437 Lincoln's Inn had decreed that 'no person born in Ireland should in future be admitted as a fellow of the Society of Lincoln's Inn and if anyone born there shall hereafter be admitted by any person or persons he shall be expelled'.[37] This decree was modified in 1513 so 'that from henceforth no gentlemen of Ireland shall be admitted to this company without the assent of a bencher'.[38] In 1542, shortly before Howth's attendance but while both of his elder brothers were in residence, Lincoln's Inn passed a resolution that 'no more of the country of Ireland to be admitted in the same house above the number of four at one time'.[39] The students from Ireland were soon to face a renewed illustration of English categorisation of their identity. In 1556, shortly following Howth's return to Ireland, the Lincoln's Inn students 'of Ireland' were residentially segregated by mandate in Dove House, with the additional mandate that any English students in Dove House should be relocated.[40] Records indicate that 'Irish' students had already tended to reside there; some of Howth's associates from the Pale, including Nicholas Barnewall, had been subject to the informal segregation.[41] Howth probably returned to Ireland armed not only with the cosmopolitan and aristocratic experience of ten years in London and, it appears given the references to legal tracts and authorities in *The Book of Howth*, some legal knowledge, but also with first-hand experience of the way in which the Old English were perceived by the English, an issue that would resurface in New English portrayals of the Old English, with detrimental impact.

Howth returned to Ireland some time between the summer of 1554 and early 1555, by which time he was heir to the Howth title following his eldest brother's death.[42] The brief period between Howth's return to Ireland and his succession as Baron in November 1558 coincided with the end of St Leger's deputyship and Sussex's first deputyship of 1556–8, a phase of governance that began to have greater impact on the Old English.[43] Along with his brother, the 6th Baron, Howth fulfilled administrative duties and may have accompanied his brother in the field with Sussex in 1556.[44] The 6th Baron seems at this time to have maintained the position of influence he held formerly under Croft's and St Leger's deputyships, appointed Marshal of the Field in 1556 against the Scots in spite of Sir Nicholas Bagenall's complaints and in spite of what we know to have been Sussex's increasing displacement of the Old English in military posts in favour of newly arrived Englishmen.[45] However, the 6th Baron was soon to suffer similar displacement, reduced first to Pale defence and ultimately replaced even there by Stanley.[46] His untimely death in the autumn of 1558, with no heirs, left his younger brother, Christopher, the new 7th Baron of Howth.

Howth quickly surpassed the position of his two elder brothers. He had already begun to receive routine commissions of local administration upon his return from London as noted, and he would continue to do so throughout his tenure as Baron even in the aftermath of later political and legal difficulties.[47] Upon inheriting his title, which coincided with Elizabeth's succession, Howth began immediately to attend council sessions, reversing his brothers' low attendance, again a pattern he would retain throughout his career.[48] He was, in fact, in attendance at the council session of 11 December 1558 when the memorandum of Elizabeth's succession arrived, in what may have been one of his first sessions – if not his first session – as Lord of Howth.[49]

There is no evidence that Howth attended the 1560 parliament at which Elizabethan religious reforms were passed, though it seems likely he would have, given his pattern of regular attendance at council sessions and his attendance at the parliaments that met under Sidney and Perrot. Nor is there conclusive evidence regarding his reception of those reforms, though again it seems likely that he agreed to them given his subsequent increasing influence with Sussex.[50] Loyalty to the administration is suggested by the augmentation of his commissions for local judicial and military administration and by his appointment, within months of the 1560 parliament, as general captain for County Dublin in the summer mustering of 1560. Later that year he was commissioned to attend Sussex against O'Neill, reversing his brother's removal from that position.[51] His rapid advancement under Sussex put him in the company of many of Sussex's recently appointed favourites, including William Fitzwilliam, George Stanley, Henry Radcliffe, John Plunket, Jacques Wingfield, Thomas Cusack, Francis Agard and John Chaloner, and set him apart from an emerging Old English group critical of Sussex.[52]

Criticism of Sussex centred on two issues: his campaigns against Shane O'Neill and his imposition of the cess, the exaction of supplies for the maintenance of troops and the deputy's household. Howth had already acquired a military position of some standing under Sussex, and as Sussex's continuing efforts to reduce O'Neill became a central objective of his administration, Howth was positioned to contribute to that effort.[53] In the summer of 1561, while lords such as Baltinglass, Dunsany and Gormanston were left to defend the Pale, Howth accompanied Sussex into the field against O'Neill again.[54] When arrangements were concluded for O'Neill's trip to London, Sussex reported that Howth had been instrumental in those negotiations.[55] This placed him squarely at the centre of Sussex's political objectives, distinguishing him yet further from emerging opposition.

Opposition to Sussex continued to intensify in the late winter of 1562, following O'Neill's return from court, concerning the second issue of importance: complaints against Sussex's cess and his slow payments. This culminated in 1562 when many refused to agree to a composition in lieu of the cess (the replacement of in-kind payments with a tax) and a group of legal students in London presented their 'Book of 24 Articles' to the privy council.[56] Howth continued to ally himself with Sussex, signing into effect the cess of October 1562 along with staunch supporters such as Fitzwilliam, Stanley, Cusack and Agard. As difficulties ensued and Sussex attempted to defend himself, Howth took an even more supportive position, dispatched to London in December 1562 along with Plunket and Fitzwilliam to represent Sussex and his supporters on the Irish council. The letters they carried suggest that Howth was privy to information regarding Sussex's administration at the highest levels, noting that they were sent 'with instructions of all matters comprised within your letters and for that we have chosen them as men for their knowledge and experience able to satisfy your lords in all matters that may fall in question'.[57] Howth was perceived to be – and most likely perceived himself to be – now operating at the centre of English administration. However, a curious event occurred while Howth was at court: to his great dismay, he was asked by Elizabeth 'whether he could speak the English tongue'.[58]

Howth certainly felt frustration, if not anger, and lamented in *The Book of Howth* that Ireland had been so misrepresented.[59] Perhaps renewing his resolve to assert his loyalty, Howth returned to Dublin and continued to support Sussex in the midst of intensifying criticism. In Howth's absence opposition to Sussex had escalated further; lords such as Slane denied that they had agreed to support aggressive measures against O'Neill and debate over garrison provisions intensified.[60] Howth, though, continued to support Sussex, accompanying him into the field against O'Neill yet again in the spring of 1563, an exploit about which even some members of the Irish council now had reservations, while other Old English lords refused even to fulfil the requirements of the general hosting.[61] His support for Sussex would soon change.

The precise role that Howth played in the final year of Sussex's deputyship, as Sussex came under increasing censure from both the Irish council and London, cannot be reconstructed. His signature does not occur on extant council documents again until Nicholas Arnold replaced Sussex in May 1564.[62] Failure to attend was atypical for Howth, but it is clear that his political allegiances underwent a transformation during this brief period of archival silence. As Howth returned to his former practice of regular council attendance once Arnold took office, this shift became evident in his position on military policy. Within days of his return to council Howth signed a council memorandum requesting a reduction of the garrison.[63] This was a departure from his earlier assent to Sussex's military programme. The signatories justified their request on the grounds that any danger that had warranted an established military presence had been rectified, citing an extensive list of Irish opponents who had been subdued. The groundwork for opposition to lord deputies, focusing on their military policies, practices and expenses, had begun in the late 1550s, at which point Howth disagreed with that opposition. Now he was in league with that opposition on precisely the points over which he would emerge as spokesman in the later 1570s. Howth's new alliance accorded with the generally amicable relationship Arnold nurtured with the Old English.[64] Although it suggests a reversal in his position on policy, it was not unlike Howth's relationship with Sussex in that its substance was one of loyalty. In other words, transferring loyalty to Arnold when Sussex's departure became clear did not place Howth in a precarious position; rather, it preserved the position he had achieved with the Dublin administration. And, alone, it did not constitute opposition; Howth was supporting a lord deputy. Critically, though, it did entail a new stand on the cess. Howth's stand on the cess would thereafter serve as the guiding rationale for either his loyalty or his opposition to lord deputies. Hence, he continued to support Arnold – with whose reduced cess and garrisons he agreed – even as Arnold also came under criticism.[65]

Howth's new stand on the cess, though, was more carefully constructed. It was not merely that he was opposed to the cess: he was opposed to the cess when he believed it was levied unnecessarily. As the document cited above stated, the Palesmen, including Howth, perceived no need for the cess at that time and supported Arnold against detractors. When Howth believed that increased military efforts were warranted, he would support governors' increased garrisoning and its attendant expense, as he had during the period of Sussex's attempt to reduce Shane O'Neill and would do again when Sidney later renewed raids against O'Neill in 1566.[66] This same principle directed Howth's opposition to Sidney's attempt in 1570 to convert the cess into a composition, a move he argued was not warranted.[67]

Howth not only emerged in league with other Old English opponents to Sidney's proposed composition, he took the role of spokesman.[68] This new conflict with Sidney, whom Howth had only recently supported during the period preceding O'Neill's death, erupted at a council session in 1570. Howth informed Sidney that his group believed the composition 'was contrary to the laws and good orders of England'.[69] Sidney, responding 'in a great rage' according to Howth, threatened Howth and his allies with imprisonment though he recanted the following day, confessing that 'he and the counsel did commit an error and so promised upon his honour the like should not be in his time'.[70] Howth's stand on the cess and composition had undergone its final transformation. He now questioned not only its necessity, but the legality of its imposition, the terms on which Howth would oppose Sidney more aggressively during his second term as lord deputy.

The Cess Controversy of 1577–8

In spite of early opposition to Sidney's composition plans, Howth continued throughout the later 1560s and early 1570s to support the Dublin administration in other ways, fulfilling the aristocratic functions of Pale defence, executing martial law, serving in the local judiciary, and even playing an instrumental role in negotiations with O'Reilly, finally receiving a knighthood in 1569.[71] The conditions that gave rise to Old English grievances, however, had not been ameliorated. When Sidney returned as governor in 1575 with a renewed platform to lessen Ireland's fiscal burden on the English treasury, again through the commutation of the cess, Old English distrust and opposition quickly re-emerged.[72] Howth reassumed a role as one of the leaders of opposition as the issue of its legality came to a head, for composition meant not an ad hoc collection grounded in royal prerogative but a standing tax imposed without parliamentary or conciliar assent.

The debate between Sidney and the opposition escalated in November 1576 when Howth and others requested licence to travel to London to plead their case before the privy council.[73] Though Sidney refused their request for licence to travel, he ambiguously informed them that they were 'at liberty to go or tarry at [their] will', whereupon a delegation of lawyers, Barnaby Scurlocke, Richard Netterville and Henry Burnell, was appointed to represent the case in London, armed with seven specific issues for resolution.[74] In three separate letters addressed to Elizabeth, her privy council and the Irish privy council, all dated 10 January 1577, Howth, Delvin, Baltinglass and sixteen others expressed their concern regarding the cess to Elizabeth in legal terms, noting that 'diverse intolerable exactions [were] levied and taken . . . contrary to your majesty's laws and the ancient usage of this realm'.[75] In response Sidney wrote immediately to Elizabeth, portraying the Pale as more peaceful than 'in the memory of man', excepting the 'wilful repining at the cess which is stirred up by certain busy-headed lawyers and miscontented gentlemen, who indeed bear not themselves the burden of it, but the farmers and husbandmen who willingly would contribute toward it, if the gentlemen would suffer them'.[76] Seditious in their alleged pressure on others to resist, Sidney further defined the opposition as a conspiracy of recusants who 'do conspire . . . to complain of cess, and of me, and my government'.[77]

In May Elizabeth wrote to Sidney advising him of the proceedings following the Pale delegation's arrival in London. After examining Scurlocke, Netterville and Burnell, Elizabeth and her council concluded that the core of the issue was not 'a matter against law and the ancient customes of that our realm', but that it 'tendeth manifestly to the over-throw of our prerogative'.[78] Once the contentious accusation of a challenge to the royal prerogative had been made against the opponents, they became disloyal subjects. Scurlocke, Netterville and Burnell were imprisoned in the Fleet, and Sidney was instructed to meet with their colleagues in Ireland to ascertain whether or not they maintained that the cess was against law and tradition. If they did, Sidney was to 'proceed against them with all severity'.[79] Sidney's return letter to Elizabeth fuelled fears that the opponents harboured ulterior motives and needed only the slightest provocation to enter into open revolt. Scurlocke was identified as one who ever since 'the time of my Lord of Sussex government . . . never ceased to impugn English government'. Netterville was noted to be 'as great an impugner of English government as any this land beareth'. Sidney closed by invoking fears of French and papal assistance, noting

> I have real cause to mistrust the fidelity of the greatest number of
> the people of this country birth of all degrees. They be papists, as I
> may well term them, body and soul, for not only in matter of reli-
> gion they be Romists but for governement they wish change and to
> be under a prince of their own superstition.'[80]

The cess opponents would be compelled henceforth to assert repeatedly their claims of loyalty to Elizabeth.

Sidney also, as he had been commanded, called the Palesmen
before a council session on 1 June. Following a heated argument
between Sidney and Howth, Sidney produced copies of the January
1577 letters that had been sent to Elizabeth and her privy council,
demanding to know whether they maintained their position. Howth,
Baltinglass, Delvin and others stated that they did, and that furthermore
they would do so until the matter was resolved by Elizabeth. After
further debate and their refusal to subscribe to the cess in the presence
of the council, Howth and the others left the council session, following
which their imprisonment was debated.[81] When the cess opponents
were recalled to council chambers they were presented with Elizabeth's
letter of 14 May 1577 instructing Sidney to proceed against them if their
opposition continued. The opponents stood firm even in the face of
this pressure and were confined to Dublin Castle.[82]

In the early weeks of their incarceration two submission statements
were presented by the imprisoned to Sidney and the Irish council, both
of which were unsuccessful in achieving their release.[83] Sidney had
also at some point during this period confiscated a letter sent by
Netterville from the Fleet to Howth.[84] Though it is unclear whether the
letter was intercepted before reaching Howth, or taken from him, the
letter's contents suggest that Howth, if not others among the imprisoned, were aware of its nature even before the council session of 1
June. Netterville wrote that although the delegates had been imprisoned, he thought 'your message was not evil thought of . . . I doubt
not the cause will do well'. The assurance of hope that their grievances
would receive remedy at the hands of Elizabeth is perhaps what led
the group to resist Sidney's attempt to force their compliance at the 1
June council session. They seem to have been aware of the letter's
contents by the time several submission statements were prepared later
in June. The early submission statements persisted in a refusal to
acknowledge Sidney's right to levy cess for his household and
expressed surprise that their grievances had been perceived as a challenge to royal prerogative, categorically denying this was their intent.

These statements also reiterated the grievances as outlined in the initial letters of January 1577 and reveal the crystallisation of key issues for both sides: accusations of disloyalty on Sidney's part and assertions of loyalty and legal right from the imprisoned. Perhaps aware now of Sidney's belief in a disloyal conspiracy against him, the imprisoned asserted not only their loyalty to Elizabeth, but also contextualised their status historically by outlining their long-standing and ancestral loyalty to the English conquest dating to the reign of Henry II.[85]

Sidney was concerned that those imprisoned in Dublin had been able to maintain contact with Scurlocke, Netterville and Burnell imprisoned in the Fleet through an intermediary, Thomas Talbot, and that Howth was serving as leader of the opposition.[86] Sidney ordered the individual examination of the imprisoned in Dublin Castle on 1 July 1577. Although the questions of interrogation are no longer extant, the signed examinations are. They reveal that each was questioned specifically as to whether he had met with Talbot, recently arrived from England. Precisely what information Talbot was suspected to have carried is unknown, though it is possible it was he who carried the letter from Netterville to Howth. Several of the imprisoned responded only briefly that they had not met with Talbot and some denied even knowing Talbot (as Edward Plunket and Lavalen Nugent claimed). Others, however, reiterated the belief that they would receive assistance from Elizabeth in their grievances, suggesting familiarity with Talbot's letter.[87] Under interrogation Howth insisted he had not spoken with Talbot, even when informed by the examiners that Talbot had confessed otherwise.[88]

The imprisoned were examined a second time regarding their position on the cess and the opposition more specifically. In this case, the questions of interrogation are extant.[89] The imprisoned were asked 1) how they came to believe that the royal prerogative did not extend to the cess, 2) whether they still held that belief, 3) who had allied with them in sending agents to England, and 4) what bonds and sums of money had been promised to finance their agents in England.[90] Interestingly, based on the responses recorded, a fifth question – though not recorded – seems to have been asked in the attempt to ascertain possible accomplices on the English privy council. To the first question Howth responded that 'he had seen the chronicles and read of the laws of this realm and because he could not find in any of them such cess so laid down therefore he was of that mind that except by parliament he could not be lawfully charged', a position he maintained in response to the second question. Howth claimed to be unaware of financial pledges others had granted, but confessed that he had given '£5 or 6'. Howth further asserted that he had granted financial assistance of his own means, without levying additional charges on his tenants for this cause. His expanded response indicates the underlying motive for this line of questioning and bore the graver assertion of insubordination, for if the opponents had raised funds by levying the cost on their tenants, they created a situation that only further burdened their tenants and compromised their ability to fulfil the administration's cess obligations. Throughout the examination, Howth claimed a patchy memory of specifics, refusing as before to incriminate any of his peers, asserting in particular that he could not say specifically how many had consented to sending delegates to London. To this he also appended a further response which suggests that a much more specific, and critical, question had been asked though not documented. To the third question, Howth stated also that he was unaware of anyone 'of her majesty's privy counsel that consented . . . to the said letters' and that he knew of no one 'in England who encouraged them to complain or consented to their complaint'.[91] This suggests that not only were the imprisoned questioned about accomplices, but specifically about accomplices with influence in England who had the ability to further damage Sidney.

The imprisoned were released at some point in July; however, this was just as probably in response to Elizabeth's letters requesting Sidney to reach a compromise with the opposition as it was due to Sidney's acceptance of the sincerity of the opponents' concession.[92] Sidney by now was concerned that in spite of the fact that he had followed Elizabeth's directive to imprison the opponents, she would oppose his levy of the cess as Howth and the others requested. Sidney may have now also feared his imminent recall, having already been requested to return to London in May of 1577, and thus began, as Elizabeth requested, to negotiate with his opposition following their release. Throughout the summer a series of documents outlining grievances and proposed alternatives were drawn up.[93] The negotiations were not successful, and by September the opponents were once again refusing to sign a cess agreement. Their persistence in awaiting resolution from Elizabeth was revealed in a statement given to Gerrard as he was dispatched to London. Among other concerns, he was specifically to address the renewal of opposition to the cess. He was instructed to:

> declare how wilfully many of the noblemen of the Pale, as namely
> the Viscount of Baltinglass, the Barons of Delvin, Trimleston, and

Howth are bent to oppose themselves against the state: how loth they were to make any submission; which although it carried appearance in writing and show of words to be very dutiful and from the heart, yet within a few days after, being called as in former times to yield their consents to . . . agree to cess by consent of nobility they refuse to sign the council book, alleging that the cause was before her Majesty, and that they expected resolutions from her. . . . You shall move therefore that they be specially sent for over to yield their opinions there of liking or disliking of the matter for the example in punishing of them will breed both a great honour to the state and a contentment and quiet to the country . . . for if their wilfulness be borne withall it will make a general discontent and mutiny among the people.[94]

Gerrard's report on Sidney's insistence on the necessity of the cess, a key foundation for his policies as governor, was well received by Elizabeth. She now directed Sidney to recall the opponents to obtain their submission to a cess.[95]

As Sidney was on progress, not returning until 22 January, Howth and the others were not called to a session of the Court of Castle Chamber until 31 January 1578.[96] Sidney initially demanded a submission to the cess during that day's session, but agreed to wait an additional day (after denying their request for more time to confer). They returned the following afternoon with a submission which Sidney refused to accept, proffering instead a submission drawn up for them to which only Richard Missett, Christopher Fleming, Nicholas Taaffe and Barnaby Scurlocke subscribed. Those who refused to sign were fined and imprisoned a second time.[97] As during the previous year's imprisonment, the opponents formally requested release, a request again refused by Sidney after the failure of the two sides to agree on the terms of bonds in payment of their fines.[98]

In March Sidney was again called to London. Warned by Walsingham of his imminent recall and the need for an immediate resolution to the cess dispute,[99] Sidney resisted, excusing his attendance on the grounds that he needed to remain in Dublin in order to resolve the matter of cess.[100] Dispatches from London encouraged punishment of the imprisoned as an example, but warned against a retaliation so harsh that it might aggravate their opposition rather than accomplish resolution, privy council's ultimate objective. Even following the release of Scurlocke, Netterville and Burnell from the Fleet in the spring of 1578 and directives to resolve the dispute, the imprisoned would spend another four months in Dublin Castle, during which time they presented several statements of submission, before finally achieving their release on 30 June 1578.[101] Negotiations on the cess were renewed, and despite the failure of resolution on all issues, proposals for alternate provisioning were accepted as an interim solution.[102] A provisional fifteen-week cess began in November 1578. However, difficulties surfaced yet again when this agreement expired in February 1579 and renewed negotiations continued into the late spring. Howth's participation in those negotiations would be precluded by his imprisonment on charges of another nature.

Howth's Domestic Abuse Trial

Concurrent with the concluding cess negotiations, Howth was investigated by the Court of Castle Chamber on four charges of domestic violence brought against him by his wife, Elizabeth.[103] Howth would ultimately face fines (later reduced) and a nineteen-week term of imprisonment for the beating of a servant, two beatings of his wife, and the beating of his thirteen-year-old daughter, Jane, which resulted in her death. During the course of the trials, allegations of Howth's disreputable personal life were expanded upon. Adding to the political discredit from which he had not yet fully emerged as a result of the recent cess difficulties, resolved only temporarily and tenuously, Howth now stood to suffer personal discredit, and as he would later claim, financial ruin.

Only two court examination records are extant for Howth's domestic abuse case. In the first of these his servant, Nicholas Tyrrell, was questioned by the Court of Castle Chamber in late May 1579 regarding Howth's association with Elizabeth Bermingham. Though Tyrrell had apparently earlier confessed to Gerrard – corroborating Elizabeth Bermingham's testimony – that he had been sent by Howth to bring Elizabeth Bermingham to him the previous weekend, Tyrrell now proved an uncooperative informant before the court, denying the allegations.[104] Charged with perjury, Tyrrell was imprisoned in Dublin Castle.[105] The seriousness with which the Court of Castle Chamber viewed this case, or the seriousness with which they intended to pursue Howth, is suggested in part by the punishment inflicted on Tyrrell. Though the court rarely enforced the pillory as a form of punishment, they did so in this case.[106] Tyrrell was sentenced to have first his right and then his left ear nailed to the pillory on the following two Saturdays, from which he could be removed only by tearing away or cutting free with a knife his own ear.

The court, however, was willing to forgo this portion of the punishment upon payment of a £10 fine for each ear, though Tyrrell was to remain imprisoned pending the court's further orders.[107]

The second of the records extant for the case against Howth details his July 1579 trial for the beatings of his servant, wife and daughter.[108] Without denying the veracity of the charges, it is important to note the manner in which the court reported the details of the events and to consider as well the larger political context in which the case took place. Characterisation was an essential part of the proceedings, and Howth was portrayed as one whose temper was easily roused to vindictive behaviour with little or no provocation.[109] He was reported to have first 'cruelly beaten his wife without cause (as himself upon examination confessed)', which left her confined to bed for two weeks. Upon her recuperation, Howth 'came to her with two sally rods and whipped her with them to the stumps upon her bare skin'.[110] Reportedly, during this second recuperation, Howth ordered the household staff to keep her 'in a close chamber like a prisoner', allowing her only minimal food and drink. When one of the servants disregarded this order, Howth punished the servant as well. The court recorded that Howth 'stripped him naked, tied him to a post and whipped him with two sally rods one after another . . . in such sort that it had like to have cost the poor man his life'.[111] The final and more serious charge against Howth involved his thirteen-year-old daughter Jane, an episode in which Tyrrell was again involved. Here the court recorded that Howth

> sent his man Tyrrell to Dublin to bring home his daughter Jane . . . and upon her coming home he caused the said Tyrrell to take her upon his back who did so and having her arms about his neck the said Lord of Howth caused a woman that was by to take up her clothes and hold her legs which being done he with two sally rods provided for that purpose beforehand gave her about three score blows which caused her to fall into an ague and then into a flux and a fortnight after died.

Howth's physical cruelty was then allegedly matched by emotional cruelty. The court proceedings related that

> in the time of her sickness [he] caused her to be removed from her accustomed bed to . . . a yielding house and never all the time of her sickness came to visit her or sent to her to see how she did, she being kept and comforted all her sickness by poor neighbours, and after her death would not see her buried.[112]

These events were recorded as occurring a year and a half earlier, placing them at some point between Howth's two incarcerations for his cess opposition. Though there is no explicit reference to this chronology in the court's report, it would have been known to the judges, some of whom had also been sitting during the recent cess trials, including Dillon, John Chaloner and John Garvey. Howth was committed to Dublin Castle, remaining there for nineteen weeks, and fined £1,000 (£100 for the first beating of his wife, £300 for the second, £100 for the beating of his servant, and £500 for the beating of his daughter) and reminded by the court in no uncertain terms that he was responsible for the death of Jane, for which he deserved the sentence of death, a sentence that was not within the court's powers.[113]

This case tells us more than what may have been the disturbing and violent nature of Howth's character; the way in which it was represented and prosecuted by the court reveals an additional manifestation of the way in which Tudor domination affected the Old English. A comparison of Howth's case with the work of Susan Dwyer Amussen, Frances E. Dolan and Anthony Fletcher on domestic violence in the Tudor–Stuart period and Cynthia Herrup's study of the case against the 2nd Earl of Castlehaven illustrates the way in which domestic violence was perceived in early modern England as a phenomenon of three integrally linked areas: legal, political and social/cultural. These precepts would have particular significance when applied in the context of Howth's recent cess opposition and the deteriorating position of the Old English.

This prosecution for domestic violence offers another example of the effort to establish, enforce and extend English law in Ireland, a principal element of successive governors' programmes for reform, and the strict application of which Howth had only so recently insisted upon regarding the legality of cess impositions, an irony unlikely to have been lost on the judges. The most significant factor which sets this case apart from prosecuted cases of domestic violence in England is that the Court of Castle Chamber did not hold the power to hand down a sentence of execution. Howth's case rested fundamentally upon the distinction made in English law and in proscriptive literature between beating, a force 'administered in anger' with little or no reason, and the household patriarch's obligation to correct his spouse, children and servants, using physical force, within limits, if necessary.[114] Howth was repeatedly shown guilty of beating which, as he confessed, was 'without cause'.[115] He had abrogated his responsibilities as a husband, father and master by transgressing conventions and law governing the nature of physical force against those beneath him. What the court exhibited to Howth were the limits of his authority and, simultaneously, their authority over him: their legal authority to define, limit and censure his behaviour.

The distinction between beating and physical correction was crucial not only legally, but culturally and politically as well, for it reflected fundamental Tudor precepts about order/disorder, stability/instability and the proper balance between the prerogatives and obligations of power within a hierarchy of relationships. An ordered household, like the kingdom of which it was a reflection, was dependent upon this hierarchy. Though a household patriarch might be obligated at times to correct his spouse, children or servants, it was to be done within the constrictions of just cause and restraint. A beating implied that the husband/father/master was unable to control himself; he had abrogated his responsibilities, the household was in disorder, and by extension the order of the larger community threatened. For an aristocratic household in the Pale in particular, which should have been a model of English civility, an internal hierarchy in disorder compromised the stability of the state. Similarly, Howth's recent opposition to the cess had also reflected his failure to uphold the established hierarchy of authority.

While it is difficult to quantify the prevalence of domestic violence in early modern Ireland, and hence to quantify the percentage of incidents which came to trial, certainly some cases, if not many, as is suspected, were never brought to trial. We must ask then why Howth's case was prosecuted. Herrup has argued that trials or indictments for cases which incorporated charges of domestic abuse at one level or another usually incorporated larger socio-political issues associated with disorder and political unrest.[116] Each of the cases cited by Herrup share a triad of characteristics with Howth's case – spousal abuse, sexual transgression and, perhaps the most critical issue, political disloyalty – each used to corroborate the others. Lord Hungerford, whose indictment and execution in 1540 for sodomy relied heavily on character denigration, citing spousal abuse and, as in Howth's case, the imprisonment of his wife, had been an ally of Thomas Cromwell, whose own trial had concluded only two days before Hungerford's began, though they were executed together. Hungerford was also charged for harbouring a participant of the Pilgrimage of Grace. In the early 1580s, political opponents who accused the 17th Earl of Oxford of treason also relied heavily on character denigration, citing spousal abuse, sexual transgression and compulsive behaviour.[117] In Howth's case, this triad of behaviours was reversed. Domestic violence constituted the formal charges (the beatings themselves compulsive, exhibiting a lack of self-control), while sexual transgression was used as character denigration to build a case against him. The court documentation refers repeatedly to his 'dissolute life', his 'consorting with whores for twelve years', his 'filthy conversation' and, cryptically, 'other secret causes known to council not fit to be remembered'.[118] To complete the triad, Howth was not yet entirely free of the political difficulties arising from the recent cess controversy, an issue still in negotiation at the time of Howth's domestic abuse trial, as noted above.

Howth's domestic abuse case provided another opportunity for the administration to reiterate to Howth – if the cess imprisonments had failed – the ultimate power and authority of English government over him, or an opportunity, where the cess proceedings had also failed, to remove a contentious individual. This case, though only temporarily, did discredit Howth politically and perhaps socially among his Old English colleagues as well, for in the midst of the proceedings against him the Barnewalls sued for the dissolution of a marriage contract arranged between their son, Patrick, and Howth's daughter, Mary.[119]

In spite of the severity of this case, Howth suffered only a temporary setback, suggesting further that the court's proceedings had been of a retributive or reiterative nature rather than a real attempt to punish him. By October, Howth was sitting on the Irish council and had been reinvested with judicial and military powers, including the power of martial law.[120] His reinvested status and release from prison seem to have had much to do with Gerrard, by now critical of Sidney, in spite of the opposition of the new lord deputy, William Pelham.[121] Pelham later wrote to Gerrard:

> For the Lord of Howth I am glad I am resolved of your lordship's dealing with him, for as there were reports in the worse sent to me so was it verified that he was clearly delivered without fine, and because I saw no new service in him to merit so great a commission, I marvelled at it. Nevertheless for the credit of your lordship I neither called the matter in question nor returned him back to prison, neither any way dealt with him but in courteous manner though his demeanour after your departure deserved it, only to save the honour of your word (which was all that the constable could allege for his enlargement) I forbear to have any dealing with

him or to suffer others to do it, though his wife's complaints were
of late as grievous in manner as at any time heretofore.[122]

Notwithstanding objections such as Pelham's, following a two-year
period for which there is no extant evidence regarding Howth, in June
1582 the court reduced Howth's 1579 fine from £1,000 to £500 and,
moreover, he was elevated to a position he had never before held: a
seat on the Court of Castle Chamber.[123]

This two-year period was one of renewed opposition from portions
of the Old English community with the Baltinglass Revolt and Nugent
Conspiracy in the midst of the Desmond Rebellion. There is scant
evidence from which to draw conclusions regarding Howth's reception
of these events. Neither of these rebellions gained widespread support
within the Pale; hence if, in fact, Howth did refrain from collusion, that
alone would not support the conclusion that Howth had fully reconciled himself to the Dublin administration.[124] Crawford has argued that
the nature of the Court of Castle Chamber was altered substantially once
Sidney's control of it abated, which might account for Howth's release,
but the timing of Howth's emergence on the court also suggests that
other factors of a political nature were at work.[125] Howth only emerged
in this significant position following the end of Grey's oppressive
response to the rebellions with a series of arrests, interrogations and
executions and his own departure, replaced by Loftus and Wallop.
Howth not only returned to political life but, though there is no
evidence that he had held the position before, came back as a regular
member of the Court of Castle Chamber, sitting routinely throughout
November 1582 when at least twenty cases were heard.[126] Howth's
elevated role and apparent loyalty to the administration did not include
relinquishing his former position on the cess, for he would lead the
opposition to composition plans again under Lord Deputy Perrot.

Howth's Later Career

As at the beginning of his political career, the extant evidence indicates
that Howth again entered this round of opposition to the cess under
Perrot in 1582 belatedly.[127] Opposition had been developing for three
years before there is clear evidence that Howth aligned himself with it.
Perrot's policies reintroduced a number of issues that posed renewed
threats to Old English political, social and economic viability in addition
to the cess, principally enforcement of reformed religion and the
attempt to suspend Poynings' Law.[128] Once more, it was Old English

opposition that thwarted a viceroy's administrative proposals. Howth ultimately joined Slane and Louth as leaders of the resistance. Perrot wrote to Walsingham in January 1586 that, in spite of the general amenability of the Old English to his composition plans, three of the lords – Slane, Howth and Louth – were again working to undermine the administration.[129] As in earlier cess disputes, Slane, Howth and Louth sought the assistance of Elizabeth by writing to her in July 1585.[130] Howth and Slane ultimately relented, according to Perrot, voluntarily.[131] Louth, however, writing in his own defence to both Walsingham and Burghley, asserted that they had been forced to recant under threats to cause their 'disgrace and utter undoing' and under the threat of arrest (and Louth was ultimately arrested for his refusal to recant).[132]

There is no evidence to indicate whether Howth recanted under threat, as Louth insisted, or voluntarily, as Perrot asserted. Now in his mid seventies, Howth's age might have made imprisonment on a stand of principle less appealing, but more likely he was unwilling to relinquish the position of political influence he had long sought. Importantly, too, Perrot – in spite of his general dismissal of the Old English – had shown a willingness for conciliation where Sidney had not.[133] Under Perrot the issue of the cess was tied to attendant issues, religious and political, and it was on these issues that Perrot was willing to negotiate, though under some pressure from London. Perrot had, for instance, initially sought to enforce religious reforms. His attempt to require the Oath of Supremacy for all justice of the peace commissions threatened not only Old English religious sensibilities, but one of the last remaining avenues of political control to which they retained routine access.[134] Perrot's acquiescence in this issue permitted the retention of what had become a central issue for the Old English, the practice of Catholicism, tied now to their political survival.[135] Howth's recantation of opposition to Perrot, whether enforced or voluntary, indicated his willingness to negotiate when it meant he was able to maintain that for which he had worked throughout his career: a politically viable role for the Old English.

The remaining three years of Howth's life prior to his death on 24 October 1589 were spent in service to the English administration through the fulfilment of commissions of local military and judicial office.[136] Opposing rebellion, Howth had no wish to detach himself from crown government; rather, he sought to participate in it. His attempts to preserve the status of the Old English had ranged from displays of loyalty to the administration while disregarding his peers' opposition, to his own opposition and imprisonment, and, finally, negotiation. His efforts bore only temporary – and personal – results, however, and had neither substantial nor permanent impact in stemming Old English displacement. Both his son and grandson, as well as the Old English community at large, would face similar predicaments during the Nine Years War and its aftermath.[137]

Religion

Confessionalism became an increasingly key issue over the closing two decades of Howth's life as religious affiliation was bound to political survival. New English disparagement of the Old English frequently incorporated reference to their Catholicism, a pattern exacerbated by events such as the Baltinglass Revolt and Desmond Rebellion. In spite of assertions that Catholicism precluded loyalty to the crown, many members of the Old English, including Howth's son as 8th Baron, would maintain their Catholic faith while insisting upon their loyalty. However, individuals and families maintained various degrees of recusancy. Though Sidney frequently portrayed Howth as a recusant throughout the cess controversy, and this may have reflected Howth's religious practice accurately, its greater purpose in that context was one of rhetoric, as Sidney sought to discredit his political opponents more generally.[138] There is no evidence that Howth maintained a markedly Counter-Reformation recusancy though circumstantial evidence suggests that he maintained a steady, if less than zealous, adherence to Catholicism.

Howth's father had perhaps offered only the necessary support of the Act of Supremacy, as had other members of the Old English aristocracy in the early phases of the Reformation, but did not acquire any land following the dissolution of the monasteries. His eldest son, Edward, later to become the 5th Baron, gained only nominal interest through his wife's inheritance of tenements within the manor of Donnamore formerly leased by St Mary's Dublin, worth 23s 4d.[139] However, the family continued to maintain a private chantry on at least one of their holdings, Kilbarrack.[140] It is through a pattern of marriages that we gain the best insight into Howth's religious practice. This evidence suggests that the 7th Baron was at the very least sympathetic to, and more likely practising, Catholicism. Marriages were arranged for one of his children, Leonard, to Anne Eustace, and for two of his children, Mary and Nicholas, to two of Christopher Barnewall's children, Patrick and Margaret, both families with known Catholic sympathies.[141] Howth himself married, as a second wife, Cecilia Cusack, also of a known recusant family, who would later harbour her brother, Henry, a Jesuit, in her home.[142] Additionally, his eldest son, Nicholas, the future 8th Baron, was reputedly openly Catholic, intimating the religious environment maintained at Howth Castle.[143] Lennon has illustrated that throughout the period 1560–1630, and particularly after 1580, Catholicism was maintained among many of the gentry through the practice of holding mass in their residences.[144] While there is no conclusive evidence that the 7th Baron did so, records indicate that his grandson, Richard, younger son of the 8th Baron, regularly engaged a priest to perform mass at his residence, Corr Castle.[145]

Religion does not appear to have played the central role for Howth that it played for some Old English families, the Eustaces or Nugents, for example. Although Howth had been only recently closely involved with the Eustace and Nugent families in opposing the cess, he did not participate in either the Nugent Conspiracy or the Baltinglass Revolt, influenced heavily by attachment to Catholicism, suggesting that he maintained some distance from flagrant displays of recusancy as it intertwined with political opposition. As Howth had concluded work on *The Book of Howth* before these rebellions occurred (see Chapter Three), his compilation does not provide evidence of his response to those events. However, even before this more significant phase of Counter-Reformation influence, Howth had not used his text as a forum for religious discourse although it provides some clues as to his Catholic sympathies. Whether Howth refrained from public displays of religious sentiment because he perceived its potentially damaging ramifications, or simply did not find it in discord with his political loyalties, remains speculation. It seems more likely that in the 1570s, the period during which Howth compiled *The Book of Howth*, he did not perceive religious affiliation to compromise political loyalty, a position many Old English would maintain even in the midst of the Nine Years War.[146] Howth's willingness to reverse his opposition to Perrot's composition once Perrot relented in enforcing the Oath of Supremacy, though, does suggest Howth's concern to protect freedom of practice when it came under threat.

Howth defies easy categorisation, the framework into which New English figures from Sidney to Edmund Spenser tried to place them, and the complexity of his own identity can enhance our appreciation of the forces with which the Old English were forced to contend. He neither assented unwaveringly to successive viceroys, nor did he fit easily into William Gerrard's identification of the 'two kinds' of 'English rebels': those who 'enter into the field in open hostility and actual rebellion', or those who 'refusing English nature grow Irish in such sort as (otherwise in name) not to be discerned from the Irish'.[147] Though Howth would have identified himself as English, he was identified as Irish while a student at Lincoln's Inn and questioned by Elizabeth about his ability to speak English while on Irish council business in London. Nor did Howth fit easily into Tudor assertions of Ireland's factional division; though never unreservedly pro-Butler, he would at times shun subservience to the Kildare faction.[148] He would assert steadfast loyalty to the conquest, but oppose its policies, though never to the point of rebellion. Though Catholic, he did not display the Counter-Reformation zeal of others in his community. In spite of his many difficulties with the Dublin administration, when serious threats to the stability of English control arose Howth ardently defended England's right to Ireland. That the 7th Baron does not fit easily into any of these clearly delineated groups signals the need for a more nuanced assessment of the impact of intensified conquest on the Old English community in order to clarify their reception of that process. In Howth's case, the archival records permit us only to track him intermittently, identifying his position and its underlying causes at various times only generally. His manuscript compilation, *The Book of Howth*, however, provides far more evidence, revealing specifically why he responded as he did.

3. Compiling Opposition:
Manuscript construction
and contents

In 1569 Howth began to compile material for 'his book', as he signed the manuscript upon its completion. It was a project that commenced in the context of Howth's emerging opposition to the policies of Sidney and continued throughout the 1570s, a period that saw his opposition culminate in the cess controversy of 1577–8 and his incarceration on charges of domestic abuse in summer 1579. The compilation was abandoned soon after his release in the autumn of 1579, coinciding with Sidney's final departure as lord deputy and the restoration of Howth's relationship with the Dublin administration. The decade of the 1570s was a pivotal era for Howth and for the Old English, book-ended by the Butler and first Desmond rebellions at the beginning, and at its end the renewed Desmond Rebellion, the Baltinglass Rebellion and the Nugent Conspiracy. As the period of its production suggests, *The Book of Howth* is of value for the perspective it offers on the Old English community's position in this tumultuous period, a value enhanced by the paucity of other written sources from within the Old English community during the 1570s.

Although Howth's manuscript was sought out by collectors, historians and administrators throughout the later sixteenth and seventeenth centuries, it fell increasingly out of use thereafter. Concerns that *The Book of Howth* represents little more than the sum of random collection activity of uncertain date and authorship, and is therefore of dubious merit, have left it to languish underutilised. This impression of the compilation is a false one, largely imposed on the work by its only printed edition, as calendared by J.S. Brewer and William Bullen in 1871. In that edition the editors' lack of attention to the manuscript's structural and organisational details, their identification of thirteen unknown scribal hands and their failure either to date definitively or provide authorial attribution is compounded by mistranscription. Any analysis of *The Book of Howth* is dependent, of course, upon careful attention to its contents. However, the collective difficulties of the printed calendar preclude productive assessment of Howth's work by concealing the very elements essential to contextualisation of its contents and consequently assessment of its purpose. Therefore, it is essential to return to the manuscript itself.

This chapter necessarily begins then by undertaking the first detailed consideration of the manuscript's construction. This begins with more careful attention to the contributing scribal hands than accorded them by the calendar editors. That process brings to light new and funda-mental information about this text on which to base its assessment, principally the methodology employed as the work was in creation, its definitive attribution to the 7th Baron of Howth, and, finally, dating of the compilation. It is only once these elements have been unveiled that the contents Howth chose to include can be assessed more construc-tively, revealing ultimately the compilation's purpose.

PART ONE

The Construction of *The Book of Howth*

Strategies of Compilation

As it is now bound *The Book of Howth* contains 201 vellum folios in two sets of numberings.[1] At the heart of the compilation is the set of folios numbered 1–178, probably inscribed at the compilation's incep-tion by the initial scribe. This set contains, though, 179 folios, for folio 103 is followed by an unnumbered leaf (hereafter referred to as folio 103i), a point of importance later.[2] Within this set, folios 138–45 and 148, though foliated by the same hand, contain no text.[3] Preceding these folios are another twenty-three leaves that appear to have been numbered later (hereafter referred to as folios A1–A23).[4] Folio A23 is an errant folio, however, having been bound into the manuscript by a later owner; hence, the first set contained only twenty-two folios as compiled by Howth.[5] The entire compilation thus actually contains 201 folios, 192 of which contain text and nine of which were left blank, also a point of importance in understanding how the manuscript was constructed, as discussed below.

Not unreasonably, the 1871 calendar editors transcribed the folios in the order in which they are now bound: A1–A23 followed by 1–178. A roman numeral was then assigned to each of the thirteen hands based on the sequence in which that hand first appeared on the folios in their bound order. This numbering of the hands suggested that the folios were compiled in the order in which they presently stand, that the various scribes contributed in the sequence suggested by their numbering and, critically, that the passages were entered consecutively in the order in which they now stand. These implications are, however, erroneous and are exacerbated by the editors' inaccurate and inconsistent attempt to note each hand change, which they identify only vaguely by notational comments such as 'This last sentence is in a different handwriting' or 'From here to f. 158 the chronicle is continued by several different hands,' suggesting that a confusing array of scribes contributed entries to the manuscript.[6]

This editorial practice, which noted merely that a hand change occurred, rather than taking into account specifically which hand concluded, which commenced, and the locations within the text at which earlier scribal hands reappeared, created what seems, incorrectly, to be the chaotic nature of *The Book of Howth*. It also fundamentally damaged the compilation's integrity by obscuring the organisational strategies that directed the manuscript's construction, an organisation essential to analysis. *The Book of Howth* was created, not by the consecutive addition of entries as they now stand, but in carefully controlled stages. That the manuscript was constructed under a guiding set of strategies that directed each scribe's placement of entries is revealed by attention to the location of each hand, many of which reappear throughout the work. Identification of each hand easily permits the reconstruction of specifically which passages each scribe entered. By noting the utilisation of folio space left blank by previous scribes, we can see where each newly retained scribe placed his entries, sometimes by completing a section of text on a folio where the previous scribe had stopped, sometimes by beginning another section either on the same or a new folio, and sometimes by adding shorter entries to existing folios as blank space permitted where the new content was relevant to the old, either chronologically or thematically. It permits, in other words, a reconstruction of the manuscript as it was created (see Appendix B).

In addition to ascertaining that the manuscript was constructed in stages that sometimes entailed a return to pre-existing folios for the placement of new material, more thorough attention to scribal analysis also reveals another important principle that guided the placement of entries: the concern to compile information in what are in fact two distinct collections on which each scribe worked simultaneously. The first of these, contained on folios 1–137, clearly displays the purposeful creation of a history of the English conquest of Ireland from its Anglo-Norman inception to 1579. This was accomplished by collating into chronological order transcripts of and selections from available though formerly discrete sources, each covering on its own only a limited period of that history. In order, the sources utilised for this were: 1) the *Polychronicon*, a universal history compiled in the fourteenth century by the Benedictine monk Ranulf Higden and popularised in England by William Caxton's 1482 publication; 2) *The English Conquest of Ireland*, a fifteenth-century English translation and abridgement of Giraldus Cambrensis's *Expugnatio Hibernica*; and 3) *Pembridge's Annals*, a chronicle of events in Ireland to 1370; to which were appended entries from chronicles maintained by Sir John Plunket, Chief Justice of the Queen's Bench, and Walter Hussey, a clerk in the Irish Exchequer. Where Hussey's chronicle concluded in 1554, Howth appended passages of original composition to bring the history up to 1579. Passages of original composition were also incorporated into the copies where Howth found that his source failed to adequately support his presentation of the history of the conquest, usually passages relevant to the history of the Old English. Analysis of the scribal hands reveals furthermore that what appear in the calendar edition to be illogically placed passages interwoven with the historically ordered passages were, in fact, marginal notations appended by later scribes as they complemented previously entered content with supplemental information cross-referenced to sources such as *Hall's Chronicle*, Edward Hall's 1542 history of England from Henry IV to Henry VIII. Much of the confusion in the calendar edition of *The Book of Howth* arises in locations where the editors transcribed the supplemental information as text integral to the initially placed passage.

The second distinct set of entries on which each scribe worked simultaneously is contained on folios 147–78. These folios contain a collection of entries which, though they might appear miscellaneous in nature, were of no less relevance to the manuscript's overall concern with the history of conquest. This 'miscellaneous' collection contains items such as poetry, modified selections from documents such as Patrick Finglas's 'Breviate of the Getting of Ireland and the Decay of the Same', an early sixteenth-century Anglo-Irish treatise addressing failed conquest and proposals for its reform, excerpts from Edmund Campion's *Two Bokes of the Histories of Ireland*, a history of Ireland to 1571 written during his brief stay in Dublin, and lists of rebellions, giants and prophecies. Here isolation of the scribal hands among the collection of miscellaneous entries is of particular importance, for it reveals not only that each scribe worked simultaneously on both the historical and miscellaneous collections, but that they were specifically concerned to lodge the miscellaneous entries in a separate location where they would not compromise the integrity of the chronologically ordered history on folios 1–137. That the intent was to maintain these items separately is further suggested by the inclusion of nine foliated but blank leaves following the last entry for 1579 on folio 137r, indicating the intent to continue to chronicle contemporary events as they occurred (which, as it happened, never took place).

To summarise, as *The Book of Howth* was constructed each newly retained scribe contributed to the historical section on folios 1–137 by picking up chronologically where the former scribe had concluded, completed that section and/or added new sections, and occasionally returned to an earlier section to cross-reference or supplement it with additional information from the source with which he now worked. Entries which, due to their length, content or nature, would have interfered with the chronological framework of the historical narrative on folios 1–137 were maintained as a separate miscellaneous collection on the manuscript's concluding folios.

The contributions of three of the manuscript's principal scribes, identified as Hands III, VII and IX by the 1871 calendar editors, illustrate the manner in which *The Book of Howth* was constructed. These scribes did not, however, work in the order which their roman numerals suggest. Hand VII was retained first, followed by Hands IX and III, respectively. Hand VII created the foundation of the manuscript, possibly foliated its leaves (many of which he left blank for future addition) and entered the bulk of its contents – 132 of the manuscript's 192 folios of text (ff. 1–14, 17–101r, 104–20r, 154v, 159–73 and 176).[7] The entries in this hand indicate that Hand VII was employed principally as a copyist; none of his contributions address contemporary events. He created a history of the conquest from its Anglo-Norman inception to 1552 by copying and collating into chronological order formerly discrete works: selected chapters from the *Polychronicon*, followed by *The English Conquest of Ireland* and selections from *Pembridge's Annals*, John Plunket's collection and Walter Hussey's chronicle. This scribe's contribution to the historical portion of the manuscript concluded with events of 1554, the point at which his last source, Walter Hussey's chronicle, ended. Hand VII also laid the foundation for the miscellaneous collection. Leaving thirty-eight folios blank for the future addition of material, Hand VII moved to the manuscript's latter folios (ff. 159r–176v) to make copies of items such as the stanzas on the Knights Templar, the life of Muhammad, and selective annalistic entries dealing principally with Arthurian lore and prophecy taken again from the *Polychronicon*, but also from works such as Robert Fabyan's 1515 *New Chronicles of England and France*. Hand VII also left blank space on various folios within his set of miscellaneous entries. For example, his entry on the Knights Templar concluded midway down folio 160r. He then turned the leaf over to begin a series of annalistic entries on the verso. Similarly, where these ended on folio 162r, he turned to folio 163r to begin the lengthier and separate entry on England's right to Scotland taken from the *Polychronicon*, leaving space later utilised by Hand IX. All of the items entered by Hand VII are in Elizabethan secretary, suggesting professional training, and, as his entries constitute by and large a fair copy, Howth may have begun his compilation intending its circulation, though whether strictly within the Old English community or for a larger reading audience is unknown.[8] The subsequent stages of entry are less formal and reflect patterns more closely resembling those of commonplace books for personal use.

Hand IX was Hand VII's successor. Where Hand VII concluded his contribution to the history of conquest midway on folio 120r, Hand IX picked up the work on the verso, beginning the entry on the deputy-ships of Sussex, Fitzwilliam and Arnold (ff. 120v–127v). This hand also contributed to Howth's miscellaneous collection, clearly subsequently to Hand VII, for it was this scribe who utilised the folio space left available by Hand VII on folios 160r and 161r to make an entry on King Arthur. Hand IX seems to have been employed only briefly; his only other contributions were an entry on folio 162v regarding battles between the Danes, Normans and Irish, entered there for its thematic rather than chronological relevance (as indicated by the marginalia, a consideration of the number of warriors pre-conquest Ireland was capable of raising), and the entry on giants on folios 146v–147r.[9]

Hand IX was replaced by Hand III. Hand III added to the historical portion of the manuscript by picking up where Hand IX had ceased near the bottom of folio 127v, contributing a passage to cover the succeeding period, 1566–72, addressing issues such as Shane O'Neill, Carew's land claims regarding Idrone (1568), the Butler Revolt (1569–70), the campaigns of Sir John Perrot as Lord President of Munster against Fitzmaurice (1572) and the campaigns of Edmund

Fitton as Lord President of Connacht against Clanrickard (1571). The events chosen for inclusion here suggest a concern with the causes of unrest and rebellion, administrative attempts to quell unrest among the Irish in Ulster and, just as significantly, among the Gaelicised Old English in Connacht and Munster. It is perhaps not coincidental then that this scribe also compiled the folios on Suleiman and Islamic conquest of Christian lands, events presented as examples of the political vulnerability created when ruling forces are distracted by dissension within their ranks. This passage was entered on the two folios left blank by Hand VII between the conclusion of his entries taken from *Pembridge's Annals* (f. 101) and the commencement of his passage addressing Butler–Kildare factionalism (f. 104). Hence, Hand VII left two blank folios in the midst of his historical entry for the later inclusion of content covering the period 1370 to 1485, folios that Hand III utilised for this entry on Suleiman where, though it was placed out of chronological order, it served as an example of the dangers of factionalism and was placed to precede Hand VII's entry on factionalism in Ireland for its thematic relevance (an entry that in the end required more than two folios, hence his insertion of an additional folio, folio 103i as noted above).

Hand III also contributed all of the entries on Fionn mac Cumhaill, the Fianna and pre-conquest Ireland on folios now bound at the manuscript's beginning (A2–A13). Thus, as it is evident from above that this scribe was working well after much of the manuscript had already been compiled, we can determine that the compilation's interest in pre-conquest Ireland arose not at the manuscript's inception, but rather in its later stages of construction. Given the subject matter of these passages, it is apparent that in order to maintain the collection's chronological and structural integrity the folios were lodged to precede what had formerly been the manuscript's opening folios, where the history of the Anglo-Norman conquest began on the folio originally numbered 1 by the initial scribe, Hand VII.[10]

Manuscript Attribution

Just as more careful attention to the scribal hands reveals that a pre-planned organisational strategy guided the placement of entries, and additionally permits a reconstruction of the order in which entries were made, so too more careful attention to the scribal hands reveals another element key to the work's assessment: its authorship. Though associated by tradition with the 7th Baron of Howth, an association noted by its earliest users in the late sixteenth and early seventeenth centuries and followed since then, this attribution has never been demonstrated. The calendar editors, in fact, ascribed the manuscript to the 7th Baron only with reservation. Their hesitancy was challenged by J.H. Round in 1883, who asserted the accuracy of the traditional attribution based on personal and family information contained within the work. However, Round's preliminary remarks, while generally accurate, have not been addressed since.[11] The traditional attribution can be affirmed by the identification and analysis of Howth's hand in the manuscript. It is not only the recurring appearance of his hand in the manuscript, but close attention to the points at which it appears that reveal Howth's fundamental role in the manuscript's conception and creation.[12]

The calendar editors were cautious about attaching the manuscript to Howth, stating: 'No other evidence appears as to the title or the reasons for attaching it to the house of Howth than what is furnished by the following passages.'[13] They cited three passages, the first of which is a notation on the manuscript's final folio: 'Christopher Howth, his book'. They identified additionally the work's two references to Walter Hussey, one of which identified him as the compiler's elder brother Richard's foster-father (f. 177v), and another which identified him as servant to William Howth, brother of Nicholas, the 3rd Baron (f. 120r). Brewer and Bullen acknowledged their inability to decipher the significance or identity of the hand that entered '*finis par me* ke be he' at the bottom recto of the manuscript's last full page of text (f. 177r), potentially a fourth source of identification. They concluded that this 'would leave the question undecided whether Howth was only the possessor or whether we are also indebted to him, if not for the whole compilation, for . . . parts of it'.[14]

The cryptic closing note '*finis par me* ke be he' is open to speculation. Though 'ke be he' appears most obviously to stand for 'Christopher, Baron of Howth', the hand which entered '*finis par me* ke be he' does not bear similarity to Howth's. It has, however, been penned in a highly stylised calligraphy, perhaps by one of the later scribes if not by Howth. There is no extant evidence that Howth ever signed his name in abbreviated or cryptic form, nor is there extant evidence, although he signed his name with variant spellings, that he ever spelled Christopher with an initial K. It may well refer to Howth, for he certainly entered at least one if not both of the items on the last folio. However, as Round suggested, the other evidence is more conclusive in establishing the identity of the 7th Baron. Though

Christopher was a name commonly used by the St Lawrence family, shared by the 4th, 7th and 9th barons, the family relationships identified within the manuscript establish the writer as the 7th Baron. His elder brother was Richard, 6th Baron of Howth, and Nicholas, the 3rd Baron, was his grandfather. Having thus established the central role of the 7th Baron, one can see that the hand of the entries cited by the calendar editors is evident throughout the manuscript. That this was indeed the 7th Baron's hand can be further confirmed by comparing his signature on the manuscript's final folio to his signature on various state papers and letters.[15] Thus, with the possible exception of the cryptic *'finis par me* ke be he', the other three pieces of evidence the calendar editors provided as potential identification of the 7th Baron do in fact confirm his identity.[16] Having confirmed the identity of Howth's hand, one can see its prevalence throughout the manuscript, appearing on 178 of its 192 folios of text.[17] It is the location of his hand that establishes his authorial role.

One of the forms in which Howth's hand appears in *The Book of Howth* is in marginalia. The manuscript contains extensive marginalia in several hands. Carew later annotated the manuscript heavily, for instance, but many of the initial marginalia were entered by Howth.[18] Identification of his hand here substantially advances assessment of his relationship to the compilation. Some of Howth's marginalia served as information to complement the text when no other space permitted, or as a locating device for a text which has no index, and on occasion as a means of noting his sources. More significantly, Howth's marginalia identify for the reader the importance he attached to passages. For example, to a section on problems that confronted the twelfth-century conquerors, Howth entered in the margin, 'The country ill guided as it hath been since many times' (f. 50v). The ability to securely identify commentary such as this as Howth's is fundamental to the entire compilation's assessment.

The manuscript also contains periodic interlining. Identification of Howth's hand reveals that all of it was made by him. As with some of the marginalia, the interlining on occasion serves to append supplemental information to the text. For example, to the series of entries made by Howth's scribe taken from Plunket's chronicle Howth later interlined additional information to six of the entries.[19] The 1871 calendar noted in a footnote only that these additions were in another hand, obscuring evidence of Howth's hand here, and more substantially concealing Howth's active engagement with the text.[20] His engagement with the text is evident in other interlineations in which Howth amended the scribe's work by the insertion of words or phrases to clarify the passage. In one such instance, Howth inserted 'saith the Lord of Howth' to clarify the various speakers within a dialogue.[21] There is no evidence to suggest whether Howth proofread or annotated folios upon their completion or during later periods of reading; however, that he did so at some point reveals his concern with the manuscript's content and clarity.

While identification of Howth's hand in marginalia and interlining might only suggest that he was one-time owner of a completed manuscript who annotated it as did its later owners, evidence of his hand elsewhere in the manuscript indicates rather that he played a fundamental role in its creation, present alongside the scribes as they worked. For this reason the identification of Howth's hand is even more critical in other locations throughout the manuscript. In these locations his hand reveals the authorial contribution and direction he provided both by making his own entries and by contributing to passages otherwise entered by scribes. For example, there are several instances in the manuscript in which the scribe stopped mid-sentence, Howth continued the work for several lines before also stopping mid-sentence, at which point the scribe resumed the entry. This can be seen in the following passage where the lines in Howth's hand have been italicised.

> Sir John saw the host coming to town. He was but 700 men; nevertheless they were full hardy and manfully of kind. He chose sooner to assay the adventure of battle in the field rather than he would be kept in a cave within *like a bird in a cage. He came out of the town and did put his men in good order and divided them in three companies. He put his* brother Sir Amorey St Lawrence with the horsemen which was 140 and every horseman had a bowman behind him . . . (f. 34r)

On other occasions Howth took advantage of blank space where the scribe had stopped to continue a passage, as he did, for example, with the passage on the Field of Fentra in Munster begun by Hand III (f. 13r). However, in the passage cited above, as in other locations within the text, the point at which Howth's hand commences occurs not in available blank space on the folio's foot or in its margins, but in the middle of the folio and in the midst of text. Here Howth takes up the writing during what appears to have been the scribe's brief absence (one of only a few by this scribe). Thus these are clearly not additions to an acquired text, but indicate that Howth worked alongside scribes as the manuscript was in progress.

Howth's role in the construction of the passage cited above is of yet greater significance. Up to the point at which Howth's hand commences, the scribe had been copying from *The English Conquest of Ireland*. Importantly, Howth's version of this document begins to deviate from its source precisely at the point at which he takes up the writing. In this case Howth entered the first few lines of what would become a six-folio addition to his source, the remainder of the addition completed by the scribe. In this addition, the first of only four such additions to this particular source, the roles of John de Courcy and Howth's ancestors in the Anglo-Norman conquest are extolled. Given Howth's initiation of the additional information, it appears that he was responsible for the editorial decision to augment his source with this additional detail.

Regarding the calendar editors' question as to just how much of the text we are indebted to Howth for, evidence such as this indicates that we are indebted to Howth not merely as owner, but as editor and contributor to the work in its formation. Entries in his hand are scattered throughout the manuscript, and while the location of many suggests that they may have been later appended to previously entered text, the location of others indicates that Howth actively engaged in the manuscript's production both by making his own entries, some of them extensive, and by directing the scribes in his employment.[22]

Dating the Compilation

The Book of Howth does not provide a date for either its inception or its termination, and only one passage, a brief item on Pope Joan made by Howth, is accompanied by a note indicating the date of its entry as 1579 (f. 160v). It is possible, however, to ascertain a range of dates during which the manuscript was compiled based on the above reconstruction of the manuscript's stages of compilation. Having identified the order in which Howth's scribes were employed, by identifying contemporary events to which specific scribes alluded, Hand III in particular, it is possible to isolate the period of their employment and reconstruct a range of dates both forward and backward during which each of the scribes worked. This suggests initially that the manuscript was compiled over a period ranging from the late 1560s until late 1579, with slightly earlier opening or later concluding dates possible. However, the bulk of the manuscript had been compiled by 1572 and

Howth would return to it only intermittently between 1573 and 1579 to make brief additions. Reconstruction of the stages by which the manuscript was constructed in tandem with identification of each stage's dating permits the isolation of specific periods of time during which Howth was interested in particular subjects, interests reflected in the manuscript's content for that period of compilation. This heightens the significance of the manuscript's contents for their conveyance of Howth's response to contemporary events.

As noted above, reconstruction of the manuscript's compilation indicates that Hand VII was Howth's first scribe as well as the scribe who contributed the majority of its entries. He provided the work's foundational layer by collecting into chronological order copies of documents addressing the history of the conquest from the twelfth century until 1554, leaving blank folio space intermittently for later entries, and entered items of a miscellaneous nature on the manuscript's later folios. None of his entries address contemporary events. However, Howth appended a header note to Hand VII's selection of entries from Plunket's chronicle indicating that he had acquired this item in 1569 (f. 61v). This indicates only, though, that Hand VII worked at some period either during or subsequent to 1569; however, as he had already compiled at least folios 1–60 before copying from Plunket, if not also the miscellaneous entries made to folios 159–76 on which he worked simultaneously, he may have begun work slightly earlier. He had certainly concluded his work on the manuscript by 1571, as evidence internal to the passages made by Hands IX and III suggest that they had taken up the work by that date. Based on this evidence alone, we can surmise that Hand VII worked at some point ranging between the late 1560s and 1571, probably in a concentrated period of time, as suggested by the uniformity of his hand and the style of entry, particularly when compared to the remainder of the manuscript.

Though Hand IX followed Hand VII, there is nothing more conclusive by which to date his employment other than his tenure between Hands VII and III. He commenced with a discussion of Sussex on the verso of folio 20 where Hand VII had concluded with the end of Hussey's chronicle. As with the entries of Hand VII, these entries also addressed past events though of more recent date – the deputyships of Sussex, Arnold and Fitzwilliam – but were certainly entered subsequent to their occurrence, for he notes that Sussex was 'better beloved three years after his departure then he was at his being there' (f. 124r). Thus he was working at some point after 1567, if his reference to three years is accurate, but also clearly after Hand VII (discernible by his use of blank space left by Hand VII on folios 160r, 161r and 162r), hence after 1569, but before November 1571, after which date Hand III had been retained.

The period of Hand III, successor to Hand IX, can be determined with more accuracy. Hand III commenced with a discussion of Sidney on folio 127v where Hand IX concluded, contributing passages to cover the events of 1566–72. These events are out of chronological order, though. He returned to the subject of Shane O'Neill several times, for example, a matter then of concern in light of O'Neill's recent posthumous attainder in the parliamentary session of 1569, rather than integrating his discussion of O'Neill into one passage. Hand III was certainly working on the manuscript subsequent to late 1571, for he mentions specifically that Ormond's routing of Desmond's men occurred on 18 November 1571 (f. 132r). This scribe's term of employment may have ended soon after, perhaps by March of 1572. Though he alludes to difficulties with the Clanrickard Burkes in Connacht, notice of Clanrickard's arrest in March of 1572 (identified only as 1572 in the text) was appended later to the verso of this folio by Howth, suggesting that this event had not yet occurred when Hand III concluded. As noted above, it was Hand III who also at this point compiled many of the passages relevant to pre-conquest Ireland appended to the front of the manuscript.

Therefore, based on structural analysis it appears that by early 1572 much of the manuscript had been compiled, at least 161 of the manuscript's 192 folios of text, if not more. It appears that Howth returned to the manuscript after 1573 in intermittent sessions to make only brief entries. Only five folios can be identified clearly as having been entered after 1573: folios 133–7, comprising short notices of land claims in Ulster, the death of the 1st Earl of Essex, and copies of two of Howth's submission statements for his terms of imprisonment during the cess controversy of 1577–8. The chronological portion of the history ends on folio 137v, where Howth entered notice of the murder of Henry Davells on 1 August 1579 and the proclamation of Desmond as traitor. Though its date of entry is not noted, as this proclamation occurred on 2 November 1579 this entry would have been made during or after November 1579, following Howth's release from his third term of incarceration in Dublin Castle.[23]

Howth seems to have abandoned work on the manuscript soon thereafter. In what may have been his final return to the manuscript, Howth entered an excerpt on Pope Joan from John Lydgate's *Fall of*

Princes, an English translation of Boccaccio's *De Casibus Virorum Illustrium* taken from Laurence de Premierfait's French translation of that work (f. 160v). To this item he appended: 'written in this book 1579'. This is the only item in the manuscript that provides its date of entry. Suggestively but inconclusively, Howth may have felt compelled to note the date of entry for this item as it was appended to a folio that had been entered as much as ten years earlier by Hand VII. There is, however, no reference within the manuscript to any event after 2 November 1579 by which to surmise its continuation beyond that date. Howth seems to have laid aside his compilation in the wake of his final release from prison and to have chosen not to return to it in the aftermath of the Baltinglass Rebellion and Nugent Conspiracy, a period that for him, conversely, coincided with a reconciliation with the authorities in Dublin.

Reconstructing the stages by which *The Book of Howth* was compiled corrects former misperceptions of this work as a composite of random collection activity and establishes it as a collection purposefully created by the 7th Baron of Howth. Though work continued on the compilation over the ten-year period of his opposition to the policies of the Dublin administration (1569–79), much of it was compiled in the concentrated period of 1569–72 – 161 of its 192 folios of text – as Howth first registered opposition during Sidney's first term as lord deputy. Such dating provides a more solid context within which to consider the contribution Howth's text makes to our understanding of the Old English community's varied responses to its threatened position in this period. The manuscript responds to a central question in Tudor Ireland: where did the conquest fail and why? Howth, in fact, specifically lodged this question in the manuscript, asking: 'What was the stay or let of the conquest that Ireland was not made one or belonging to one?' (f. 5v). *The Book of Howth* challenges charges levelled against the Old English as both the source of the historical failure to have completed the Anglo-Norman conquest and as the source of contemporary impediments to its completion. Howth's search for the causes of failed conquest and his simultaneous defence of the Old English laid the organisational framework upon which the manuscript was maintained, in particular its unique creation of a comprehensive history of the conquest accomplished by bringing together into chronological order formerly discrete works, each of which on its own had addressed only a portion of that history. The contents Howth chose for inclusion as he considered these issues are the subject of the next section.

PART TWO

The Contents of *The Book of Howth*

The array of information Howth collected as he considered the history and state of conquest in Ireland can appear perplexing, ranging from versions of episodes from the Fenian cycle and Arthurian legend, to poetry, unnatural phenomena, political prophecy, errant women and extensive excerpts from medieval annals. In spite of what might seem to be the initial irrelevancy of some of the entries, they were all collected by Howth because they served the collection's purpose, yet they have never been addressed in any detail. Just as, in the previous section, more careful attention to the manner in which Howth's manuscript was constructed revealed factors that prove central to its analysis, so too more systematic attention to the contents of *The Book of Howth* reveals elements that prove essential to its analysis.

Cataloguing Howth's entries is not only helpful in sorting out what can appear to be a confusing collection, but more fundamentally it reveals the compilation's rationale as the consistency and currency of Howth's concerns become quickly apparent. Cataloguing Howth's entries also reveals that he relied heavily on sources available in both print and manuscript, a common practice in the early modern period, but more importantly a factor that proves essential to the collection's overall assessment in several ways.[24] Some of Howth's sources, such as Edward Hall's *Chronicle*, the *Polychronicon* and the chronicles maintained by Plunket and Hussey, are cited by Howth, who occasionally even referenced specific folios from these works. Importantly, where his referenced sources remain extant comparative assessment can be carried out. This reveals that Howth often copied very closely as items were entered into his collection. Once that practice has been discerned, its application elsewhere in the collection permits the identification of unnamed sources used by Howth, including works such as John Lydgate's *Fall of Princes* and Edmund Campion's *Two Bokes of the Histories of Ireland*. Identifying as many of Howth's sources as possible provides a more secure foundation on which to base assessment of the collection's purpose. For example, once we know that Howth used Campion as a source, comparative assessment can be used to detect the subjects in which he was interested by identifying those items he chose to extract from Campion and, just as importantly, the items he chose not to extract. Howth did not always duplicate his source verbatim, however. Where comparative assessment can be carried out we can also see that on some occasions Howth modified sources as they were entered into his collection. On these occasions we can distinguish between passages that replicate his source's presentation of events and, critically, passages that were altered to create a new presentation of events, the determination of which again contributes substantially to the entire collection's analysis. Finally, the ability to identify those passages that depended to one degree or another on existing source material permits the isolation of passages in the text that represent composition original to Howth. Identifying composition original to Howth is, of course, also essential to identification of his position.

Following Howth's organisational structure, this section outlines the contents of *The Book of Howth* in two parts. Part One addresses that portion of the compilation that comprises a relatively chronologically ordered history of Ireland from the Anglo-Norman conquest to 1579. Part Two addresses the entries that Howth maintained as a separate but equally relevant miscellaneous collection. It applies the comparative methodology set out above in demonstration of his use of sources and offers preliminary analysis of them. This reveals Howth's reassessment and rejection of representations of failed conquest and proposals for its completion, particularly as set out in the Act for the Attainder of Shane O'Neill. His collection offers instead an alternative presentation in which it is the newly arriving colonial community, rather than the existing colonial community, that has historically impeded successful conquest. Systematic attention to the contents of Howth's collection lays the groundwork for the following chapter's more detailed analysis of his compilation.

I: The History of Ireland from the Anglo-Norman Conquest to 1579

As outlined above, folios 1–137 of *The Book of Howth* contain a history of Ireland from the Anglo-Norman conquest to 1579. That history was created in four principal stages of construction. During the first and most intensive phase of construction Howth retained the scribe identified by the calendar editors as Hand VII who worked *c*.1569–71 compiling copies of and extracts from existing texts. They were placed in the compilation in the following order: two variants of a document entitled 'Description of Ireland', excerpts from the *Polychronicon*, *The English Conquest of Ireland*, augmented with lengthy passages purportedly taken from a work Howth identified as Archbishop George

Dowdall's translation of a Latin text, *Pembridge's Annals*, and, finally, items taken from the collections maintained by Plunket and Hussey. This first phase introduced Ireland and covered the history of conquest to 1554, the year in which Hussey's death brought his work to an end. The second phase of compilation was entered by Hand ix at some point *c.*1571 and lasted only briefly. This phase consisted of the creation of seven folios of original composition addressing the deputy-ships of Sussex, Arnold and Fitzwilliam. The third phase of compilation was also brief, probably occurring at some point between November 1571 and March 1572, during which Hand iii entered five folios also of original composition covering Sir Henry Sidney's first term as lord deputy. The final stage of entry took place between 1573 and 1579. Its nature suggests an alteration in Howth's attempt to chronicle events, for here the pattern of narrative adopted in the second and third phases was abandoned. The six folios of this last stage contain a set of rela-tively short entries, not all of which address contemporary events, entered primarily by Howth but also by two other hands. The entire composite history also contains extensive marginalia entered through-out by Howth, as well as supplemental information gathered from additional sources including Campion and Hall, as noted above, along with John Stow's *A Summary of the Chronicles of England* and Robert Fabyan's *New Chronicles of England and France*. Howth ceased work on the history late in 1579, making a final, brief entry in which he noted the onset of the Desmond Rebellion.

An Introduction to Ireland

Howth began his history with a preface introducing the subject of Ireland. The first folio of prefatory material contains two variants of a document entitled 'Description of Ireland'.[25] Each of these documents identifies Ireland's geographical division by province, and more specif-ically, by its number of shires, ploughlands, cantreds and acres. These were copies of documents that appear to have been drawn up for the purpose of calculating potential revenue, though their respective calcu-lations do not agree. The remainder of the prefatory material contains excerpted passages from a William Caxton edition of the *Polychron-icon*. Following a description of Henry ii, Howth then drew selectively on this work's other chapters describing Ireland's geography, flora, fauna, its inhabitants and their customs. Howth's version generally replicates the *Polychronicon* closely, with a significant exception: while he included many of this source's negative depictions of the Irish as uncivilised in behaviour, noting, for example, their infidelity in matters social, political, martial and sexual, Howth consistently excised all reference to the purported Irish practice of drinking blood. Following these omissions Howth's copy ends abruptly where the *Polychronicon* continued on to further develop its derogatory portrayal of the Irish, noting, amongst other characteristics the prevalence of witches and misshapen children. Howth may have found this line of inquiry unproductive, for where these excerpts conclude Howth entered: 'What was the stay or let of the conquest that Ireland was not made one or belonging to one?' (f. 5v). His response unfolded over the remainder of the manuscript.

The Twelfth-Century Conquest

Following the introductory description of Ireland the scribe next began what would become the lengthiest section in *The Book of Howth*, an entry on the twelfth-century conquest (ff. 6r–59v).[26] At its core is a nearly complete copy of *The English Conquest of Ireland*. Howth's copy expands upon its source with an additional seventeen folios of material that address the roles of John de Courcy and Howth's ancestors in the Anglo-Norman conquest.[27] According to a note Howth appended to the close of the entry, all of the material he added to *The English Conquest of Ireland* was taken from Dowdall's text noted above. Howth created this entry by collating these two sources – if his attribution of the Dowdall source is correct.[28] Identifying the role each of these sources played in the entry's creation permits determination of the manner in which Howth modified *The English Conquest of Ireland* by adding the additional information. Importantly, this reveals his rejection of that document's representation of the conquest, and his re-presentation of the origins of failed conquest.

Howth's copy of *The English Conquest of Ireland*, cited by him only as 'Cambrensis', is one of five extant copies of this text.[29] Howth's copy is unique among the extant versions in three principal ways. Firstly, Howth's copy is unique for the scribe's frequent though inconsistent adaptation of his source's syntax and vocabulary to sixteenth-century usage.[30] While the scribe's updated language is of value to linguists, his inconsistencies are also of value. They reveal that Howth probably used as a source the copy now bound as Trinity College Library, MS 592 or a close variant, for several of Howth's passages replicate the language of this manuscript.[31] Secondly, Howth's copy is unique for it is the only extant copy that omits the passage on Thomas Becket's murder. This is the only passage Howth omitted from his source, apparently an editorial decision on his part, as he inserted instead, 'see the chronicles of England and the rest shall appear of this matter' (f. 15r), though whether Howth chose to omit this passage as it was largely irrelevant to his primary concern to address the history of Anglo-Norman affairs in Ireland, or because its omission permitted him to side-step the dangerous issue of church and state, is open to speculation. Thus, as far as Howth's copy of *The English Conquest of Ireland* stands, its representation of events matches that of its source; for example, its pro-Geraldine stance. However, the final way in which Howth's copy is unique – its addition of material on John de Courcy and Howth's ancestors – is more critical. These additions *do* alter the entry's presentation of the conquest, and it is from Howth's altered presentation of events that we can glean his purpose and perspective. It reveals his assessment of the problems that confronted the Anglo-Norman conquerors and his assertion that these problems continued to confront their descendants, the Old English community.

Howth's additions to his source simultaneously exonerate de Courcy's role in the conquest and glorify the roles of Howth's ancestors, de Courcy's companions in arms, in particular Sir Tristram Amorey St Lawrence.[32] Howth's presentation of their activities includes details of their morale-building speeches to their fellow conquerors and details of their hard-fought battles won with sacrificed lives (as on f. 52v). Their successes are ultimately to little avail, not because of their own failures, but because they are undermined by conquerors newly arriving from England. Howth here begins to posit alternative reasons for failed conquest to which he returns in subsequent portions of the compilation: misgovernment, misrepresentation of the older colonial community by those newly arrived from England, the consequent displacement of the older colonial community, and the difficulty of completing the conquest because of discord between what emerge as two distinct colonial communities.

To demonstrate these themes, having expanded upon the successes of de Courcy and his entourage, Howth then expands upon the conflict between de Courcy and de Lacey. He emphasises that de Courcy's initial successes were thwarted by de Lacey's 'evil, false, feigned and envious tales' (f. 55v). De Lacey was not alone in maligning the older community of conquerors, and this resulted almost immediately in the displacement of those who had first effected the conquest:

King Henry sending his son John as L[ord] of Ireland into Ireland bringing with him such a company of young gentlemen nothing careful of the country but given their mind always to disdain those that was before them as old soldiers which was, is and shall be the common usage of all those that to Ireland come as though they all had with one mind sworn this same custom to observe from the beginning to the ending . . . at length the country that was well stabilised with great civility, riches and quietness became at length through their misgovernment so far out of order that no man could travel in safety without slaughter, robbery or imprisonment throughout the country . . . (f. 51r)

Howth elsewhere refers to the 'misgovernment' of the 'new men' under King John (f. 50r-v), and as the above passage conveys through its conflation of eras, it was a situation that continued to impede completed conquest. It was furthermore a situation that compromised stability in Ireland. Howth also attributes the inception of this to the discord that had emerged between the two conquering communities of this period: the 'rancour, grudge, malice and displeasure which grew between [de Lacey and de Courcy] . . . was the undoing of themselves and also the realm' (f. 55r). At this point in the text Howth's additional passages do not call necessarily for the return of control by the Old English as much as they call for co-operation between the established and newly arriving colonial communities. This is suggested by the text's illustration of the detrimental effect that discord between the two communities had on successful conquest. For example, he includes a litany of slaughters visited upon the Anglo-Normans by the Irish who take advantage of colonial dissension to rebel (as on ff. 51v–52r and 55r).

As noted above, Howth appended a note to the close of this section identifying the source of the material additional to *The English Conquest of Ireland*: 'this much that is in this book more than Camerans did write of was translated by the Primate Dowdall in the year of our Lord 1551 out of a Latin book into English which was found with O'Neill in Armagh' (f. 59v). As other copies of *The English Conquest of Ireland* are extant we can determine the specific points at which Howth altered that text by inserting new material. However, because no work has been identified that seems to represent either this reference to O'Neill's book or Dowdall's translation of it, what we cannot determine is whether Howth copied as closely from that text as he had copied from *The English Conquest of Ireland*. Therefore, whether the text purportedly once in O'Neill's possession did, in fact, contain the information regarding Howth's ancestors or, more fundamentally, the themes of failed conquest and Old English displacement that Howth suggests it did, is unknown. Howth may have merely utilised episodes it contained, embellishing them or moulding them to his own concerns, suggested by the fact that many of the themes here, their commentary and the language in which they are expressed recur in several of the compilation's later entries.

The Later Medieval Period

Following his entry on the Anglo-Norman conquest, Howth continued to retain Hand VII who maintained the chronological structure of this portion of the history by next including entries addressing the period subsequent to the initial conquest up to the fifteenth century (ff. 60r–101v; several of these entries address slightly earlier and later events). In general, this section is entered in annalistic format, the format of the sources from which Howth worked. The core of this section (ff. 62r–99v) contains English translations of excerpts from *Pembridge's Annals* covering the period 1162–1370. These extracts are preceded by genealogical and obituary information in Latin for the earls of Kildare, Ormond and Desmond (ff. 60r–61r), as well as a short series of brief entries in English (f. 61v), the earliest of which refers to St Patrick's arrival in 432 and the latest a reference to Walter Burke's creation as Earl of Ulster in 1264. The extracts from *Pembridge's Annals* are followed by another short series of brief entries in English (ff. 100r–101v) addressing events ranging from 400 to 1567, the last folio of which was entered by Howth (f. 101v). This section of the manuscript excerpts only items relevant to the history of Ireland and continues to develop the preceding section's principal themes of failed conquest, false representation and misgovernment. They display as well the continuing concern to demonstrate the history and loyalty of the Old English. As with Howth's version of *The English Conquest of Ireland*, many of the passages in his version of *Pembridge's Annals* that address these themes constitute additions to his source. However, Howth's choice of entries from *Pembridge's Annals* also introduces another concern: the history of a Scottish presence in Ulster.

The passages excerpted from *Pembridge's Annals* trace the loyalty of the Anglo-Norman descendants as they attempted to sustain and further the conquest. To develop this Howth excerpted only those episodes that demonstrated the difficulties facing the medieval colonial community in the form of resistance by the Irish, incursions by the Scots, factionalism that compromised the security of conquest, and misgovernment by representatives of royal authority. As a function of their annalistic source, many of the entries record in abbreviated format the terms and deaths of civil and church officials, and they record as well the role played by the Anglo-Norman descendants as they literally built the conquest by constructing castles and abbeys (ff. 62r, 63v, 65r, 69r, 93r, 100r *inter alia*). Other entries emphasise the many battles between the Anglo-Normans and the Irish. While this implies attempted Gaelic encroachment (see, for example, ff. 95v and 96v), Howth does not entirely concede the success of those attempts, stressing rather Anglo-Norman success in repulsing them (as on ff. 71v–73v, 83v, 88r, 90v, 91r).[33] Significant attention is also devoted to Anglo-Norman resistance to Scottish incursions in Ireland. Entries on the Bruce invasions (see ff. 69r–84r *passim*) permitted Howth to further develop the anti-de Lacey motif begun earlier in the manuscript as this family colluded with the Scots (ff. 75r, 78v). Other entries note that not only did the Anglo-Normans repulse Scottish incursions in Ireland, they also demonstrated their loyalty to England by travelling to participate in English battles against the Scots (as on ff. 66r, 72v and 73r) and by participating in the acquisition of Calais (ff. 91r and 96r). These passages convey additionally Howth's representation of his community as vital not only to control of Ireland but to England's larger policies of security and defence.[34] Howth also included entries that record misgovernment by governors sent from England. Ralph Ufford's administration (1344–6), for example, is characterised as one of disregard for the established colonial community, an issue of particular concern to Howth (ff. 94r–95v).

While excerpting from *Pembridge's Annals*, Howth again took the opportunity to add substantially to his source by introducing passages that further demonstrated several of the themes introduced earlier in his additions to *The English Conquest of Ireland*. These later additions are similar to those made in the manuscript's previous section in length, style, concern, commentary and level of detail regarding Howth's ancestors and thus probably represent composition original to Howth. For example, an entry for 1329 in *Pembridge's Annals* recorded the slaughter of John Bermingham, Earl of Louth, and over 200 members of the Bermingham and Talbot families.[35] To this entry Howth added three folios (ff. 85v–87v) of additional information identifying the perpetrators more specifically – the Verdons and Gernons – and their motivation, and attributing the retaliatory murders of the Gernons (in the wake of the authorities' failure to indict them) to his ancestors, Walter and William Howth, sons-in-law to one of the murdered Talbots. Much as in Howth's earlier descriptions of de Lacey's jealousy of de Courcy's success and his consequent misrepresentation of de Courcy's motives, with the instability caused in Ulster by de Courcy's removal, Howth here noted Louth's success as a stabilising force and attributed the slaughter of the Talbots and Berminghams to the jealousy of the Gernons and Verdons, who were 'evil contented that the earl should in all affairs have the commendation of all service' (f. 86r). Howth later notes that had Louth not been murdered, 'Ulster had been civiler than Leinster' (f. 86v). However, the Verdons and Gernons suffer no legal retribution; they are 'winked at' by the authorities (f. 87r), for the 'magistrates for indignation or some other fond opinion never revenged such like facts but always did permit this same as though they were of counsel thereunto' (f. 86v). Here then Howth returns to the themes of factional misrepresentation of those who *are* advancing the conquest and of misgovernment as a cause of impeded conquest, as well as the problems of securing control in Ulster. Howth again asserts central roles for his ancestors, placing them on the side of those who were initially successful, though thwarted, in securing conquest. The Howth brothers' murders of the Gernons are dramatised with speeches and personal descriptions of a type included nowhere in *Pembridge's Annals*, but mirroring very closely the descriptions and speeches Howth earlier attributed to Tristram Amorey St Lawrence during the twelfth-century conquest.

Precisely how much of this passage was fabricated is unknown. At the point in the text at which the additional information began, Howth added a marginal note indicating that he had seen the Verdons' and Gernons' pardon (f. 85v). If he did, this is the only evidence in *The Book of Howth* that Howth had access to official papers. A footnote appended to folio 86v suggests he may have. This note indicated that the pardon exonerated the Verdons and Gernons by citing the Berminghams for 'manslaughter, burning, robbery and felony', thus effectively charging the Berminghams, rather than the Verdons and Gernons, for creating instability. The pardon also apparently implicated unidentified members of the Howth family in the activities of the Berminghams, charging them with murder, a charge Howth claimed was false as that crime had been committed by 'three of the Irish'.[36]

Not only is this information not contained in *Pembridge's Annals*, Howth in fact never cites *Pembridge's Annals* as a source for any of the passages in this section of the manuscript, though that was clearly the source from which either he, or the text from which he worked, had drawn many of the entries.[37] Howth did, though, cite a source for the short list of entries on folio 61v: 'more of the chronicles as appeareth in this book found with Justice Plunket 1569'. Neither those entries nor the short list of entries appended to the final two folios of this section reference events included in *Pembridge's Annals*. This header implies that Plunket's collection had been used elsewhere, but the structure of the manuscript suggests that the short list to which the note was appended was added later utilising blank folio space. Comparison to Howth's cited source is precluded by the loss of Plunket's collection, or its failure to be identified as yet. It is therefore unknown whether it was Plunket or Howth who augmented *Pembridge's Annals* with these two brief lists, or in what other section of the manuscript Howth had employed Plunket's work. The silent expansion of excerpts from *Pembridge's Annals* with additional information integrating Howth family history with themes of factional misrepresentation and failed conquest thus probably also represent composition original to Howth.

The Early to Mid Tudor Period

Following the collection of annalistic entries, *The Book of Howth* reverts to narrative form as Hand VII, still working in the manuscript's initial stage of construction, next made entries covering a very limited selection of events from the late fifteenth to mid sixteenth centuries (ff. 104r–120r). According to a note Howth appended to its close, Hussey's chronicle served as the source for this section of the manuscript, another of Howth's sources unfortunately either no longer extant or as yet unidentified. The first fifteen folios of this section seem less concerned to create a sequential history of events – its passages, in fact, record events out of chronological order – than to address the issue of factionalism (ff. 104r–119r). It attends to this theme by addressing factionalism briefly as related to the Butler family and the execution of the 7th Earl of Desmond, but principally by presenting the rise and fall of Kildare power. This is achieved through passages on the Battle of Knockdoe, the Lambert Simnel affair, an anti-Kildare faction on the Irish council under Surrey, problems between the 9th Earl of Kildare and Robert Cowley, and the Kildare Rebellion. This section integrates substantial detail regarding Howth's ancestors once more, in this case his grandfather, Nicholas St Lawrence, 3rd Baron of Howth. The composite effect of incorporating the position of the 3rd Baron of

Howth at each stage of the rise and fall of Kildare hegemony and of relating this period's events out of chronological order creates a simplified and false pattern both of Kildare history and of the Howth family's developing independence from the Kildare faction. Howth's attempt to extricate his family from charges of allegiance to the Kildare faction, and hence disloyalty, may in fact have served as the rationale for this section of the manuscript. Following the Kildare Rebellion, this section's final two folios shift in structure, tone and presentation (ff. 119r–120r). Rather than address episodes and situations at some length and with some detail, as the previous folios had done, the closing passages address events chronologically within an administrative framework.

As noted above, the section as a whole relates events out of order, creating a simplified and historically false pattern in which the earls of Kildare receive, wield responsibly, and then abuse their position of authority in Ireland, ultimately losing it in rebellion. It opens with a lengthy discussion of Kildare–Ormond factionalism, the inception of which Howth dates to 1485. In spite of its subject matter, the role this passage plays in the manuscript as a preface to the Battle of Knockdoe should not be unduly deflected by the header Carew appended to the passage, 'A Discourse of the Variance between the Earls of Kildare and Ormond' (f. 104r), and exacerbated by the artificial break in the passage Carew created by entering a second header, 'The Battle of Knockdoe', midway through the passage (f. 108r).[38] This passage does demonstrate the detrimental effects of factionalism, as the inhabitants of the Pale suffer the worst of its consequent fighting, but in the context of Howth's presentation it lays a foundation for the Battle of Knockdoe by demonstrating that Kildare's position was royally granted. The role that Kildare takes, then, by engaging his network of Old English and Irish allies in battle against the Clanrickard Burkes, is presented as one in which Kildare places his power in the service of the English conquest. Several brief entries follow this in which Howth records Ormond–Desmond factional fighting, Ormond–Lancastrian alliances and the execution of the 7th Earl of Desmond in 1468 (ff. 112v–113v), entries that draw attention to the fact that factionalism was not a phenomenon specific to the earls of Kildare, or even to Ireland. These entries also draw attention to the fact that much of the factional fighting in Ireland was bred by factionalism in England. This is evident in the episode Howth next recorded, the Lambert Simnel affair. Though this had occurred thirteen years before the Battle of Knockdoe, Howth's presentation of Geraldine support for Simnel distorts it as an emerging challenge to Tudor authority. Howth then moves ahead thirty years to address Surrey's appointment as lord lieutenant.[39] Surrey is lauded for restoring civility to Ireland (f. 116r) and, in spite of his reduction of Kildare power, Howth praises Surrey in particular for his concern that the Old English in general not suffer displacement at the hands of newly arriving administrators (ff. 116v–117r). Surrey's successful efforts to overcome factional alliances and preserve the position of other members of the Old English community are reversed by his successors in the following passage where problems facing the 9th Earl of Kildare are sympathetically portrayed as the result of Old English displacement. Kildare is called to London in response to Robert Cowley's 'evil disposed purpose', an event that leads directly to the Kildare Rebellion (f. 118r–v). There is absolutely no sympathy, however, for Silken Thomas or his allies, whose execution is described as their 'reward according their dessert' (f. 119r).

Although the relationships of the 8th and 9th earls of Kildare to English policy and authority provide a framework for this section of the manuscript, the manner in which substantial detail regarding the 3rd Baron of Howth is integrated into the presentations of events suggests that ultimately these passages were less concerned to outline the history of the Kildare faction than to demonstrate Howth's position relative to the Kildare faction. The text's representation of events is not consistent in its approval of Kildare's use of authority, nor does it reflect unwavering Howth family loyalty to the Kildare faction. What it does represent consistently is Howth loyalty to the Kildare faction *only* when Kildare's use of power benefited and did not challenge the crown's ultimate authority, in other words that the Howths were loyal always to the crown and not to Kildare. This was a loyalty that perhaps gave the appearance of adherence to the Kildare faction, for when Kildare's power advanced the objectives of the crown Howth supported Kildare, as at the Battle of Knockdoe. The text is clear in demonstrating the detrimental effects of Kildare's abuse of power and that Howth opposed Kildare on such occasions, as the 3rd Baron did by informing Henry VII of the support for Simnel in Ireland. Here the distortion of chronological order, while it creates an illogical portrait of Kildare history, is central to a portrayal of the history of Howth family loyalty. Immediately following Howth's presentation of his grandfather's role in thwarting the Simnel affair *The Book of Howth* next moved, as noted above, to Surrey's deputyship, a period in which an anti-Kildare faction's attempt to remove the 3rd Baron of Howth from the Irish council was stopped by Surrey who recognised that attempt as a 'dissimulation or craft' (f. 116v). Surrey not only restored Howth to the council, but 'placed him as one above all other worthy to be of the king's privy council' (f. 116v).

Following the passage on the Kildare Rebellion, the compilation shifts from a structure in which events are presented out of chronological order but with a significant amount of detail to a structure in which events are organised chronologically by vice-regal administration and with far less detail (ff. 119r–120r). The very structure of this portion thus reflects the new political climate in which it was now the activities of successive lord deputies, rather than the earls of Kildare, that determined the course of the conquest. The four administrations – Grey's, St Leger's, Bellingham's and the term shared by Thomas Cusack and Gerald Aylmer – are addressed far more briefly than the events of any of the previous passages and the focus is on two new issues that arose in the aftermath of the Kildare Rebellion: the rise of O'Neill power in Ulster and the issue of financing the conquest through the cess. Grey's term receives the most attention of the four (thirty-one lines of text as opposed to only nine devoted to St Leger, who receives the least attention), and each administration is characterised by identification of its principal developments. Grey's administration is noted for addressing the rise of O'Neill and O'Donnell, a threat he had nearly contained when, the text makes clear, he was executed on false charges of treason (f. 119v). St Leger is lauded for the success of his conciliatory strategy with the Irish, and the text is specific in stating that St Leger was responsible for initiating the cess though it offers no commentary on its implementation or reception.[40] While the text returns to the subject of the need to contain rising O'Neill power in its description of Cusack's and Aylmer's administration (this is, in fact, the only subject to which the text refers in its address of their administration), it is the cess that takes centre stage in the intervening description of Bellingham's administration. The passage on Bellingham's administration addresses almost exclusively his implementation of the cess; its only additional reference is to the establishment of forts in Laois and Offaly. This passage makes clear that Howth was not opposed to the cess itself, but rather to its abuse. The text notes that though Bellingham's exactions were heavier than St Leger's, his compensation was responsible and fair; that Bellingham was a 'true payer' and always 'paid for all he took' is repeated four times within a twelve-line description (f. 119r–v).

The loss of Hussey's text precludes assessment of Howth's use of it, and thus we cannot determine the extent to which Howth copied from, excerpted, modified or reflected the concerns of his source in this case. Critically, we cannot determine whether Hussey's text contained such detail regarding Howth's grandfather, displayed an overriding concern to address factionalism and the decline of Kildare power, or had only contained a core of information that was embellished or modified by Howth as elsewhere. The passages concerning the 3rd Baron of Howth bear marked similarity to the manuscript's earlier passages regarding Howth's more distant ancestors and their role in the conquest, suggesting that Howth was responsible for the composition of these passages and not merely copying from Hussey. However, Hussey occupied several positions that would have given him particular insight regarding Howth family history, as well as administrative concerns and the pressures placed on the Kildare faction. Howth entered two biographical notes regarding Hussey. According to his first note (f. 120r), Hussey lived to the age of 107 and had served in the Irish Exchequer's office over sixty years. Howth made a later entry on Hussey (f. 177r) in which he noted that Hussey died on 9 March 1554 (though Howth here indicated his age as 100). Hussey's official capacities thus spanned fundamental changes in the Dublin administration in a position that would have afforded him particular insight into the evolution of the cess in Ireland, an issue reflected in the section's concluding passages. Additionally, Hussey had intimate connections both to Kildare factionalism and the Howth family. Howth also recorded that Hussey was foster-father to his brother, Richard, the 6th Baron of Howth, whose wife was an illegitimate daughter of the 9th Earl of Kildare, and that Hussey was servant to Howth's great-uncle, William (brother to the 3rd Baron), when William 'slew James Earl of Ormond's brother and seven of his men at the bridge of Kilmainham' (f. 120r). Hussey was then in a position to comment on Kildare affairs and factionalism, its effect on the Howth family, as well as administrative and financial matters.

Hussey's death in 1554 brought his chronicle to an end. The conclusion of this source also brought to an end the first stage of construction on *The Book of Howth* in which Hand VII, Howth's initial scribe, had entered modified copies of and excerpts from existing texts. The termination of Hand VII's scribal work also coincided with the close of the parliamentary session of 1569–71. The two principal subjects with which this section of the manuscript closed – security in Ulster and the cess – reflected Howth's estimation of the concerns of Sidney's term as deputy and set the stage and subject matter both for the second phase of the manuscript's construction and the central episodes of this stage of Howth's political life. With no further sources on which to rely, it also necessitated composition original to Howth in the compilation's next sections.[41]

The Period 1554–79

The latter segments of Howth's creation of a history of Ireland continued where Hussey's work had ended in 1554 and concluded with the onset of the Desmond Rebellion in late 1579. With the exception of copies of two submission statements dating to Howth's imprisonments in 1577 and 1578, the passages in this section were composed by Howth and/or his scribes. They are not consistent in structure, however. Initially, Howth retained two scribes in perhaps relatively rapid succession, Hands IX and III, who worked from 1571 to early 1572. Each of these scribes retained the structure with which Hand VII had concluded by addressing events within the framework of vice-regal administration. Hand IX first contributed an entry covering the period 1556–66 (ff. 120v–127v), covering principally the deputyship of Sussex but also including brief passages on Fitzwilliam and Arnold.[42] Hand III commenced where Hand IX concluded on folio 127v, contributing an entry covering Sidney's first term as lord deputy (ff. 127v–132r).[43] Both of their entries trace conflict between the Old and New English communities and its threat to Old English security. Following their entries, the latter of which had ceased by early 1572, Howth seems to have abandoned the attempt to chronicle events in detail. He returned to the manuscript only intermittently over the remainder of the 1570s to make annal-style entries, some of which referenced much earlier events of the fourteenth and fifteenth centuries (ff. 132v–137v). The majority of the entries made between 1573 and 1579 are in Howth's hand, and their subject matter indicates that his primary concerns continued to be Old English displacement. Surprisingly, given Howth's key role in the cess controversy of 1577–8 he made relatively little reference to that period of open opposition aside from the inclusion of copies of two submission statements, one for each of his imprisonments in 1577 and 1578, and very brief commentary. In what was probably his final return to the manuscript late in 1579, Howth made a brief entry noting the onset of the Desmond Rebellion.

The first entry in this section of the manuscript is devoted largely to Sussex's attempts to subdue Shane O'Neill, presented through detailed descriptions of battles and military strategy. In spite of emerging opposition to Sussex from other members of the Old English community in this period, Howth's presentation of him is positive, noting 'no evil did he ever commit to none that under his power was' (f. 124r). He attempts to minimise both Sussex's conflict with the 11th Earl of Kildare and emerging opposition to the cess.[44] While Howth does note Sussex's abuse of the cess, he attributes opposition to it to the 'many evil disposed doers under him and of his council' (f. 124r). He instead portrays Sussex as one who initially attempted to preserve the position of the Old English, frequently granting them military positions rather than New English officers, attributing his later disregard for the Old English to the legal students' complaint against the cess (f. 125v). Before returning to a discussion of efforts to subdue O'Neill, with which this entry concludes, Howth included a resounding note of support for Sir Nicholas Arnold as lord deputy for his fair use of the cess and his restraint of abusive behaviour by English troops (ff. 125v–126r).

The history continues as Hand III commences where Hand IX had concluded by making an entry covering Sir Henry Sidney's first term as lord deputy. Following its opening brief and generally positive description of Sidney, the scribe makes abbreviated reference to problems with the Scots in Ulster, the first Desmond Rebellion, and the Butler Rebellion which Howth, in a marginal note, attributes to Peter Carew's challenge to Butler landholdings (f. 128v). The text then returns to describe Sidney in greater detail and far more negatively. This description attributes the destruction of the Pale to Sidney's abuse of the cess and criticises Sidney for repeatedly promising but failing to deliver on policies for the improvement of deteriorating conditions in the Pale. This passage is also highly critical of Sidney's attempt to abolish coign and livery. Howth identifies Sidney's attempted abolition, in combination with excessive cess exactions, as the cause of the Pale's economic deterioration and the related deteriorating position of the Old English. He digresses to provide commentary on Old English displacement, stressing that those who have 'experience learned with bloody hand' (ff. 129v–130r) were better able to determine and administer efficacious policies for Ireland. This assessment of the ruinous nature of Sidney's policies was affirmed, he believed, by supernatural events. Following this commentary the scribe noted two events that occurred while Sidney was in office, a hill that purportedly moved 'a good quantity of ground' in 1571 and the destruction of the 1567 harvest by worms (f. 130v). That Howth had joined the opposition to the cess by this time is reflected in the text as it records Howth's role as spokesman for that group (ff. 130v–131r). In spite of the detail with which the previous entry had addressed Sussex's efforts to subdue O'Neill, the entry on Sidney makes limited reference to O'Neill (ff. 128r and 130v) and no reference to O'Neill's death. Howth offers no explicit commentary on provincial presidencies, one of the measures usually regarded as a key policy of Sidney's administration, but the disorder he records in both Connacht and Munster suggests Howth believed they incited rather than prevented disorder.

With the conclusion of this entry early in 1572, Howth abandoned the attempt to chronicle events in detail and does not seem to have retained a scribe for any substantial period of time thereafter, though the next set of brief entries made primarily in Howth's hand indicates his continuing concern with the causes of unrest. In the first of these entries, Howth returned to the subject of Ufford's misgovernment. Howth's perception of the dire state of Ireland is made clear here, for this entry closed by noting that even though the lords in Ireland had complained to the king of Ufford's behaviour, they 'had never so much cause as now is offered and yet we write not nor complain to our prince; God help poor Ireland that is fatherless. Amen' (f. 133r). This is followed by another brief entry on the destruction of Ireland under Steven Scropt as lord deputy in 1399 due to his 'violent extortions'. These were followed by two entries made in 1573 that reflect Howth's continuing concern with instability, but in this case due to the recent plantation efforts in Ulster. While only the second of these, on the attempted schemes of Walter Devereux, Earl of Essex, and Lord Rich, refers directly to their failure, the first contains details of the grant made to Thomas Chatterton, which had also caused concern to Lord Deputy Fitzwilliam, who feared it would destabilise the region.[45] Howth did not return to the manuscript thereafter until his release in 1577 from the first of his incarcerations for opposition to the cess. A copy of one of the cess opponents' submission statements is included, accompanied by commentary reiterating that abusive cess exactions had left Ireland 'utterly decayed and impoverished' and emphasising that the opponents had not challenged royal prerogative as charged (f. 134v). Another submission statement dating to the cess opponents' 1578 imprisonment was later added. Between these two statements, Howth included a note attributing the arrest of Kildare in 1575 to the 'malice' of Robert Dillon and his accomplices (f. 136r). Late in 1579, following his imprisonment on charges of domestic violence and coinciding with his reconciliation with the authorities in Dublin, Howth returned to the manuscript to make what was probably his final entry. In this very brief passage Howth noted Drury's appointment as lord deputy, the murder of Henry Davells and the onset of the Desmond Rebellion (f. 137r).

This entry brought to an end that portion of his compilation in which Howth had created a narrative history of Ireland from the twelfth-century conquest to 1579 by compiling into roughly chronological order extensive excerpts from existing sources, augmented with passages of original composition. The contents of this section indicate Howth's overriding concern to reconsider the progress, successes and failures of English conquest to that point. His portrayal of events conveys moreover an express desire to defend the historical loyalty and success of the Old English. As Howth and each of the scribes contributed to this history they also contributed entries to the miscellaneous collection maintained separately on the manuscript's latter folios. These miscellaneous entries confirm Howth's concern with the misrepresentation of conquest and its failures as they isolate and expand on questions such as England's right to Ireland. They underscore Howth's perception that threats to Old English security were a function of Sidney's policies designed to advance conquest.

II: Miscellaneous Contents

It is perhaps Howth's collection of miscellaneous entries, concentrated in the manuscript's opening and closing folios (ff. A1–A22 and 146–78), that has most misled readers regarding the cohesive nature of the compilation. Here Howth compiled shorter excerpts from the *Polychronicon*, Robert Fabyan's *New Chronicles of England and France*, John Lydgate's *Fall of Princes* and Edmund Campion's *Two Bokes of the Histories of Ireland*, recorded poetry, versions of tales from the Fenian cycle and political prophecy, and made lists of giants, rebellions and landholdings. Though little rationale for their inclusion is provided within the compilation, the subjects of these entries indicate that they were gathered for their relevance to the themes Howth developed elsewhere as he reassessed the history of conquest. Because of their nature, Howth's miscellaneous entries are addressed by grouping them into subject categories.

Howth's Use of Printed Histories: Fabyan, Hall, Stow and the Polychronicon

In addition to using the *Polychronicon* as the source from which to draw excerpts for the introduction to his history of conquest as outlined above, Howth also used it, as well as John Stow's *A Summary of the Chronicles of England*, Robert Fabyan's *New Chronicles of England and France* and Edward Hall's *Chronicle*, in two other ways.[46] He drew from them longer excerpts for inclusion in the miscellaneous collection and also used them to cross-reference entries throughout the entire compilation. Use of these sources also permitted Howth to place events in Ireland into larger English and European contexts. Comparative assessment reveals that Howth used the 1575 edition of Stow, a discovery important in revealing that Howth continued to seek out new sources in later periods of compilation and that as he acquired them he returned to supplement previously entered text.

One of the compilation's earliest examples of Howth's cross-referential use of these four histories is evident in the header he appended to his copy of *The English Conquest of Ireland*. There Howth noted the three conflicting dates assigned to the Anglo-Norman conquest by various authors, one of which was Fabyan.[47] Fabyan's *New Chronicles* would become the most frequently used source for cross-referential material.[48] Howth cross-checked its information against *The English Conquest of Ireland* elsewhere: for example, regarding the rebellion of Henry II's sons (f. 23r–v). Howth also utilised these print histories to trace the historical relationships between Ireland, Scotland and England as a vehicle through which to illustrate Old English loyalty and ties to England. Where the *Polychronicon* had already provided a ready-made historical relationship between the Irish and Scots and a justification of England's 'right' to Scotland, a passage Howth included in its entirety in his miscellaneous collection (f. 163r–v), Howth used Fabyan on several occasions to affirm their integrated histories (ff. 4v, 22v, 163r).[49] He was also able to draw on these sources to further demonstrate the history of Old English loyalty to England. Howth had already used extracts from *Pembridge's Annals* to demonstrate their efforts to repel the Scots in Ireland, thus affirming their loyalty. This loyalty was re-emphasised on a larger stage as Howth extracted a passage from Hall which asserted that forces sent from Ireland were responsible for an English victory in France in 1419.[50]

Howth also drew on Hall for a lengthy excerpt on Suleiman and the Siege of Rhodes (ff. 102r–103iv). Its inclusion in the manuscript conveys Howth's awareness of European concerns regarding Ottoman expansion, but more to the point it was a context he was able to deploy in consideration of problems in Ireland. Many of the newly arriving English came to Ireland having fought against the Ottomans in eastern Europe, and Sidney had already drawn a comparison between Shane O'Neill and the Turks.[51] Howth's excerpt opens by emphasising that the Ottomans were able to expand because of the discord among European rulers, thus drawing a parallel to earlier episodes in *The Book of Howth* in which Howth had explicitly attributed Irish rebellion to opportunities provided by the conquerors themselves as they fought with each other.[52] Though the placement of this passage in Howth's manuscript between the excerpts from *Pembridge's Annals* and Hussey's chronicle might seem illogical, it is probably no coincidence that the scribe responsible for its inclusion – Hand III, who also made the entry on Sidney – saw the opportunity to utilise blank folios there where this episode concerning factionalism in Europe and its detrimental effect could be placed to precede the passage on factionalism in Ireland entered by an earlier scribe.[53] Howth's awareness of and interest in the Islamic world appear again in his inclusion of the life of Muhammad (ff. 168r–173r). Though this excerpt was drawn in its entirety from the *Polychronicon*, and hence its portrayal of Muhammad cannot be attributed specifically to Howth, here too Howth crossreferences that version to Fabyan, noting that Fabyan at one point provided a conflicting date (635 as compared to 620).[54] Interestingly, Howth's version adds commentary to the end of his copied passage that describes Muhammad in terms highly reminiscent of Shane O'Neill (f. 173r). Muhammad is described as given to drink, as was O'Neill both in his attainder and in Campion's history, a characteristic identified as causal in the death of both men and used to denigrate each.[55] Driving home the comparison that he – and Sidney earlier – made, Howth perhaps hoped to use this image to highlight for Sidney the dangers of exacerbating division in Ireland.[56]

Edmund Campion's Two Bokes of the Histories of Ireland

Howth's miscellaneous collection also contains a number of extracts from Edmund Campion's *Two Bokes of the Histories of Ireland* (ff. A13v–A19v, 58v, 103iv, 113v, 133r, 152v–154v and 175r–v). Campion is never cited as a source, but the near-verbatim nature of Howth's excerpts, including even Campion's use of the first person and his chapter headings, reveal it as his source. Most of the excerpts taken from Campion were entered into the set of folios later appended to the manuscript's start (ff. A13v–A19v). Those folios contain copies of Campion's first and second chapters, excerpts on the lives of Saints Patrick and Brigid, and Campion's reproduction of a 1407 letter from the inhabitants of Cork outlining their grievances. Two other items from Campion's work were copied into the miscellaneous contents on the manuscript's latter folios, a 1458 letter from the Duke of York to his brother, the Earl of Salisbury (f. 175r-v), and an entry outlining England's right to Ireland (ff. 152v–154r). Campion's text was also used, as were the print histories discussed above, as a source from which to cull supplemental information to append to the collection's central history (as on ff. 58v, 103iv, 113v and 133r).

With the exception of the entry outlining England's right to Ireland entered by Hand x at some point after September 1573, all of the other excerpts from Campion were entered by Hand IV.[57] Based on this scribe's utilisation of blank folio space, he was probably employed at some point in mid to late 1572. Both hands generally copied very closely from Campion. England's nine-fold right to Ireland and its accompanying commentary, as included in Howth's text, for example, is a verbatim copy of Campion.[58] There is, however, one exception to this practice. Hand IV made several significant modifications to the first two chapters of Campion's work as he copied them into Howth's collection.

Campion's first chapter outlined Ireland's geography by province, county and city. His regional descriptions incorporated lists of principal Irish and Old English inhabitants.[59] Howth's copy made two modifications that altered Campion's portrayal of the Irish in a manner similar to Howth's modification of portrayals of the Irish in the *Polychronicon*. Where Campion recorded the legend that Lough Neagh had been created as punishment 'for the beastial incest committed there', Howth altered the phrase to read 'for the beastial thing commited there', distracting attention from sexual misconduct.[60] The second alteration created a nonsensical, though important, re-presentation of Scots in Ulster. Campion described them as descendants of 'the old Scythian Pict', curiously altered by Howth to read 'the old citizen Pict'.[61] Howth also made alterations to two of Campion's descriptions reflecting Old English behaviour. While he retained Campion's lists of names in this geographical outline, he omitted some of the commentary. From Campion's description of Kilmallock, for example, Howth omitted 'lately sacked by James Fitzmaurice', thereby eliminating reference to rebellion, and he similarly omitted Campion's commentary that Cork contained 'some of Irish blood, some degenerate and become Irish', thereby eliminating reference to Gaelicisation.[62] In copying Campion's second chapter, however, in which Campion listed those who held titles in Ireland and identified each by their degree of Gaelicisation, Howth retained his descriptions. For example, he retained Lord Bermingham's identification as 'now degenerate become mere Irish' as well as Campion's description of Lord Courcy as 'not very Irish'.[63] Howth also took the opportunity to augment Campion's entry on him which had stated only 'Saint Lawrence, Baron of Howth'. Here Howth reasserted his lineage and his ancestral association with John de Courcy adding: 'which came before the conquest in company with Sir John de Courcy earl and president of Ulster . . . ut ait Galfredus Rodebuc St Laurens fuit viri strenui atque fortes et robustissimi in bello.'[64]

Campion's holograph is no longer extant, though A.F. Vossen speculated that Howth may have acquired it.[65] He offered no evidence other than Howth's relationship with the Barnewalls, in whose home Campion hid while composing his history in the spring of 1571, and the fact that the periods of Howth's and Campion's collection activities coincided. Having asserted this relationship, however, Vossen did not undertake a critical comparison of Howth's excerpts with the extant copies of Campion's work. If not the original, Howth had obviously gained access at the least to a copy of it. Campion's departure in the spring of 1571 coincided with the later phases of Howth's most intensive compilation work, and if Howth acquired his work soon after, it was not utilised until the following year, by which point most of Howth's text had already been compiled, possibly accounting for his relatively limited use of it. Based on Hand IV's utilisation of blank folio space, none of the entries taken from Campion were entered before mid 1572. However, one piece of internal evidence suggests that Howth may have seen Campion's original. Howth's version of Campion's first chapter contains a passage regarding Ireland's ecclesiastical hierarchy that none of the extant versions consulted by Vossen contains:

> the primate of Ireland's place in the great convocation at Rome is 22 degrees or seats afore the bishop of Canterbury in England as Sir Henry Sydney reported, being told him by one that came from Rome being an officer for placing of bishops there and the name of his office was called servus serimmonarium [sic].[66]

Such a privileging of the Archbishop of Armagh over the Archbishop of Canterbury may well reflect Howth's religious preference, and thus constitute an addition on his part. More significantly, this passage contains Campion's characteristic reference to Sidney as a source of information, a reference copied by Howth elsewhere, suggesting that Campion's original may have served as Howth's source.[67]

Pre-Norman History

Howth's manuscript included in its entirety a copy of Campion's list of England's nine-fold right to Ireland (ff. 152v–154v). Seven of these items identified events of the conquest and after. Two of them, however, asserted England's pre-Norman right to Ireland, the first based on the Spanish ancestry of the Irish who settled there and were 'subjects to the crown of Brittany' at the time (f. 153v) and the second based on the tributary status of Ireland's king under King Arthur (f. 154r).[68] Howth further investigated Ireland's pre-Norman history by turning to Arthurian legend and episodes from the Fenian cycle.

References to both of Campion's pre-Norman 'rights' had actually already been included in Howth's manuscript as copied from *The English Conquest of Ireland* (f. 48v). Howth consulted Arthurian sources to verify this information, citing 'The Book of King Arthur' in a marginal note accompanying the entry.[69] While the passage itself cites Ireland's submission to Arthur, Howth's marginalia reference the Irish king's resistance but ultimate loss in battle to Arthur, following which the Irish king attempted to force tribute from Cornwall.[70] This episode is addressed further in an entry in Howth's miscellaneous collection (ff. 160r and 161r), where Hand IX (who also made the entry on Sussex) excerpted in greater detail events following that attempt. The two kings agreed to have the matter settled by a fight between their best champions. In that battle, the Irish champion, Sir Marhaus, was defeated by Tristan, thus restoring Ireland's subordinate position, though Howth notes elsewhere that the 'Irish chronicles denied' Tristan's victory (f. 10r–v). In turning to Arthurian lore to explore England's right to Ireland, Howth was in keeping with contemporaries who increasingly utilised this justification as proof of Ireland's long-standing submission to England in the wake of the Reformation when *Laudabiliter*, with its assertion of papal authority, could no longer be invoked.[71]

Howth continued to investigate Ireland's pre-Norman history by addressing its relationship to Denmark. He drew a historical connection between the episodes from Arthurian lore and Danish incursions into Ireland in two locations in the manuscript. The scribe who made the above entries followed his final Arthurian reference with an entry on Danish invasions (f. 162v). The next scribe Howth employed, Hand III (who made the entry on Sidney), returned to this connection. Here he adapted the Fenian *Cath Fionntraghe* to Danish invasions and Arthurian lore by attributing Danish invasions explicitly to the Arthurian episode in which Ireland continued to extract tribute from foreign regions, including Denmark, in spite of its champion's loss to Tristan (f. A10r–v).[72]

Hand III was also largely responsible for the construction of folios A2–A13 on which he entered modified versions of episodes from the Fenian cycle. His passages address various battles between the Irish and the Danes, such as the battles of Gabhra (Garryston) and Fionntraghe (Fentra).[73] The contents of these passages again suggest extensive modification by Howth. They contain Howth's characteristic addition of pre-battle speeches and detailed battle scenes much like those inserted in passages on the twelfth-century conquest and the Battle of Knockdoe. Unusually, Howth assigns a Danish heritage to Fionn mac Cumhaill's band of warriors (ff. A1r and A8r) and attributes further Danish invasions to the Fianna's abuse of the Irish, as a result of which the Irish kings attempt to expel them and the Fianna call for Danish assistance (f. A2r).

Another of the items Hand III excerpted from the Fenian cycle is the episode known as 'The Colloquy of Old Men' in which Oisín survives to tell St Patrick of the Fianna.[74] Howth's version relates a passage in this episode in which Oisín tells of a foreign giant who landed at Howth and proceeded to challenge a succession of Irish kings and champions to battle. He is finally defeated by one of the Fianna after Fionn mac Cumhaill devises a plan to exhaust the giant by keeping him awake at night with stories (f. A9r–v).[75] In an earlier passage Howth's version of the Battle of Gabhra had also made use of this image of a defeated giant when, in a pre-battle morale-building speech, the warriors were called upon to remember the story of David's victory over 'the great Goliath or giant' (f. A3v).

Howth references both Goliath and Irish giants again in a list of giants included in the manuscript's miscellaneous collection (ff. 146v–147r). This list asserts the existence of giants and draws on what he no doubt understood to be an impressive list of authorities as supporting evidence, including Moses, St Augustine, Greek history, Arthurian lore and Boccaccio. Howth was not anachronistic in his belief in the historical existence of giants. Though some had come to challenge the existence of giants by the sixteenth century, references to them continued into the eighteenth century.[76] Both Jewish and Christian writers, including figures in the early Italian renaissance such as Guido da Pisa, Benvenuto da Imola and Jacopo della Luna, no less than Boccaccio, had turned to classical sources to validate their references to giants.[77] Howth, however, does not seem to address giants as a manifestation of unnatural births in the manner in which they usually appear in medieval and early modern discourse as a reflection of crisis.[78] Rather, he seems to reproduce the notion as asserted by Homer and Pliny that the extinction of giants reflected diminution in human size.[79] If so, as with Howth's references to unnatural phenomena, it was this diminution in human stature that reflected an increasingly disordered society. Read alternatively, Howth's list of giants might also have served to affirm the veracity of Irish legends he recorded elsewhere, in particular his versions of Fenian and Arthurian lore. By asserting the existence of giants he implied the veracity of these tales, thus affirming Ireland's historically subordinate status to England.

Gaelicisation, Gaelic Recovery and Failed Conquest

Howth's miscellaneous collection also includes four items that address the contentious issues of Gaelicisation and Gaelic recovery as they related to the question of completed conquest. The first of these is a highly abbreviated version of Finglas's 'Breviate' (ff. 149r–151r).[80] Howth appended to this a list of rebellions in England, probably in response to the document's defamation of the Old English (ff. 151r–152r). Another of the items in this category drew on a document of early sixteenth-century origin to which Howth added the header 'What Ireland is and how much,' containing four lists: a list of Irish chiefs, a list of Gaelicised Old English, a list of loyal counties and a list of regions that paid tribute to Gaelic lords (ff. 173v–174v).[81] The final item provides a much older regional list of landholders and knights' fees owed under Edward II (ff. 155r–158v).[82]

Howth's copy of Finglas's text is in a hand that occurs nowhere else in the manuscript (Hand XII). While it may represent a copy that Howth acquired rather than made, it contains substantial omissions that follow patterns of omission and inclusion exhibited by Howth in copying other documents such as *Pembridge's Annals* and *The English Conquest of Ireland*. Howth's version includes Finglas's opening description of early successful and stable conquest under Strongbow and his immediate successors, his son-in-law, William Marshall, and grandsons. Howth's copy, however, then omits a substantial and lengthy passage that 1) detailed the failure of their successors to sustain English control by retaining Irish captains to oversee their territories, 2) identified Gaelicisation and Gaelic recovery as a problem, and 3) outlined the Statutes of Kilkenny. Howth's version instead skipped to Finglas's list of successive landholders in Meath, Westmeath, Connacht and Ulster, the latter of which addressed de Courcy's successful conquest there, the conflict between de Courcy and de Lacey, and de Lacey's betrayal of de Courcy and subsequent acquisition of Ulster. Howth's copy ends at this point, omitting the remainder of this source in which Finglas laid out proposals for reform and charged the Old English with having failed to accomplish completed conquest. The three other documents in this category are also of relevance to the issue of the conquest's successful completion.

Probably in opposition to Finglas's charges of Gaelicisation and its attendant disregard for English laws, a list of rebellions that had occurred in England since the eleventh century was appended in Howth's hand to the close of the abridgement (ff. 151r–152v). Though it is unclear whether this list was Howth's creation or a copy (though no similar document has been identified), whoever compiled it devoted significant time to its construction, for it culls a list of nearly 200 individuals in England who had rebelled 'against their natural prince' (f. 151r). That number swells considerably when the list of entire towns and regions that rebelled against the monarch are included (Kent, Cornwall, Yorkshire), its note that over 100,000 had participated in a rebellion against Henry III, and its prefatory remark that thousands more were omitted for 'tediousness of time' (f. 151r). The list also identifies kings who engaged in 'dissension and discord' with each other, including Richard II and Henry IV, Henry VI and Edward IV, and Richard III and Henry VII, amongst others (f. 152v). The list is prefaced by a rationale that returns to the subject of misrepresentation: 'the occasion of this remembrance is for that when any of England birth come to Ireland they report and brag that all that therein is are traitors as who would say and affirm that there was nor is any treason ever in England committed' (f. 151r).

In spite of this passage's acquittal of Ireland from charges that rebellion there is either unique or ubiquitous, and the previous passage's omission of reference to Gaelicisation, Howth's miscellaneous collection does include a copy of a document dating to the 1540s that outlines in table format the existence of Gaelicisation and Gaelic recovery (ff. 173v–174v). This list was entered by Hand III, who worked at some point between late 1571 and early 1572, and who also made the entry covering Sidney's first term as lord deputy, as well as the entries relating tales of the Fianna.[83] It first lists the 'chief Irish captains' by region, followed by a regional listing of 'those English noble and worshipful captains was degenerate from the English laws', identifying sometimes individuals and sometimes entire families (f. 173v). In companion format, its final folio first lists obedient English counties, followed by a list – with amounts due – of English counties paying yearly tribute to the 'wild Irish' (f. 174v). This document closes with a return to one of the subjects of Finglas's treatise, the loss of Ulster. It attributes that loss, as did Finglas, to the early conquerors' lack of surviving male heirs and the subsequent partition of the territory among non-resident landholders, a situation that facilitated Gaelic encroachment (f. 174v).

The final document in this category is one in Latin that also lists by region knights' fees owed to Edward ɪɪ in the first year of his reign (1307). The hand of this document (Hand xɪɪɪ) occurs nowhere else in the manuscript, and although difficult to determine, may have been incorporated into rather than copied into the manuscript.[84] It is also difficult to determine precisely why Howth included this document in his collection. It serves at one level to demonstrate the extent of English settlement and landholding by the early fourteenth century, as well as the historical roots of many Old English families in Ireland, and it does so, perhaps not coincidentally, for the period Finglas identified as the final era of stable conquest.[85] However, whether or not it was Howth's intent, when balanced against the above sixteenth-century list, it also serves to demonstrate the 'failure' of their descendants to resist Gaelic encroachment. Unlike many other sections of the manuscript, Howth appended very little marginalia to this document from which to ascertain his interest. The only marginalia of substance address Peter Carew's claim to Butler lands in Munster (f. 156v). This was a subject in which he had expressed interest elsewhere in the manuscript in marginalia attributing the Butler Revolt to Carew's claims (f. 128v).[86]

Poetry

Howth's manuscript includes four items in poetic form, two in Latin and two in English. These items were entered at various points over the course of compilation by Hand ɪv, Hand vɪɪ and Howth. Howth did not cite a source for any of these entries, and no source can be identified definitively for the Latin items. However, the verbatim nature of the two English pieces reveals them to be excerpts from John Lydgate's *Fall of Princes*, an English translation and transformation into poetic form of Laurence de Premierfait's French prose version of Boccaccio's *De Casibus Virorum Illustrium*.[87] Only one of the four pieces, a sixteen-stanza excerpt on the Knights Templar copied from Lydgate, contains commentary and marginalia that permit immediate identification of

Howth's rationale for its inclusion. Although the rationale for the inclusion of the other three items is not made apparent within the text, careful attention to the hand and date of entry for the second item excerpted from Lydgate, a stanza on deceit, reveals this item to be of particular significance in conveying Howth's position at the time the entry was made.

Howth's excerpted entry on the Knights Templar taken from Lydgate was entered in the miscellaneous portion of the manuscript during the initial phase of compilation by Hand VII (ff. 159r–160r).[88] While Lydgate's stanzas describe the demise of the Templars, Howth seems to have been less concerned with the Templars themselves than with the transfer of their lands in Ireland to the Knights Hospitaller following their conviction for heresy. At the entry's start Howth made a marginal cross-reference to the manuscript's earlier mention of the Knights Templar (on f. 69v) where notice of the 1314 transfer of their land in Ireland to the Knights of St John the Baptist (the Hospitallers) had been copied from *Pembridge's Annals* (and he made a similar marginal cross-reference there to these stanzas on the Knights Templar). Following this entry, Hand VII appended additional information expanding upon the earlier reference in *Pembridge's Annals* to identify specifically the lands transferred, land that was later transferred from the Knights Hospitaller to the crown by a 1560 Act of the Irish parliament.[89] Howth's marginal note, 'Templars' possessions given', corroborates that his concern was land transfer, a concern expressed in other locations within the compilation.

As noted above, the other item Howth excerpted from Lydgate was a single stanza on the subject of deceit:

> Deceit deceiveth and shall be deceived
> For by deceit who is deceivable
> Though his deceit be not out perceived
> To a deceiver deceit is returnable
> Fraud quit with fraud is fit reward
> For who with fraud fraudulent is bound
> To a defrauder fraud will always rebound[90]

This entry serves as a pre-eminent example of the critical importance that hand analysis and date of entry play in assessing Howth's compilation. There is little initially by which to assess to whom or to what Howth attached this ominous passage. It contains no accompanying marginalia and was placed on an originally blank folio between the excerpts from Campion and a section on the Battle of Clontarf.[91] While either of its surrounding entries might possibly suggest context, there is nothing definitive to support its attachment to either Campion or Brian Boru. If Howth had seen a full copy of *The Fall of Princes*, which he seems to have, given the other, lengthier excerpt from that work on the Knights Templar, he would probably have been aware of this stanza's full context in Lydgate. The stanza's context there offers other possibilities. Lydgate included this stanza as a moralising conclusion to the story of the fall of Metius, king of Alba Longa, who failed to honour his submission to the Romans by assisting their enemies, for which he suffered death by dismemberment as punishment for his 'divided allegiance'. Lydgate's commentary advises princes to 'never let it be said that your words are contrary to your deeds', and his succeeding lines draw attention to the detrimental effects of a ruler's use of deceit to purposefully mislead 'the unwary . . . folk most prudent in their estate notable'.[92] Howth very likely had Sidney in mind when he chose this item for inclusion. The hand that made this entry worked at some point after mid 1572, following Sidney's first term as lord deputy. The other passage this scribe entered was highly critical of Sidney, noting in particular his failure to implement promised policies (f. 129r), and it was likely as he made that entry that he turned to this blank folio to enter this stanza on deceit.[93] Use of this passage as political commentary was common among Lydgate's readers. As Nigel Mortimer has noted, 'manuscripts containing excerpts from the *Fall* . . . are often the result of a careful selection of thematically similar passages, or of excerpts that contribute meaningfully to other texts in the manuscript'.[94] Howth likewise carefully selected and entered this passage as he considered the detrimental impact of Sidney's first term as lord deputy.

The first of the two Latin pieces in Howth's collection is also ominous in tone and more substantial than the 'scribbling' or 'book rhymes so dear to schoolboys', as it was described by St John Seymour:

> *Sorti supernorum scriptor rubri societur*
> *Morti malignorum raptor libri copuletur.*[95]

This item was entered very early in the manuscript's compilation by the main scribe, Hand VII, where it was placed between the conclusion of the excerpts from the *Polychronicon* and the modified copy of *The English Conquest of Ireland* (f. 5v). Though it seems unlikely that such a warning should be attached to either of those works, precisely which 'red book' this references is unknown. Several works in this period were known as such, including *The Red Book of Ossory*, *The Red Book of Ormond*, *The Red Book of the Exchequer* and *The Red Book of Kildare*, the collection maintained by Philip Flatsbury. In addition to their more formal or administrative function, each of these collections also contained various scribal entries, including poetry. Two of these in particular, *The Red Book of Kildare* and *The Red Book of the Exchequer*, may be the source for Howth's couplet. *The Red Book of the Exchequer* contains numerous couplets of a similar genre and is a work to which Hussey, a clerk in the Exchequer and one of Howth's sources, may have had access, and though there is no evidence that Howth had direct access to Flatsbury's compilation, several of his excerpts such as the Kildare genealogies and obituaries (ff. 60r–61r) parallel those contained in TCD MS 581 where that scribe cited his source as 'The Red Book', presumably Flatsbury.[96] However, while there are several likely sources for this couplet, it is not extant in any of them.

The second of the two Latin pieces was entered at the bottom of the verso of the manuscript's last folio by Howth:

> *Non bene venit homo*
> *Nisi bibat ad ostium stando.*[97]

As with the item above, no source can be identified for this, and there is little surrounding context by which to gauge its meaning or the rationale for its inclusion. The folio's verso contains only one other item, a short note at the top entered by Howth providing further biographical information on Walter Hussey. While there is no evidence as to the date of its entry, its placement at the very end of the manuscript suggests it may have been entered at or near the work's completion in late 1579. If so, this would have coincided with Howth's reconciliation with the Dublin authorities and, as the couplet may be of Howth's composition given its elementary style, it may reflect an autobiographical allusion to that reconciliation after a decade of opposition.

Political Prophecy

Howth regarded political prophecy seriously, as did many of his contemporaries and forebears.[98] Inclusion of this genre permitted him to consider further the question of failed conquest. Among the items in the manuscript's miscellaneous collection are copies of two political prophecies entered by Hand VII during the initial stage of compilation (f. 176r–v). The inclusion of these items alone signifies their importance to Howth, and it is emphasised by his appended list referencing earlier folios on which prophecies had been copied from *The English Conquest of Ireland*. Howth confidently asserted their legitimacy, stating 'many prophecies of Ireland are fulfilled as appear in Camerans' book' (f. 176v).[99] The prophecies Howth cited foretold the difficulty of completing the conquest and suggesting it would not be achieved until shortly before 'Doomsday'.[100] Howth's act of copying these prophecies into his manuscript was in contravention of the 1563 statute against promulgation of political prophecy in all of 'the Queen's dominions', particularly as their content suggested seditious intent by challenging the efficacy of Tudor policies in Ireland.[101]

Collections of political prophecy had circulated since the twelfth century, and it is perhaps from one of these, identified by Howth only as 'the Latin book', that the first was acquired.[102] It made use of time and animal symbolism to reference individuals and events traditional to medieval prophecy, beginning 'the bull shall come to Ireland and begin to be a conqueror', also foretelling that '30 years after the killing of the said calf there shall come from the parts of Scotland the bear with the dog'. Though the language of prophecy was designed to be cryptic, it was not so cryptic as to defy meaning for those who utilised it, and it was indeed this symbolism that gave political prophecy resiliency by permitting succeeding generations to reinterpret prophecies as needed.[103] This same prophecy of Howth's, however, makes uncharacteristic reference to specific locations and families. It includes references to the Field of Mullaghmast, Saint Thomas Court in Dublin, the 'city of Brid' and the Geraldines. Howth's second prophecy, attributed to the Irish 'prophet' St Brechan, also utilised animal symbolism as in the following passage: 'the swan shall swim the river along and trouble the water with his toe; the antelope shall chase the wolf's whelp when the old wolf is gone.' This prophecy made use of another trait common to prophecy, numerology. It begins: 'In Ireland the matter shall begin at the number of seven and it shall be made an end by the number of an eleven.' Howth certainly contravened the 1563 statute by deciphering the prophecy, noting in the margin that its reference to the sun ('the sun shall fade and lose his light') referred to the Duke of York (f. 176r).[104]

Recurring episodes of the promulgation of political prophecy were associated with periods of rebellion or crisis in England, as during the fifteenth century, and their prominence rose again from the 1530s on in tandem with opposition to religious changes, hence the first of the Tudor injunctions against them in 1542.[105] Many of the prophecies were understood to reference political conflict, either affirming or challenging those in power, hence government fears of prophecy's power to incite rebellion. They also often contained references to the social and economic instability that accompanied periods of conflict or signified an illegitimate ruler, in the form of references to disturbances in the natural world, particularly occasions of famine.[106] The second prophecy Hand VII copied into Howth's manuscript had closed with such a reference. It stated that following a transition of power ('the sun shall shine out of the northeast; then the moon shall change at the full') 3,000 would be killed in one day and during the ensuing anarchy there would be no grooms to keep the horses whereupon they would destroy the fields of corn (f. 176v). Howth may have perceived Ireland to be in such a period of crisis, a crisis reflected in the natural world. It was soon after the above prophecy was entered, in the midst of his entry on Sidney, that Hand III recorded the two unusual events noted above, the 1567 destruction of the harvest by worms and the hills that purportedly moved of their own accord in 1571, one in Ireland and one in England (f. 130v). Howth's belief that disturbances or unusual occurrences in the natural world reflected political contexts occurs yet elsewhere in his compilation. The same scribe who entered these two prophecies, Hand VII, also copied into the manuscript's miscellaneous collection a list of unnatural phenomena excerpted primarily from Fabyan (ff. 165r–167r). This included a list of the regnal years during which comets had appeared, to which Howth added: 'which is a sign of the change of the prince or pestilence' (f. 165v). Other items on this list included raindrops in the form of crosses of blood, windstorms and the appearance of two moons.

Women in The Book of Howth

The final category of items in Howth's compilation is references to women. These entries are scattered throughout the manuscript, drawn from a number of sources, including Stow, Fabyan and Boccaccio, and occur both as embellishments to passages within longer entries and as brief, independent entries (ff. A1r, A13r, A20v–A21r, 9r–v, 66r, 160v, 162r, 166r). Each of the entries references a woman either in a position of power over men or positioned closely enough to powerful men to effect pivotal events. With one exception, each also integrates some element of female sexual behaviour. Though Queen Elizabeth appears directly in *The Book of Howth* only in the context of Howth's assertions of loyalty to her as contained in the copy of his submission statements relating to the cess oppositions of 1577–8 and as he recorded her query regarding his ability to speak English, the composite nature of the entries on women suggests that Howth used them to explore covertly the issue of female rule, an issue of immediate and central concern to his contemporaries in Ireland and England.[107] Those who had expressed their fears, concerns and resistance to Elizabeth as a female monarch often suffered severe punishment. John Stubbs, for example, had his right hand amputated for composing a pamphlet against Elizabeth's proposed marriage to the Duke of Alencon.[108] Ambiguity was thus essential.

Four of Howth's references to women represent embellishments to passages within larger entries copied into his collection. Each of these addresses an episode of foreign incursion in Ireland, all of which are attributed ultimately to women who followed their sexual desires. The first two examples address Danish invasion. In the first episode the Danes arrive as a result of the king of Ulster's desire for the king of Connacht's wife. In their ensuing strife the Danes are called to assist Ulster (f. A8r). The second embellishment occurs in Howth's version of the Battle of Clontarf. This battle was precipitated, according to Howth, when the liaison between Brian Boru's son, Murrough, and the wife of a Dublin merchant was discovered. Brian agreed to the cuckolded husband's request for battle, and the husband called for Danish assistance (ff. A20v–A21r). In the third episode, Howth embellishes *The English Conquest of Ireland* by elaborating on the story of the affair between O'Rourke's wife and Dermot MacMurrough with explicit sexual detail (f. 9r-v).[109] Howth emphasises that this affair led to MacMurrough's need for outside assistance when O'Rourke gathered forces against him, assistance granted by Henry II. In the final episode the situation is reversed, as an unnamed foreign queen and her seven female attendants – all dressed in male clothing – travel to Connacht because the queen has fallen in love with their prince. When they arrive several battles ensue in which the queen and her ladies are victorious initially. Eventually unhorsed and defeated, the queen's gender is discovered. Order and peace are restored when, subsequent to her return to health, she and the prince marry.

Howth's shorter entries on women address Zenobia, Elfleda (wife of Edward I), the lesbians Havycya and Lucya, Joan of Arc and Pope Joan. While specific sources for the four embellishments above cannot be identified, and like much else in the collection they may have been Howth's creations, Howth was certainly also searching out information on women, for these shorter entries were obtained by turning again to works readily available in print. Howth cites Fabyan as the source for the entry on Elfleda, Stow for the entry on Havycya and Lucya, and Boccaccio for the entry on Zenobia. Boccaccio was probably also his source for the entry on Pope Joan. Howth's entry on Zenobia is anomalous for its omission of reference to sexual behaviour, for it notes only that Zenobia 'was the best and hardiest of women that ever was in martial feats of arms' (f. A1r). Elfleda is singled out for her abstinence, a vow she took as it was 'not seemly to a king's daughter to use such fleshly liking' (f. 166r). Howth's other two examples, Pope Joan (f. 160v) and Joan of Arc (f. 162r), note that each of these women conceived children illegitimately. Howth's final item references Havycya, a noble woman who had already borne several children when she 'beget upon another woman [Lucya] three sons one after another' (f. 66r).

Elizabeth's rule as a woman was of concern to many, and Howth may have found consolation in the example of Zenobia. His other references resonate with contemporary concerns regarding Elizabeth's gender, particularly the issues of sexuality, marriage and childbearing.[110] There were recurring rumours that Elizabeth and Leicester had conceived several illegitimate children, to which Howth's entries on Joan of Arc and especially Pope Joan – as illicit head of the church – might have been in reference.[111] The legend of Pope Joan, which had arisen in the thirteenth century, was frequently used by Catholics and Protestants alike in England to challenge Elizabeth's position as head of the church.[112] Of course, Elizabeth was also represented as the Virgin Queen, possibly the persona Howth had in mind when recording the entry on Elfleda.[113] Though Howth certainly did not intend to challenge the legitimacy of the Anglo-Norman invasion, each of his embellished passages illustrated the reality of foreign intervention as a result of intimate relationships, and Howth may have been aware of concerns circulating in England that should Elizabeth marry the Duke of Alencon England would be open to French intervention.[114] Alencon's first visit to England took place in August 1579, and Howth was certainly interested in the subject of powerful women at that time, entering the item on Pope Joan in autumn 1579 (if not also the other brief entries on women scattered throughout the collection at that time).[115] The entry on Havycya and Lucya, however, fits less easily into concerns attendant upon Elizabeth's gender, the question of her marriage, and her position not only as monarch but as head of a reformed church.

Though Howth did not organise the results of his research into a polished treatise, structural analysis opens its contents to decipherment. It reveals the care exercised in the placement of entries as successive scribes employed by Howth over the ten-year period 1569–79 each purposefully lodged their respective contributions either in the creation of the chronologically ordered history of conquest or in the collection of miscellaneous entries maintained on the manuscript's latter folios. In this case, because Howth maintained the compilation in stages over an extended period of time, the use of multiple scribes is actually an advantage rather than a disadvantage. It is the isolation of each hand that permits delineation of precisely which entries were made by each scribe, allowing reconstruction of the stages by which the work was compiled. Building on this, evidence internal to each scribe's entries permits us to determine within a relatively confined range of dates the period during which he worked. From this attention can then be directed to the subject matter of each scribe's entries, permitting the identification of Howth's concerns at specific points in time and their placement within the historical context.

It is only by accommodating all of these elements that Howth's compilation can be productively assessed. Of greatest importance is the revelation that much of Howth's work on the manuscript took place between 1569 and 1572. This period, within the context of and immediate aftermath of Sidney's first term as lord deputy, was critical in the formulation of Old English identity. It saw two distinct colonial communities emerge in competition for ownership and control of the conquest. What Howth's compilation conveys of his response to that development is expanded upon in the following chapter's more detailed contextualisation and assessment of its contents.

4. Colonial Conflict and Positioning:
Assessing *The Book of Howth*

Howth's compilation was driven by competing perceptions of failed conquest. This issue had been central to Tudor administrators' and analysts' policies for the transformation of English governance in Ireland since its first clear articulation in Patrick Finglas's 'Breviate' in the reign of Henry VIII. The question resurfaced with particular intensity early in the Elizabethan era during Sidney's first term as lord deputy when the 1569 Act for the Attainder of Shane O'Neill used a portrait of failed conquest both to laud Sidney for having at last achieved this centuries-old objective and as the premise on which to predicate his proposals for reform. This dual purpose had dual implications for the Old English: it implied their historical failure as colonial administrators and thus could be used as grounds on which to justify their displacement. Howth's collection countered such presentations of failed conquest and its implications, positing instead an alternative presentation of events in which successful conquest had been impeded historically not by an established colonial community, but by succeeding waves of newly arriving landholders, administrators, military officers and soldiers who, he argued, misrepresented the history and state of conquest in the service of advancing policies to their own benefit. Howth's extended portrait of conquest and its failures simultaneously defended a threatened Old English community and challenged the efficacy of Sidney's reforms.

Attention to the structure by which Howth's manuscript was compiled is an essential prerequisite to assessing its contents. Attempting to read the entries in the order in which they are now bound is futile; without dating or context it becomes even more difficult. The tendency is to look first at what seems to be the work's central focus, a reconstruction of the history of conquest, as suggested by that history's length and coherency, for clues as to the compilation's rationale and meaning. This is misleading, for it is assessment of the miscellaneous collection within the context of dating permitted by structural analysis that proves to be the most beneficial first step in assessing the entire collection. With the exception of several brief entries, all of the miscellaneous contents were collected during the first phase of compilation, the majority of them during its foundational stage. They appear initially to be one of the manuscript's most perplexing elements, with little apparent cohesion in subject matter, which ranges from lists of giants, Irish captains, prophecies and rebellions to passages on the Knights Templar, Arthurian lore and women. Along with their seemingly random nature, the placement of these entries on the manuscript's latter folios further encourages their dismissal. Though there is no concrete evidence from which to deduce whether the history and miscellaneous collection were initiated simultaneously or whether one was conceived before the other, certainly both were begun by Howth's first scribe and both respond to the same stimuli. When the miscellaneous contents are assessed first and used as a framework within which to assess Howth's history, as opposed to use of the history as a framework within which to interpret the miscellaneous contents, we find the dating of phase one not only confirmed but refined by consideration of the miscellaneous entries' subject matter. From this subject matter we can see that as Howth began to compile the miscellaneous entries he was not collecting randomly: he collected items specifically in response to the early parliamentary sessions of January–March 1569. These parliamentary sessions give clarity and cohesion to Howth's miscellaneous contents and provide the rationale for his particular presentation of the history of conquest.

Phase One: 1569–72

The era in which the early parliamentary sessions of 1569 took place was a turbulent one for the Old English and was described by Canny as 'traumatic' for them.[1] A number of events induced considerable anxiety among members of the Old English community regarding the security of their position and resulted in a variety of responses, some in the form of parliamentary opposition and some in the form of rebellion. The anxieties of this period induced a transformation in Howth's position that is revealed in his compilation. The first of the threats of this period came in the form of challenges to Old English landholdings when Sidney blatantly intervened to secure Peter Carew's claim to Butler holdings in Munster and to land in Meath held by Sir Christopher Cheevers, Howth's cousin and a leading figure in the complaint against Sussex's cess.[2] Sidney's intervention was perceived by some as indication of his intent to privilege New English colonial interests even against two influential Old English families; his intent to secure land in Ireland for New English groups was evident elsewhere in his support for plantation schemes in Munster and Ulster, schemes that severely destabilised those regions.[3] While those plans ostensibly involved only lands under Irish control, Sidney's partisan support of Carew's rival claims to Old English lands suggested that this was not the case. Fears regarding loss of land left a significant portion of the Old English community in the throes of 'incipient hysteria', as described by Victor Treadwell, by the time parliament opened only weeks after Carew's case was settled.[4]

This atmosphere contributed substantially to the manner in which some members of the Old English responded to the next threat confronting them. When parliament opened in January 1569, debates arose immediately as a group led by Edmund Butler and Christopher Barnewall, father-in-law to two of Howth's children, challenged the legitimacy of newly seated New English members in the commons, including John Hooker, Carew's solicitor in his recent land case settled only weeks before parliament opened.[5] Treadwell suggested that this exacerbated Old English concerns as New English arrivals now had not only land, but a legislative base as well, thus facilitating the passage of bills that might otherwise have been defeated by Old English opposition.[6] Carew's appointment to the Irish privy council weeks after parliament's opening must have compounded this fear, for here Carew gained the opportunity to effect reforms without parliamentary consent, such as the implementation of provincial councils, another perceived threat to Old English authority at the local and regional level.[7]

Contention was rife in the debate that followed regarding parliamentary membership and in the opposition that quickly developed to some of the first bills proposed.[8] Much of that legislation was designed, as G.A. Hayes-McCoy has argued, 'to promote the policy of conquest'.[9] Fully half of the bills addressed economic and military reforms, two central and related planks in Sidney's programme for completed conquest. These measures also threatened Old English security, and it was in regard to these bills that some of the most significant opposition arose.[10] Three of the bills directly served Sidney's plans to centralise and regularise military forces, the bills exempting Sidney from the prohibition on retaining Scots mercenaries and the abolition of captainries, while another, the Act for the Attainder of Shane O'Neill, addressed Sidney's plan to abolish coign and livery.[11] All of these measures contributed to Old English displacement by limiting their former exercise of military roles.

The rectification of Ireland's economic problems as perceived by Sidney served as the focus of other legislation designed to regulate mercantile practices and increase revenue. These issues were addressed in the bills concerning fisheries, tanning, import duties on wine, the production of hemp, and export duties on wool, linen and hides (the latter of which simultaneously served Sidney's military programme by keeping provisions in Ireland), regulation that would be extended to new areas through the shiring bill.[12] These bills generated further opposition in the commons.[13] In particular, debate between Hooker and the Butler-Barnewall group intensified as the Old English members opposed the wines bill, a significant plank in Sidney's proposals for fiscal policy. The debate that followed created yet other challenges for the Old English, and reflected the intensifying conflict between the new and established colonial communities, again involving Hooker.

In response to their opposition to the wines bill Hooker gave a caustic speech in the commons questioning Old English loyalties. He compared their behaviour to that of 'the unthankful Israelites against Moses, the unkind Romans against Camillus, Scipio, and others, and as the ungrateful Athenians against Socrates'.[14] This denigration of their character and intent further threatened the Old English by challenging the premise of their opposition, their loyalty, and in effect their identity, refining the distinction between the two colonial communities that Sidney's attempt to ameliorate in his final speech before parliament two years later only emphasised.[15] As the third session neared its end in early March 1569 the composite effect of these threats was evident in the rapidly deteriorating relationship between Sidney and the Old English, a situation Nicholas White noted with surprise when he returned to Dublin from London in March 1569 and reported to Cecil.[16] Within months its acceleration became apparent elsewhere as the Butlers entered into rebellion. Howth's response to this increasing tension is first revealed in his compilation's miscellaneous collection.

The contents of Howth's miscellaneous collection suggest that he was compiling information specifically in response to the bills, debates and issues raised by the early parliamentary sessions.[17] A number of Howth's entries address precisely those items singled out by Treadwell as particularly 'ominous' for the Old English, namely the bills concerning shiring and the elimination of captainries.[18] These bills would account for Howth's inclusion of the list of Irish and English captains (ff. 173v–174v) and his copy of two documents that addressed shiring, territory and potential revenues (f. 1r–v). That Howth was collecting in response to current events is also suggested by other items. As noted above, parliament opened amidst considerable tension regarding land transfer in the wake of the Carew case, a development further advanced by Sidney's attempts to transfer remaining monastic lands to Crown control not only in Connacht and Ulster but in the Pale as well, through the bill of treason against Oswald Massinberde, prior of the Hospitallers. Howth considered this bill by including various entries on the Knights Templar where, as his marginalia and cross-referential notation indicate, his concern was not with the Knights Templar themselves but rather to reconstruct a history of the transfer of their possessions to the Hospitallers (ff. 68v, 69v, 159r–160r).[19] Yet elsewhere the bill exempting the lord deputy from the prohibition on retaining Scots mercenaries may account for Howth's use of historical example to demonstrate the detrimental effect of the administration's reliance on the Scots and probably explains as well Howth's excerpt from the *Polychronicon* on England's right to Scotland (f. 163r–v). Hooker's castigation of Old English loyalties and identity noted above may account for Howth's extensive list of rebellions in England; this list was prefaced with a clear statement that the purpose of this entry was to challenge the misrepresentation by those newly arrived from England that all of Ireland's inhabitants were traitors (ff. 151r–152v).[20] Finally, elements of the Act for the Attainder of Shane O'Neill, another of the items identified by Treadwell as particularly ominous for the Old English for its references to the abolition of coign and livery, are reflected in Howth's miscellaneous contents, notably in his abridged copy of Patrick Finglas's 'Breviate', an abridgement that excerpted only those elements of Finglas adopted for use in O'Neill's attainder.[21]

All of the items gathered in Howth's miscellaneous collection, others of which are discussed further below, can be accounted for by addressing them within the context of the early parliamentary sessions of 1569. In the miscellaneous collection we can see only that Howth was concerned enough with parliamentary proceedings to compile information in response to them, but we cannot always determine his position on them with precision. However, when this context is then applied to Howth's history, which provided him with the narrative flexibility to address these issues at greater length, his opposition is evident. In particular, the Act for O'Neill's attainder may have been the single most influential factor that motivated Howth to compile: his history is an extended examination of and rejection of virtually every

point posited by that piece of legislation. These points lay the foundation for Howth's compilation and the oppositional stance he took.

The Act for the Attainder of Shane O'Neill was a document of
fundamental significance to Sidney's entire programme for Ireland, and
it therefore sought multiple objectives.[22] One of these, of course, was
the formal declaration of attainder, in the service of which the Act's
preamble outlined the history of O'Neill's treason as justification for the
redistribution of territory in Ulster. This preamble, however, unique
among attainders of the Tudor period, went well beyond the issue of
O'Neill to address far more comprehensively the issue of conquest, its
historical failures and its successful completion. To that end it included
two other overlapping histories that outlined England's right to Ireland
and a history of failed conquest using Finglas's 'Breviate' and Giraldus
Cambrensis as sources.[23] All three of these histories, which constitute
three distinct subsections within the attainder's preamble, rely heavily
on presentations of failed conquest. Ireland is portrayed as at the
threshold of a new era, its past a history of failure and its future one of
success. Sidney is lauded as the individual responsible for both; he has
brought the past to a close with the elimination of the threat posed by
O'Neill, and his reforms will take Ireland into a prosperous future. This
portrait of the past implicitly blames the Old English for failed conquest
by its twice-repeated reference to conquest now completed after 404
years. These histories also simultaneously serve to advertise Sidney and
dismiss, if not castigate, the Old English in other ways. The preamble's
history of Sidney's victories against O'Neill, for example, makes no
mention of the part played by the Old English.[24] Each of these histories
also integrates a careful portrait of Ireland's past as one of economic
decay, another failure implicitly attributed to the Old English, to be
remedied now by Sidney's new policies, described as 'good government' by the attainder for the multiple benefits they will bring.[25] These
benefits are encapsulated in the abolition of coign and livery, one of
Sidney's principal objectives, in praise of which the preamble culminated. This one measure would eradicate what Sidney perceived to be
the problematic retention of local military power and release resources
to the disposal of the administration, achieving both the centralisation
and regularisation of military forces and the economy.[26] Coign and
livery, however, was practised by the Old English as well as the Irish,
and its abolition would impact both communities. It would not only
limit Old English colonial exercise of military roles and interfere with
the economic relationship between lord and tenant by redirecting

resources and obligations to centralised institutions, it would dismantle the entire fabric of social relationship between lord and tenant, undermining Old English status and local authority.

Howth vehemently opposed the abolition of coign and livery. This position was stated in no uncertain terms near the end of the first phase of his compilation, as Howth addressed it under his entry on Sidney's administration, the chronological point in his history at which it was appropriate to do so. However, by the time Howth made this entry Sidney's intent to abolish this practice had been advertised two years earlier in O'Neill's attainder, and it was within that earlier context that Howth had begun to compile. Just as the items noted above in Howth's miscellaneous collection can be accounted for by their relevance to the early parliamentary sessions of 1569, so too can the remaining items entered in Howth's miscellaneous collection during the first phase of compilation be accounted for by their relevance to O'Neill's attainder. The two principal sources upon which the attainder relied, Finglas's 'Breviate' and Giraldus Cambrensis' *Expugnatio Hibernica*, were included by Howth. From the 'Breviate' Howth excerpted only those passages used in the attainder for placement in his miscellaneous collection, as noted above, and though there is no evidence that Howth had access to a full text of the *Expugnatio Hibernica*, he included a nearly complete copy of this work in the abridged form in which it circulated in Ireland, *The English Conquest of Ireland*, as the foundation of his history of conquest (see Chapter Three). The latter of these two items led Howth to extract from it and place in the miscellaneous collection in table form a list of its prophecies regarding the conquest of Ireland, supplemented with two additional prophecies.

Howth also included a list of unnatural phenomena, events that signified poor government as he perceived Sidney's administration to be, an association he would draw again more clearly in the entry on Sidney's administration made near the end of the history. An examination of decay is evident elsewhere in what seems to be one of the most unusual items in Howth's collection: his list of giants. Howth was in keeping with contemporaries in asserting the historical existence of giants, a belief that began to decline only in the mid Elizabethan era, and his reference to them may reflect the popular belief that the existence of giants in the past and the diminution of human size into the present reflected the general deterioration of human society.[27] Howth's assertion that giants once existed but no longer did parallels his presentation of the history of conquest as one in which Ireland deteriorated as the result of poor government by newly arrived colonials. This presentation of deterioration also countered the presentation of Ireland in O'Neill's attainder as in a state of recovery under Sidney's policies. Thus, the natural world here too reflected society's ills. When we turn again to Howth's history, we can see that not only were items in Howth's miscellaneous collection gathered in response to the attainder, but that Howth's entire history seems to have been catalysed by the attainder's presentation of failed conquest, proposals for its rectification, and the role (or lack thereof) of the Old English in both.

Howth's history of conquest was constructed entirely during phase one (1569–72) of the manuscript's compilation in three stages. Howth's marginalia are important in directing the reader's attention to his interpretation of various passages, and the question he lodged to precede his copy of *The English Conquest of Ireland*, 'What was the stay or let of the conquest that Ireland was not made one or belonging to one?', should not be underestimated (f. 5v). This is the heart of the entire compilation. The contents themselves reveal that Howth was not interested in a history of Ireland, and, in fact, he only came to consider pre-Norman Ireland during the final stage of phase one in 1572 and only within the very specific context of conquest. Rather, as Howth began to collect, his primary concern was to address a history of conquest from its Anglo-Norman inception to the present and, even more specifically, to address the question of failed conquest, the framework on which O'Neill's attainder depended. The attainder's use of history may indeed even have motivated Howth's decision to create his own history as the vehicle through which to develop his response to it.

Just as the attainder's histories had done, Howth's history integrated the issues of economic decay, administrative policy and the position of the Old English, though to very different ends than the attainder. Howth's history suggests that the history of conquest as portrayed in that document was misrepresented and that it posited inaccurate conclusions, for it was not an established colonial community that had historically impeded conquest, but a newly arriving colonial community. The issue of misrepresentation would surface throughout Howth's history as he sought to demonstrate that over the course of the conquest it had been used repeatedly by a newly arriving colonial community to displace the old. Once in a position of dominance, Howth argued, the new community's policies served only to create socio-political instability, economic decay and conflict between the colonial communities, all of which impeded conquest by permitting the Irish to gain the offensive and resist conquest. In stressing this point Howth would even turn to the example of Suleiman and the window for Ottoman encroachment on Hapsburg territory provided by conflict in Europe (ff. 102r–103iv). Many of the sources on which Howth relied already included an integrated address of failed conquest, economic decay, misrepresentation and conflict within the colonial community. However, our ability to undertake close comparison of Howth's manuscript with his sources is critical here, for it reveals that Howth modified those sources substantially in order to emphasise or expand on the integration of these issues. As Howth continued to address these issues in the entries of original composition that brought the history up to date from 1554 to 1572, he was able to address more recent manifestations of the established colonial community's displacement and its effect on policies such as the cess and the abolition of coign and livery.

The subject of misrepresentation surfaces in various guises throughout Howth's entries, always linked either to the displacement of individuals within the Old English community or to that group as a whole. The very opening of his history even conveys a challenge to the accuracy of the attainder's assertion that the conquest had begun 404 years earlier, which would have placed it in 1165 as opposed to 1169.[28] Preceding his copy of *The English Conquest of Ireland* Howth logged four conflicting dates attributed to the inception of the Anglo-Norman conquest – 1155, 1163, 1167 and 1170 – none of which accord with the attainder's dating of this event (f. 6r). Howth expended great effort in researching these dates, turning to various sources such as Fabyan to do so. As Howth proceeded to copy from his abridgement of Giraldus Cambrensis, one of the writers upon whom the attainder had relied in large part for its presentation of the conquest in justification of Old English displacement, he challenged even the reliability of that document, expanding on its passages to reinforce his own standpoint on misrepresentation and its detrimental effect on the Old English and, ultimately, a successfully completed conquest.

Howth made four major additions to his copy of *The English Conquest of Ireland*, each detailing episodes in the twelfth-century conquest of Ulster led by John de Courcy and Howth's ancestor, Tristram Amorey St Lawrence. These additions outlined de Courcy's success in establishing conquest and his ultimate displacement as the result of Hugh de Lacey's misrepresentation of de Courcy's motives as self-serving rather than in the interests of the English king. It was not only de Lacey who engaged in false representation here, Giraldus did as well, for Howth asserts that Giraldus had purposefully omitted these episodes, stating: 'you may see what the world is that vanity draweth truth aside as it shall appear hereafter of other things which the said Camerans did for displeasure' (f. 42r).[29] This further served Howth's larger point that events had been misrepresented purposely from the inception of the conquest, as portrayed by Giraldus, to its purported conclusion under Sidney, as portrayed in O'Neill's attainder, the effect of which in all cases was displacement of the established colonial community. Just as Giraldus had omitted the role of the earliest colonial community, including Howth's ancestor, in portraying the conquest's initial successes, so too had the attainder misrepresented its assertion of the conquest's conclusion under Sidney by omitting the role of the Old English, including Howth, in efforts against O'Neill.[30] Just as Howth's history supplied detail regarding de Courcy by adding to *The English Conquest of Ireland*, so would he later similarly supply the attainder's missing detail in his entries that addressed O'Neill (ff. 120v–131r). In both of these episodes Howth portrayed a situation in which the established colonial community had been successful in advancing the conquest through use of diplomacy and military force. The loyalty and ability of the established colonial community as demonstrated in these examples were re-emphasised by Howth in numerous other episodes, such as their successes in defeating the Bruce invasion (ff. 79r–80v) and at the Battle of Knockdoe (ff. 108r–112v), among others. The historical loyalty of the Old English, Howth therefore argued, did not warrant the displacement that histories which misrepresented or simply omitted these episodes attempted to justify.

Misrepresented histories had contributed substantially to the displacement of the Old English, but so too had misrepresentation of individuals and their motives. This was again an element already contained within the sources on which Howth drew, but his additions underscore its historical recurrence as a factor in the displacement of a loyal and successful colonial community. Their motives were frequently misrepresented by newly arriving colonials to serve their own ends, Howth would assert, or in the attempt to usurp royal authority. Such behaviour had occurred in one episode in *The English Conquest of Ireland*, among others, in which Hervey de Montmorency falsely accused Robert le Gros, who had been responsible for much of the initial conquest's success (f. 30r). Another of Howth's additions to this source held de Lacey similarly responsible for false testimony against de Courcy, testimony that led to de Courcy's disgrace and displacement (f. 55v). De Courcy was ultimately arrested and the territory he had acquired in Ulster given to de Lacey's son. This passage gave Howth the opportunity to address the issue of inheritance of land in Ulster, an inheritance claimed ultimately to rest with the crown. English control in Ulster was an issue of immediate concern, and a centrepiece of O'Neill's attainder, and thus Howth here recited once again the genealogy of Elizabeth's right by inheritance to Ulster as contained in Finglas's 'Breviate', as adopted for use in O'Neill's attainder. Howth was by no means contesting the crown's right to Ulster. Rather, this permitted him to demonstrate yet again that on an issue as critical as control of Ulster, history had been misrepresented and moreover in a manner that undermined the established colonial community's successes in the service of advancing new policies.

Initially, as Howth used *Pembridge's Annals* he specifically picked out items that tracked the inheritance of Ulster from the de Laceys to the Burkes (ff. 63r–v, 84r), though he also continued to track episodes of misrepresentation and the displacement of the established colonial community. Once again Howth found a number of ready-made items that suited his purpose, but he also added to this source to emphasise the effect of misrepresentation, both on a loyal community and on the success of the conquest, as he had in earlier additions to *The English Conquest of Ireland*. To one of his excerpts from *Pembridge's Annals* Howth added an incident reminiscent of his earlier descriptions of the conflict between de Courcy and de Lacey. In this episode the Earl of Louth, envied by some of the leading families of Uriel for his good character and successful leadership, is invited to a dinner party where he is traitorously killed by his hosts (ff. 85v–86v). The slaughter that was unleashed had larger ramifications, destabilising Ulster, which, Howth said, would have been 'civiller than Leinster' had Louth lived. In the legal case that ensued, the magistrates chose to accept false witness. 'No marvel', Howth lamented in commentary added to this passage, 'that Ireland could never be brought to conformity for God never did permit any to reign that ever sought earnestly the commodity thereof' (f. 86v). When the de Laceys subsequently acquired power again in 1331 with Anthony de Lacey's appointment as lord justice, that position was used to eliminate a number of leading members of the Old English community by placing them under arrest, including Desmond, Burke, and Louth's son, Walter, later executed by Anthony de Lacey (f. 90v), another destabilising period that permitted numerous Irish incursions. A similar occurrence would reappear late in Howth's history as he recorded the recent arrests of Clanrickard and his sons, John of Desmond and Kildare, falsely charged with treason (f. 136r).

Each of the examples cited above, as well as others in Howth's history, incorporate a presentation of economic decay and failed conquest caused by the ability of a newly arriving colonial community to gain dominance and impose detrimental policies. This can be seen in Howth's portrait of Ireland in the wake of Sidney's attempted abolition of coign and livery in the Pale and his opposition to that policy (f. 129r–v). Howth's presentation of his opposition to the abolition of coign and livery addressed the detrimental effect of this policy on the economy, morale and defence of the Pale, using precisely the integrated context within which O'Neill's attainder had presented the benefits of its abolition, but to very different ends. Howth presents its abolition as destructive rather than constructive because it facilitated Irish attacks on the Pale, compromising stability and secure conquest. In keeping with the pattern maintained throughout the history, Howth here integrates the issues of economic decay and impeded conquest. Old English displacement is again a central focus of this passage, most immediately in the loss of his community's ability to exercise military control as they are no longer able or even motivated to maintain a defensive, much less offensive, position. The displacement evident in this episode goes yet further.

Howth expands on that displacement in the commentary that follows his passage on coign and livery. In that commentary he draws the reader's attention from a consideration of the lost ability to exercise military power to a consideration of the lost ability to influence policy. In doing so he further directs the reader to consider the cause and effect of that loss through historical example that conflates the eras of Sidney's administration and King John's.

> See and peruse the orders taken by King John at his coming first to Ireland in this book and what sequel did follow this same when that he took new orders contrary to that was by experience learned with bloody hands for the wealth of the Pale; he, perceiving that no fruit did grow upon this new planted stock, was content to rot away these orders and left this same to the old experienced learned with bloody hand and in like manner I fear we must do before that ever the Pale shall be as it was. (ff. 129v–130r)

Here Howth provides an analogous situation in which a newly arriving colonial community displaces the established colonial community. When we turn to his passage on King John, as Howth directs, we see that there are actually two passages on King John, the first copied from *The English Conquest of Ireland.* In this passage a successful older colonial community is displaced as those newly arriving gain dominance; the result is destabilisation and economic decay. Under King John's new men 'all things [were] unprofitably wasted to the harm of peace men and not of foe men . . . they burned and slew, robbed and stole . . . through the land in all places was wailing and mourning, yelling and crying' (f. 50v). Howth wished it to be understood that this was the result of poor administration, adding in the margin: 'the country ill guided as it hath been since many times', a sentiment that, in keeping with the comparison Howth draws here, is to be applied to Sidney's policy of abolition.

Howth then modified his copy of *The English Conquest of Ireland,* adding a second passage on King John to follow the above. In this passage Howth sustains the discussion of poor administration, but expands on the destruction caused by new arrivals in a manner that draws attention to the contrast between Ireland under the authority of the older colonial community and the new:

> at length the country that was well stabilised with great civility, riches and quietness became at length through *their misgovernment* so far out of order that no man could travel in safety without slaughter, robbery or imprisonment throughout the country; as they were in riches before, so they waxed poor and in thralldom. (f. 51r, italics mine)

Howth developed this contrast further, conflating time again to press not only the comparison of Sidney and King John but to emphasise the historical existence of conflict between the new and old colonial communities:

> King Henry sending his son John as L[ord] of Ireland into Ireland bringing with him such a company of young gentlemen nothing careful of the country but given their mind always to disdain those that was before them as old soldiers which was, is and shall be the common usage of all those that to Ireland come as though they all had with one mind sworn this same custom to observe from the beginning to the ending . . . (f. 51r)

Howth also takes the opportunity to introduce an episode that had not been referenced in his source. In Howth's passage King John calls his council to discuss the 'disorder'. When the new council confess their fault, de Courcy is restored to power, stability and prosperity are

restored, and the conquest continues (f. 51r–v). The contrast is underscored in Howth's marginalia which define the restoration generated by
de Courcy as 'good government' in direct opposition to his above characterisation of the administration of King John's new men as the
'misgovernment' of 'unskilful governors' (f. 52r–v). To follow through to
completion the comparison Howth wished to be drawn between King
John and Sidney, Howth asserts that contrary to the attainder's assertion
that the elimination of coign and livery was good government, it was, in
Howth's estimation, misgovernment. In Howth's passage on the abolition of coign and livery and in his additional passage on King John,
conquest is impeded by poor counsel advanced by a new community
ill-placed and insufficiently informed or experienced to offer wise
counsel. Their new policies initially receive acceptance but bring only
instability and decay. Howth's additional passage on King John asserted
that successful conquest and economic prosperity were restored,
however, when de Courcy and his 'old friends' were restored, the very
situation for which Howth called at the close of his commentary on the
abolition of coign and livery: 'and in like manner I fear we must do
before that ever the Pale shall be as it was' (f. 130r).

The attention Howth drew to the contention between new and old
orders is neither as crudely defensive nor as simplistic as it might
appear. It employs the language of counsel, and it is within this framework that he asks the reader to compare the counsel offered by the old
and new colonial communities, the reception of each group's counsel
by Sidney and by King John, and the effect of each group's counsel.
The rhetoric of counsel, as John Guy argues, was at the centre of Tudor
and early Stuart politics, a concept that 'underpinned not only the
assumptions, but also some of the most important practices and political structures' as it 'informed public discourse and shaped political
institutions'.[31] This rhetoric was also familiar in Ireland. Rowland White,
for example, used it as the principle introducing his proposals for
reform outlined in a contemporary document, 'Discors Touching
Ireland'.[32] It was also used by Howth, providing a framework in which
he could link Old English displacement and failed conquest.

Guy identifies several precepts central to the rhetoric of counsel as
it developed over the course of the Tudor period that are relevant to
Howth's presentation of the problems facing conquest, in particular the
problem of competing colonial communities. Guy identifies two basic
schools of counsel: the feudal-baronial and the humanist-classical.
Adherents of both models agreed that the fundamental purpose of

counsel was the preservation of the commonwealth; by 'curbing human passions and mitigating misjudgements' it maintained order and prevented chaos.[33] However, these models were at odds in identifying who was best suited to offer counsel, an identification dependent on each group's definition of wisdom and the role it played in one's ability to make judgements. Those who held the feudal-baronial model viewed the aristocracy as better fit to provide royal counsel; these were the 'natural-born counsellors' who, by virtue of their birth, possessed the requisite merit to determine the best counsel. Those who advocated the humanist-classical model, on the other hand, identified those with the benefit of legal and university education as better equipped to provide counsel. The humanist-classical model, therefore, preferred appointees, contributing to the rise of a new class of royal advisors in the Tudor period that was often, though not always, able to supersede the advice of the nobility. The feudal-baronial model, on the other hand, often characterised such appointees as 'base-born flatterers' offering 'evil counsel' in the pursuit of personal and political gain rather than in the interests of the commonwealth.[34] When critics challenged 'evil counsel' they were doing so certainly to defend themselves from charges of challenging the monarch, but they were also able to defend their accusation by claiming that those who offered poor counsel were not concerned with the preservation of the commonwealth but only with advancing their own self-interest.

In spite of this difference, adherents of both schools held firmly to the notion that it was the subject's duty to offer counsel. It was a necessary component of governance, and the monarch was obliged to receive counsel as advisors and monarch worked mutually in the best interests of the commonwealth. One's duty to offer counsel, however, faced potential difficulty when it conflicted with or infringed on royal prerogative, for the monarch, though obliged to receive counsel, was not obliged to implement it.[35]

These issues are central to Howth's consideration of the problems involved in conquest, where counsel is by necessity understood in Ireland's colonial context. Howth's presentation of conflicting counsel, for example, is evident in his many passages that address conflict between an established and a newly arriving colonial community. Howth adheres to the feudal-baronial model in advocating that the established nobility are best suited to determine policy. Their bloodied hands, an image Howth uses repeatedly, give evidence of their experience, experience that constitutes wisdom, in Howth's use of this rhetoric, and validates their position. Thus, while humanism was in accord with an Old English preference for reform as opposed to conquest, humanism as employed in the rhetoric of counsel complicated this outlook, for the group in Tudor England that benefited from this philosophy, a new servitor class reflected in the New English, was the very group that Howth perceived to be the most significant threat.[36] As beneficial as humanism might have been to the long-term objectives of the Old English within the debate over reform versus conquest, employing a framework of counsel from the feudal-baronial perspective permitted Howth to integrate Old English displacement and failed conquest: both were caused by the poor counsel of a new colonial community, as Howth's examples of King John, Sidney and others demonstrated. Howth's description of King John's 'new men' as 'evil counsellors', whom the reader was directed to compare to Sidney's administrators, even fulfils the conventional rhetoric of counsel in which those who proffered advice were careful to do so by challenging administrators rather than rulers. It was their poor counsel that destroyed rather than preserved stability in Ireland; it contravened counsel's fundamental purpose and resulted in impeded conquest.

Howth's consideration of counsel would develop as the manuscript continued beyond this point. There he would consider more intensively one's duty to give counsel and the ramifications of one's failure to comply with this duty, even when faced with opposition. As the 1570s progressed Howth would also be forced to confront the potential problem inherent in counsel, its conflict with royal prerogative, made manifest in the cess controversy of 1577–8.

At the conclusion of this commentary on the abolition of coign and livery at the end of Howth's entry on Sidney, by which time we can see from the above that he was deeply concerned with the subject of counsel, Howth abandoned the attempt to narrate events in chronological order. In the final folios of this section (ff. 130r–133v), the expansion of Howth's concerns is evident in his inclusion of several brief entries that note (out of chronological order) episodes of unrest throughout Ireland which had occurred between 1567 and 1572. These items record instability in Leinster, Ulster, Munster and Connacht, the latter two regions in which provincial presidencies had been established. Though Howth did not dwell on the issue of provincial councils and made no direct statement regarding his reception of them, the unrest he detailed in Munster and Connacht suggests that, as implemented, these institutions had failed to achieve stability. Like Rowland

White, he was cautious regarding this, and also like White, Howth may be suggesting here that it was the presidents rather than the institution itself that were the cause of problems.[37] In these brief entries Howth also returned to the subject of contention between Sidney and the Old English within the context of counsel. Possibly referring to one of the sessions of parliament that met at Drogheda in February 1570 about which there is little extant documentation, Howth recorded that when he advised Sidney of the illegality of the proposed composition Sidney 'was in a great rage and threatened the gentlemen to the castle of Dublin' (f. 130v).[38] Written with hindsight after Sidney's departure, Howth maintained his presentation of Sidney's first administration as one that created new unrest rather than advancing stability and conquest. This presentation is underscored by Howth's two references to unnatural phenomena that occurred during Sidney's administration, the 1567 pestilence and the hills that purportedly moved in 1571, events conventionally understood to reflect divine judgement on human mismanagement of affairs, and thus divine affirmation of Howth's analysis of Sidney's term as lord deputy.

At some point soon after these entries detailing unrest throughout Ireland were made, Howth acquired Campion's history, the use of which signals a transitional phase in the manuscript's compilation. Campion would be the last major source from which Howth drew excerpts of any length. He made relatively limited use of Campion given the wealth of information it contained; however, the excerpts he did choose reveal again the subjects that concerned Howth in this period. In spite of the portrayal of general instability in Ireland in the entries made just prior to his acquisition of Campion, Howth now turned his attention again to the origins of conquest and the position of the Old English. Maintaining continuity, where Hand III had concluded with an entry on Osseyn's recital to St Patrick of the deeds of Fionn mac Cumhaill and the Fianna, Hand IV, the hand who made all of the excerpts from Campion, commenced work by entering selections from Campion's chapter on Ireland's saints, beginning with St Patrick. He also included passages on St Brigid and St Colmcille, perhaps for Campion's reference here to the translation of their remains by de Courcy, a figure in whom Howth had already displayed significant interest. There is, though, even more substantial continuity in Howth's concerns as displayed in his excerpts from Campion. For example, Howth continued to be interested in perceptions of the Old English, excerpting in its entirety Campion's second chapter in which Old

English families were categorised by the degree to which they had adopted Gaelic custom. As the other excerpts from Campion convey, Howth's concern to continue compiling information relevant to the Old English was directed to an even more specific purpose: his increasing interest in the subject of counsel and its relationship to the restoration of stability in Ireland. Howth's use of Campion was transitional not only in terms of the manuscript's compilation, but also for what it conveys of his evolving opposition as he considered his duty to offer counsel.

The remaining excerpts Howth drew from Campion all address situations in which individuals or groups in Ireland took up their obligation to counsel either by levying grievances against detrimental policies or advising London of the need for intervention. The first of these, an entry lodged by Howth himself, addresses the administration of Ralph Ufford. Howth paraphrases Campion's passage to draw attention to the economic decay that developed under Ufford's excessive exactions (ff. 132v-133r).[39] Here he emphasises the effect of this, as he had at great length earlier in the history, noting that Ufford's 'great and unmerciful charges' brought decay to all Ireland and to no purpose, for they failed to achieve successful conquest. He also noted the perceived need to alert London to the situation on this occasion. Howth amended Campion's entry to add that when the lords complained to the king they received redress. Howth, as on several other occasions throughout the manuscript, states directly why this entry was of importance: 'for this cause I hath written this here that none of these aforesaid had never so much cause as now is offered and yet we write not nor complain to our prince' (ff. 132v-133r). Clearly he believed that Ireland's deterioration had progressed beyond that of any preceding period, and he was aware of the option of lodging grievances (an option he would later take at the onset of the cess controversy in 1577). Howth's dismay at this point is evident in the passage's closing comment: 'God help poor Ireland that is fatherless. Amen.' Similarly, Howth excerpted from Campion a letter from the inhabitants of Cork to Edward IV's deputy and Irish council alerting them to the disastrous conditions in Cork. They beg intervention from the Dublin administration and also threaten to inform the king if their grievances are not redressed (ff. A18v–A19v).[40] Another of the excerpts Howth drew from Campion addresses the concomitant economic decay and detriment to conquest that occurred under yet another administration, that of Steven Scropt. However, this excerpt illustrates the benefits to be gained when the established colonial community is treated justly. Once Scropt amended his ways, he was restored to such good graces among the people who now 'so cheerfully served him' that together in one day they were able to 'spoil Arthur McMorrow' (a significant threat in that period), here providing a contrast to Howth's portrayal of the Pale in the wake of Sidney's abolition of coign and livery when its inhabitants had not the ability or motivation to even defend themselves.

Each of these passages addresses Ireland in a period of economic deterioration as the result of poor administrative policies and, importantly, the action of the affected community. As this first phase of compilation concluded we can see the further refinement and focus in Howth's consideration of the deteriorating position of the Old English and failed conquest. As Howth searched Campion, he sought out further information regarding the history of situations in which the Old English either had or had not pressed their counsel against detrimental policies and its effect on stability and conquest. These examples would be of significant use to Howth in the next phase of his life when he took a leading role in opposition to the cess in Sidney's second term as lord deputy. Howth's long consideration of this issue materialised in a resolve to confront more aggressively what he perceived to be detrimental policy in spite of his previous failures to convince Sidney.

Phase Two: 1573–9

Subsequent to his use of Campion Howth added very few items. Four folios were appended to the close of the history noting events that occurred between 1573 and 1579, including private colonisation efforts in Ulster, the arrest of Kildare in 1575 and the onset of the Desmond Rebellion, together with copies of two of Howth's submission statements regarding the cess controversy of 1577–8. Even less was added to the miscellaneous contents. Only one of the items in that collection can be attributed with certainty to the manuscript's second phase of compilation, the entry on Pope Joan (f. 160v), though possibly the other entries on women scattered throughout the manuscript in available blank folio space were added at that time as well. It is also possible that during the final stages of the manuscript's compilation Howth entered the passage on the Battle of Clontarf (ff. A20v–A22r) and on the final folio the closing Latin couplet and additional biographical information on Walter Hussey (f. 177v). Howth added to the manuscript only intermittently in this period, possibly in four sessions of entry. The first of the two entries on plantation in Ulster could have been added at some point between 1573 and 1576, but the second would certainly have been added after September 1576, given its reference to the Earl of Essex's death. Howth then seems to have returned to the manuscript following his incarceration for opposition to the cess in 1577, and at least once but possibly twice more following his incarcerations in 1578, again for opposition to the cess, and in 1579 on charges of domestic abuse. Curiously, the period 1573–9, during which Howth's work on the manuscript waned, was precisely the period when his political opposition intensified.

As noted above, Howth returned to the compilation at some point in mid to late 1577 following his first incarceration for opposition to the cess to enter three folios of material after a hiatus of perhaps several years. This material was concerned principally with the cess controversy. It contained a copy of one of Howth's submission statements, commentary on the cess, and a brief entry on Francis Agard that noted his deathbed recantation of support for the cess. Assessment of the cess controversy of 1577–8 has focused on the opposition's constitutional challenge and Sidney's counter-claim that this challenged royal prerogative (though he also claimed that it was part of a larger Papist conspiracy against him).[41] Howth's manuscript, as well as other extant documentation, indicates that there were other far larger issues at stake that have generally been overlooked and which warrant examination. It also suggests that Sidney's presentation of the cess controversy has been permitted to influence assessments of it.

Undeniably, a legal challenge to the constitutionality of cess provided the grounds on which the opposition presented their case. That challenge has been used as the primary framework within which to assess this period of Old English opposition.[42] However, there were more substantial issues of concern to the opposition. In their initial letters to Elizabeth and Sidney and repeatedly throughout the two-year controversy the opposition made reference not only to the implementation of this measure, but to its *effect*: economic deterioration and the inability of those affected to meet the demands of the cess. In numerous letters and submission statements the opposition noted that Sidney's implementation of the cess was an obligation that simply could not be met and that attempts to do so had exacerbated economic hardship.[43] Sidney counter-charged that this was patently untrue. The lords lived, he argued, in far greater prosperity than their ancestors had, and that at any rate it was not the lords who complained that bore the burden of cess, but their tenants, thus asserting that their claim of economic burden was disingenuous, that his opponents' interests were self-serving rather than for the welfare of their tenants, and that they again failed to co-operate in securing English control which, in Sidney's analysis, required standing military forces and the funds to support them.[44] To preserve his own objectives and policy, Sidney simply dismissed this grievance and redirected attention to the charge that the opposition's complaint constituted a challenge to royal prerogative. This charge thus became the dominant – and by its end the only – issue in the controversy as the opposition was forced to defend itself against it in the face of imprisonment. Their release, of course, necessitated denial of the charge, but this should not permit that denial to be understood – like their claims of economic hardship – as either disingenuous or self-serving. Brady has commented that:

> the Palesmen became estranged from the government they had once welcomed because of the sheer material burden which the maintenance of the government imposed upon them. More than beliefs or ideas, more than competition for land or office, it was this practical and fundamental economic resentment which inspired every agitation against the government organised within the Pale until 1580.[45]

Economic grievances were behind the complaint against the cess, but it was part of a larger constellation of displacement and lost influence. Assessments of the cess controversy must not, therefore, as Sidney did, fail to acknowledge that more substantial issues lay behind them.

Howth's commentary on the cess controversy mirrors the position maintained by the opposition in state paper documentation. He comments on its illegality, citing several legal authorities, and reiterates that their intent was not to challenge royal prerogative (f. 134r–v). However, these are not the first issues to which Howth drew attention. In both his commentary and the marginalia attached to it, the initial emphasis is on the economic decay caused by Sidney's imposition of the cess. Howth was not opposed to the cess in principle as he made clear in his address of this subject under the administrations of various lord deputies from Bellingham to Sidney. He responded in this case to its abuse. The exploitation of the cess and its consequent detrimental economic effect also served as the focus of initial attention in the opposition's earliest letters to Elizabeth and the Irish council and even in their earliest submission statements. The illegality of the cess was not the source of the complaint. The source of the complaint was its effect; challenging its legality served merely as the strategy to alleviate the distress it caused.[46] Howth identified Sidney's cess as 'great and unreasonable', leaving Ireland 'utterly decayed and impoverished' (f. 134r–v). These conditions are revealed in greater detail in letters to and from Delvin and other members of the Nugent family.[47] They portray both a suffering population and the Nugents' genuine concern for their tenants, thus calling into question Sidney's dismissal of the sincerity of the opposition's complaint. Richard Nugent, for example, wrote to Thomas Nugent in prison:

> Cousin Thomas I have no news to send you to lighten your mind and give you consolation in your imprisonment, but that Captain Collier by virtue of my lord deputy's commission or rather the sheriff in his name hath robbed our poor country . . . your poor tenants are made very poor for in every town of yours they took a prey of gearans or sheep . . . no cattle could escape them . . . they were constrained to sell their little kyne for half the value, some others to mortgage their pots or pans and other like household stuff.[48]

Similarly, Thomas, James and Lavalen Nugent wrote from prison to Sidney: 'for God's sake let our poor tenants and followers have no less favour than the rest of our neighbours . . . they are not able either to manure the ground or yet to pay their rent.'[49] The economic deterioration that led the Palesmen to lodge a grievance was a subject that Howth's manuscript reveals had long been of concern to him as he collected historical examples of its occurrence and, importantly, of its occurrence as the result of poor policy.

While we cannot be certain that Howth shared the Nugents' concern for their tenantry, Howth's manuscript does reveal that he saw in this episode of economic deterioration a larger threat. In Howth's earlier examples of economic deterioration it had also always impeded conquest. This was not a conclusion constructed by Howth in the midst of the cess controversy to justify his opposition; it was a conclusion that he had reached as many as seven years earlier as he began the compilation. The first phase of Howth's manuscript also indicates that his decision to participate in grievances against the effect of Sidney's implementation of the cess was not one made lightly or in haste, but after considered examination of historical exempla and their demonstration to him of the necessity to counsel against detrimental policy.

In the wake of his release from Dublin Castle in 1577, in what would turn out to be only the first round of the cess controversy, along with entries on these recent events Howth also made another entry that reveals the level of anxiety he now felt regarding the security of the Old English community and what he perceived to be the severity of the administration's intent to debilitate them. In this entry Howth listed the recent arrests of other, more prominent members of the Old English community: Clanrickard, John of Desmond and Kildare. As with so many other passages throughout the manuscript, Howth's rather annalistic recording of these events should not lead us to underestimate their importance to him. Reflecting on recent events, as he had done when reflecting on conditions following Sidney's first administration, a pattern of general unrest dominates Howth's entries. He singles out rebellion in Connacht and Munster and notes instability in Leinster concerning the O'Mores (also recording their capture of Sidney's nephew, Henry Harrington).[50] These entries also convey his concern with a perceived pattern of arrest, to which he had also now been subject, a pattern that suggested to him the progression of more aggressive attempts to displace the Old English by a variety of means. While Clanrickard, his sons and Desmond were arrested for their role in rebellion, a response that Howth suggests here, as earlier in the manuscript, was catalysed by the failure of provincial councils, Kildare, Howth emphasises, was arrested on false charges of treason (f. 136r). Hence this pattern of arrests was not grounded exclusively in the need to quell rebellion, but opportunities for the removal of leading Old English figures were being constructed.[51]

In the final two years of the manuscript's compilation Howth would return to it only briefly to make a few entries. To the history he added a copy of the submission statement from his second imprisonment for cess opposition in 1578, a very brief note of his fines, and notice of the Desmond Rebellion's inception. To the miscellaneous collection, as noted above, he entered the item on Pope Joan, biographical information on Hussey and the closing Latin couplet. Howth provided no commentary on the second round of the cess controversy and, in the aftermath of his imprisonment for domestic abuse, seems to have abandoned the manuscript. This period coincides with his reconciliation with the Dublin authorities in autumn 1579, a reconciliation that might account for the manuscript's abandonment, for Howth had only turned to the manuscript in periods of difficulty with the Dublin administration. He may not yet, though, have reconciled himself to a female monarch, as his entries on women suggest, for each of those entries addresses female acquisition of positions traditionally reserved for men. Though it is difficult to determine at what point Howth entered the Latin couplet lodged on the manuscript's final folio, it may well have been one of the last items entered, and, given its elementary Latin, it may have been composed by Howth. Its subject is certainly reflective of the reconciliation Howth had just achieved after a ten-year period of opposition:

> *Non bene venit homo*
> *Nisi bibat ad ostium stando* (f. 177r)[52]

Identity, Religion and Status

The period during which Howth compiled was one of crystallising identity formation for the Old English, a process forced on them as they were confronted with the loss of land, offices and, critically, influence.[53] Not only were the Old English in the process of formulating an identity for themselves, but the New English were also engaged in constructing an identity for them. While the Old English defined themselves largely by political position and their history stretching back to the Anglo-Norman conquest, in this early period of 'alienation' from the Dublin administration, as Brady defined it, New English identification of the Old English also included consideration of Old English cultural and religious identity.[54] The question of Old English cultural identity was as much a point of contention for individuals in this period as it is for historians today.[55] It had been an issue since the Statutes of Kilkenny and was revitalised by Finglas early in the Tudor period and exacerbated by reformed religion and new policies of conquest. The contexts of reformed religion and intensifying conquest raised questions regarding the reformability of the Irish.[56] Where attention was drawn to Gaelicisation among the Old English, as in Campion's history, the question of the viability of the Old English – as a function of their identity – was also necessarily raised.

Howth was generally careful to avoid references to cultural and religious identity, for the Old English as well as the Irish, though he was certainly aware of the existence and ramifications of this volatile issue. It seems reasonable to assume, for example, that he was aware of Hooker's direct challenge to Old English identity in the parliamentary debates of early 1569. Howth would have been aware of questions regarding Old English identity long before this event, however. While a student at Lincoln's Inn he would have been aware of the distinction made between English students and those 'of Ireland' in that institution's many policies and practices controlling their enrolment and their lodging. Howth had been personally confronted with questions regarding his identity again, at the very centre of power, while in audience with Elizabeth. When he was serving as representative of the Irish council sent to London to defend Sussex, Elizabeth reportedly asked Howth whether or not he spoke English. Howth lamented: 'belike such was the report of the country made to the Queen', though he did not belabour what he clearly deemed to be misrepresentation on this occasion as he had earlier, nor did he feel compelled at that point to defend the use of English as spoken in Ireland, as Stanihurst did when confronted with questions regarding language (f. 124v).[57] Howth's inclusion of Campion's second chapter reveals not only Howth's awareness of the issue of Gaelicisation and its categorisation, along with the opportunity it afforded for misrepresentation, but his awareness that this was an issue of interest to Sidney, for Campion clearly identified Sidney as the source of this information, which Howth would have seen as he copied. Howth was thus well aware that his community's identity was in question at the highest levels of power both in Dublin and in London, yet he chose not to confront it in his compilation, where it is conspicuous by its omission. Its absence may, in fact, reveal his awareness of the volatility of this issue and reflect a decision to deflect attention away from it by concerning himself rather with the identity of the Old English community in terms of their historic loyalty to the crown and to conquest.

Adherence to Roman Catholicism also presented another challenge to Old English identity. Here again Howth was cautious and refrained from confronting the question directly. Though an ardent advocacy of Roman Catholicism in Howth's collection, given its dating, would have been slightly premature, it seems difficult to believe he was unaware of the precarious situation in which the Old English were placed by *Regnans in Excelsis*, the papal bull which excommunicated Elizabeth, and which was proclaimed in 1570, contemporary with the inception of his collection.[58] While Howth may have simply believed that his religious convictions were of no relevance to his political loyalty, and the Old English insisted that this was the case as late as the Nine Years War, here again his care in avoiding assertions of religious preference may belie awareness of its potentially damaging ramifications.[59] That awareness is suggested not only by Howth's avoidance of the question of religion in passages of original composition, but more clearly in the fact that he went out of his way to omit passages that touched on issues necessarily raised by religious association as he copied from sources. For example, as noted earlier, his copy of *The English Conquest of Ireland* is nearly complete, with one exception: Howth omitted the passage on Thomas Becket's murder and its accompanying commentary on royal infringement of church authority. Similarly, when copying from Campion Howth omitted passages that referenced royal infringement on church authority, as he did when copying the passage on Ufford. Howth certainly did not accept the ultimate authority of the state over the church, for there are other clues as to the authority Howth still deemed the church to hold, though he perhaps believed that these two authorities could work co-operatively (again a position the Old English held into the Nine Years War). As Howth copied from Campion yet elsewhere he added passages asserting the legitimacy of Rome's authority. To Campion's list of England's rights to Ireland, for instance, Howth added that Pope Paul IV had affirmed England's use of the title 'King of Ireland' in 1555 (f. 153v).[60] Thus, while Howth's collection conveys that he was well aware of the factors that contributed to perceptions of Old English identity, cultural and religious, and that he maintained adherence to the authority of Rome, what he chose to address in presenting the Old English community was their loyalty. This would have preserved him from further doubts regarding his identity, but it was also strategic to the success of the collection's attempt to persuade the reader that conquest depended on the restoration of the Old English to positions of authority and influence and the restoration of their administrative strategies.

Howth would have agreed with Sidney that the conquest was in danger. He would even have agreed with Sidney that a consideration of its failures necessarily demanded an examination of the position of the Old English and the military and economic systems in place in Ireland. However, their conclusions were in direct opposition to each other and each seemed unwilling to accommodate the other's position. Sidney presented the military and economic systems of the Old English as precisely the reason for failed conquest, and thus in need of reform. Howth, on the other hand, argued that conquest was jeopardised by these reforms, that Old English administration of the conquest had in fact been successful whereas Sidney's reforms only destabilised Ireland. Though Howth's compilation does not develop either a well-formulated response to reform or alternative proposals for reform beyond the restoration of the Old English and the abandonment of Sidney's policies, his position, as well as the anxiety he experienced in the face of displacement by the New English, can be gleaned from his compilation. His manuscript contributes significantly to assessments of the 1570s, a period critical to the declining status of the Old English. Reaction against specific factors that contributed to this deterioration can be seen far more clearly in episodes of aggressive response such as the Butler Revolt or the Baltinglass Revolt, and even in the more strident attachment to Counter-Reformation Catholicism that was beginning to emerge just as Howth's manuscript concluded.[61] That Howth responded by compiling information, a rather more passive response, is no less valuable to considerations of the process of intensified conquest and Old English deterioration, and indeed his compilation helps to illuminate a formative period for Old English identity and opposition. His manuscript offers insight, for instance, on the parliamentary opposition of 1569–71, for which there is less extant documentation regarding the lords' position than the commons. Howth's manuscript certainly also indicates that the cess controversy of 1577–8 involved far more substantial issues of concern to the Old English that have generally been overlooked, of relevance not only to that immediate context but to their general decline. That decline was, of course, the catalysing factor in the manuscript's inception and the subject that maintained it.

5. Circulation of
The Book of Howth
and its Use

Little was formerly known of the history of the *Book of Howth* other than its acquisition by Carew under unknown circumstances and its ultimate deposit in Lambeth Palace Library along with other items in his collection. Lack of information regarding its early circulation generated the erroneous assumption that Howth's compilation existed only in its original form. The recent discovery of several misidentified late sixteenth-century copies of fragments of *The Book of Howth* in Lambeth Palace Library and in Trinity College, Dublin, indicates that, on the contrary, Howth's work enjoyed much livelier circulation in the decades following its completion than suggested by the relative obscurity into which it increasingly slipped over the ensuing centuries. This occurred initially in manuscript form, as the following study of the newly identified copies of Howth's work demonstrates. *The Book of Howth* received its first citation in the 1590s in Meredith Hanmer's *Chronicle of Ireland*, and was cited soon thereafter by William Camden and John Davies, evidence of the widening circulation of Howth's work within an influential circle that also included Carew and James Ussher.[1] Historians and antiquarians sought out Howth's work only periodically thereafter, James Ware in the mid seventeenth century, Sir Richard Cox in the later seventeenth century and Thomas Leland in the mid eighteenth century. A brief nineteenth-century revival of interest in Howth's work saw its first publication, in calendared form, and its first critical assessment by J.H. Round in 1883. Round's notice of the work's potential importance, however, went unheeded and failed to generate further critical study. Frequently mined for interesting or antiquarian anecdotes on episodes such as the Lambert Simnel affair, the Battle of Knockdoe or St Lawrence family history, few recognised its Old English perspective or took into account the political context of its production, obscuring the more valuable contribution it could offer to studies of sixteenth-century Ireland.

The Early Circulation of *The Book of Howth*

The former failure to identify accurately several copy fragments of Howth's compilation – the items now bound as Trinity College Library, Dublin, Manuscripts 584, 591 and 593, and Lambeth Palace Library Manuscript 248 – concealed several important aspects of this work's early history. In addition to confirming the work's early vibrant circulation, assessment of these copies is instructive in other ways, most importantly by supplying content lost when Howth's folios sustained damage. Lambeth 248, for example, contains marginalia lost in the original when its folios were cut for binding. The correct identification of TCD MSS 584, 591 and 593 gives further evidence of the circulation of *The Book of Howth*, and as a corollary advantage clarifies the identity of archival sources and therefore the history of source transmission in late medieval and early modern Ireland.

TCD MSS 584, 591 and 593 each contain excerpts from *The Book of Howth* copied by the same unidentified late sixteenth-century hand. MS 591 contains a number of items including saints' lives, excerpts from *Chronicae Annalibus Connaciensibus* and mayoral lists for Dublin. It also includes three entries taken from *The Book of Howth*: the origin of Meath's name, a list of the five ancient towns of Ireland and a brief entry on Ireland's size.[2] MSS 584 and 593 make more extensive use of *The Book of Howth*. T.K. Abbot's *Catalogue of the Manuscripts in the Library of Trinity College, Dublin* incorrectly identifies MS 584 as containing as its first item a translation of *Pembridge's Annals* covering the period 1162–1370.[3] While it is a translation of the fourteenth-century work known as *Pembridge's Annals*, more accurately it is a verbatim copy of the translation of *Pembridge's Annals* as modified by Howth for entry in his collection, including, tellingly, all of his interlining and marginalia. (Hence, scholars consulting this copy of *Pembridge's Annals* would have unknowingly consulted not this source but in fact Howth.) The scribe of MS 584 copied even more, though, than Howth's version of *Pembridge's Annals*, for where Howth's version of these annals ends, he continued to copy nearly verbatim a further thirty-seven folios of Howth's manuscript – the sections in which the history of Ireland was taken up to 1579, omitting only Howth's entry on Suleiman and the Siege of Rhodes. Thus, excepting this omission, folios 1–74 of MS 584 are an otherwise complete copy of folios 62–137 of *The Book of Howth*.

This same hand also copied other items from Howth's manuscript now bound with a copy of *The English Conquest of Ireland* as TCD MS 593.

Folios 57–182 of this manuscript contain entries taken from *The Book of Howth* that largely compensate for those entries not contained in MS 584.[4] However, unlike MS 584, in which the copied entries follow their order as in *The Book of Howth*, the entries in MS 593 are out of order and incomplete. A reordering of these entries into a sequence that matches their order in Howth reveals that, as with the missing entry on the Siege of Rhodes in MS 584, some of Howth's entries are missing here as well. The missing items fall into three categories: 1) the probably intentional omission of several of Howth's miscellaneous entries such as the poem on the Knights Templar and the entry on giants, suggesting that this copyist was interested only in items that seemed of direct relevance to the history of Ireland (perhaps the reason also for his omission of the Siege of Rhodes entry in MS 584); 2) the omission of Howth's folios 62–137, which may be accounted for by their presence in MS 584; and 3) the possible loss of folios that may have contained other missing entries. For example, MS 593 begins midway through Howth's version of *The English Conquest of Ireland* on a folio which was severely damaged and subsequently attached to a blank folio to permit its current binding. As we know this folio was damaged, its preceding folios may have been as well, possibly deemed too damaged for preservation. More conclusively, this copy of Howth elsewhere contains the beginning of Howth's adaptation of Finglas's 'Breviate'. It ends abruptly and incompletely, followed on the next folio by the concluding portion of Howth's entry on rebellions in England. In Howth's text, the 'Breviate' is followed by the entry on rebellions, and the missing conclusion of the former and introduction to the latter in MS 593 can be accounted for by the loss of a single folio. Such a hypothetical reordering of items to determine missing entries and folios also reveals that some of the entries which appear fragmented in MS 593 in fact have portions of their corresponding fragments bound elsewhere in the manuscript. Thus, MS 593 once may have constituted an ordered and more complete copy of *The Book of Howth* subsequently disturbed before or during binding.

There is further evidence that not only did these fragments of Howth's text once belong to a less disturbed copy, but that they also once comprised part of a single, more extensive copy of Howth's work that contained these fragments as well as the fragment now bound as MS 584 discussed above. The fragments are in the same hand, each displays the copyist's practice of including Howth's marginalia, interlining and footnotes (usually incorporated as part of the narrative rather than as additional material), and, as noted above, the fragments complement each other; MS 584 contains a copy of Howth's folios 62–137, the folios missing in MS 593. Each was also clearly copied from the original, for each contains a scribal note regarding the foliation of the source from which it was made, foliation that matches Howth's original.[5] The transmission and binding history of these separated fragments provides yet more evidence that they were once a single and nearly complete copy of *The Book of Howth*.

Though there is no internal evidence to indicate under whose patronage this copyist worked, the earliest identifiable owner was Carew, avid manuscript collector and provincial president of Munster (1600–3).[6] From Carew it passed to James Ussher, notable scholar and Archbishop of Armagh, then to John Madden, a seventeenth-century physician and collector of manuscripts, ultimately deposited in Trinity College Library, Dublin, in 1741.[7] What was thus once a single manuscript could have been separated for binding or rebinding at several points in its history. The folios might have been separated while still in Carew's possession, for it was his practice to separate and rebind sections of manuscripts as well as books.[8] In the case of MS 584, as noted above, another version of *The English Conquest of Ireland* has been bound with a copy of Howth's version. However, when compiling a guide to library collections in 1776 William Nicolson noted that the Bishop of Clogher had an 'old Book of Howth'.[9] Though he seems to have had outdated information, as the papers from the bishop's office had been deposited with Trinity in 1741, Nicolson's reference suggests that a copy of Howth's work, rather than excerpts or fragments bound separately, had survived into the eighteenth century, intact upon its deposit in Trinity College Library.

However, coinciding with the deposit of Madden's papers, Trinity began a rebinding and recataloguing project under John Lyon, antiquarian and canon of St Patrick's.[10] Lyon separated many of Trinity's manuscripts to rearrange their component parts with fragments from other manuscripts, a common if destructive process, then classing them as A–G.[11] As our two manuscripts in question were assigned distinct cataloguing identification at this point – MS 584 as E.3.22 and MS 593 as F.4.4 – they were certainly now separated, if not before. The order integrity of MS 584/E.3.22 was retained in rebinding, while MS 593/F.4.4 was disordered (or further disordered) in binding. MS 593 was rebound once more in 1806, though it is unclear whether either of these manuscripts was rebound yet again in 1820 when nearly half of Trinity's manuscripts underwent rebinding, destroying the provenance of many.[12] By the time a new catalogue of Trinity's manuscript collection was produced in 1900, the identity of MS 584 as a partial copy of *The Book of Howth* had been lost, and MS 593 had been so disturbed that it was described only by its component parts.[13] As no other copies or fragments of *The Book of Howth* have yet been identified in Irish archives, once Howth's original and its only other copy known to date – Lambeth MS 248 – were transferred to England among Carew's possessions, the Trinity copies may have been the only ones available in Ireland, copies unfortunately deprived of their identity.

Lambeth Palace Library MS 248 offers more evidence regarding the circulation of Howth's text. This is also a late sixteenth-century copy of Howth's compilation – or more accurately collation of copy fragments – also acquired by Carew.[14] It is in at least six hands and, like TCD MS 593, composed of disordered fragments. Though this initially obscures the nature of the manuscript as a copy of Howth, it has its advantages, for a reordering of the contents to match their sequence in *The Book of Howth* reveals information regarding the construction of Lambeth MS 248 that consequently also permits greater speculation regarding the early circulation of Howth's text. This copy begins midway through Howth's entry 'The Field of Ard-kaghe' and was originally foliated 2. Its textual content at this point corresponds to the textual content of Howth's folio 2, suggesting that its first folio is now missing. Additionally, folio 223 was originally foliated 103 and, as above, its textual content, though out of order here, matches so closely the content of Howth's folio 103 as to suggest that it once belonged to a copy nearly corresponding to the original. Both of these folios are in one hand, the hand that contributed the bulk of the manuscript. The core of this compilation seems then to have been a copy containing a significant portion of *The Book of Howth*, also probably made before Carew acquired it, for it contains much of Howth's marginalia but none of the marginalia Carew appended to the original.

As noted above, though, this copy is highly fragmented, disordered and ultimately incomplete, necessitating a hypothetical reordering of its contents for analysis. In addition to revealing what served as the core of the copy, this process also reveals that Lambeth MS 248 was constructed in stages in what appears to have been the attempt to supply missing entries for the re-creation of a complete copy (ulti-mately unsuccessful if that was the intent).[15] This was accomplished in two ways, the first of which was the addition of entries that may have either been lost through damage to the initial copy or omitted there. For example, the information on Howth's first folio, originally missing in Lambeth MS 248 due to the loss of its first folio as noted above, was later added to folio 172v by a different hand. Secondly, it was accomplished through the collation of what were distinct copy fragments, evident in the existence of at least six foliations in the manuscript; the folios now numbered 141, 167, 174, 178 and 192 had each been foliated 1 at an earlier point in their existence. This collation accounts for some of the hand changes in the manuscript. Other hand changes can be accounted for by later attempts to supply still-missing entries as noted above.[16] Whereas TCD MSS 584 and 593 once constituted a single copy of Howth, the composite nature of Lambeth MS 248 as a collation of distinct fragments indicates that it was constructed in part from existing multiple copies of Howth's work, suggesting a wider circulation than can be presumed from the Trinity copies.

The original and the copies identified here all came into Carew's possession at some point, evident in the marginalia he appended to each. The three names identified in the Lambeth collation, a Mr Edmund of Limerick City, James Fanning of Waterford and Thomas Fitzwilliam Roche, suggest Howth's work was circulating in southern Ireland.[17] It is not surprising therefore that Carew acquired the copies given his regional association with Munster, though how he came to acquire Howth's original is unknown.[18] Nor do we know whether he merely acquired existing copies, and if so from whom, or whether he patronised the creation of either or both of the copies. Copies may have been circulating already in Munster when Carew arrived to take up his post, in light of the names associated with the Lambeth copy, and Meredith Hanmer had probably already gained access to Howth's work before Carew arrived.

Using *The Book of Howth*

The years immediately following Hanmer's and Carew's access to *The Book of Howth* saw the flowering of a prominent circle of administrators and historians brought together by their collection activities.[19] As members of this group shared material, in particular Carew, Ussher, Camden and Davies, Howth's work received yet greater exposure.[20] Hanmer was the first to utilise Howth in his own work, as well as the first to cite Howth's compilation as *The Book of Howth*.[21] He was in Ireland by 1591, holding thereafter a succession of clerical posts in Ross, Waterford and the diocese of Ossory, operating under the patronage of

Thomas Butler, 10th Earl of Ormond.[22] Like Carew, this regional association with Munster may have exposed Hanmer to Howth's work. Hanmer
made occasional use of Howth for annalistic pieces of information, but
his extensive reliance on Howth's presentation of de Courcy's conquest
of Ulster would be of greater importance to the later history of Howth's
work. Hanmer's excerpted passages from Howth were copied repeatedly
by successive antiquarians and historians into the modern era.[23]

Hanmer's presentation of the Anglo-Norman conquest incorporated
Howth's version of *The English Conquest of Ireland*, including the
probably exaggerated if not fabricated role of his ancestor, Tristram
Amorey St Lawrence.[24] His uncritical reliance on *The Book of Howth* in
this case accorded the Howth family a central role in the twelfth-
century invasion. Once published by Ware it would become the
standard account. Under Hanmer's pen, however, this story was
detached from its context in Howth where it was integral to his rhetorically controlled presentation of the conquest in defence of the Old
English community. Elsewhere, Hanmer's replication of Howth's
version of pre-conquest Irish history, the history of Fionn mac Cumhaill
and the Fianna in particular, would provide his readers with a history
of Ireland that was also informed by Howth's rhetorical purpose, for
which Hanmer – and thus Howth indirectly – was roundly criticised by
Geoffrey Keating.[25] Hanmer's inclusion of lengthy passages from *The
Book of Howth* would remain the only substantial occurrence of
Howth's work in print until the 1871 calendar edition. Hanmer's history
was not published until 1633, and by that time other notices of Howth's
work, though far briefer, had already occurred in the printed works of
Camden and Davies.

Camden cited Howth's work in his 1607 edition of *Britannia*.[26] He
made far less use of Howth than Hanmer, drawing only two pieces of
information from it, one on the Irish kings' transfer of loyalty to Henry
II and the second on the bishop of Dublin under Edward II, on both
occasions citing Howth as 'Ms Pen Bar Howth'.[27] While this early print
reference to Howth is important in providing exposure to a reading
audience in England, Davies's use of Howth's text for his 1612 treatise
A Discovery of the True Causes why Ireland was Never Entirely Subdued
was of more immediate importance to the charged environment in the
aftermath of the completed Tudor conquest when Old English and
Gaelic alike were coming under the increasing pressures of plantation
and religious reform.[28] It illustrates that Howth's text could be of more
than antiquarian interest, for it contained information potentially

damaging to the Old English position, the very converse of Howth's intentions. Davies used Howth's text for precisely this purpose, turning Howth's presentation of the Battle of Knockdoe against the Old English as he considered the history of failed conquest and its successful resurrection in the sixteenth century. Howth had used the episode of the Battle of Knockdoe to diminish concerns regarding factionalism and to illustrate Old English loyalty to the crown. Davies countered Howth's representation, arguing rather that participation in this battle was yet another manifestation of factionalism and its detrimental effect, on this occasion in pursuit of a 'private quarrel of the Earl of Kildare'.[29]

Ware's 1633 publication of Hanmer's *Chronicle of Ireland* was the first time that significant portions of Howth's text were seen in print, as noted above. If Ware was not already aware of Howth's work through Davies's and Camden's references to it he would certainly have become aware of it through his work with Hanmer's text, and it may have been Hanmer's extensive reliance on Howth that sparked Ware's desire to see the manuscript himself. He seems to have been unaware that a copy existed in Ireland (or was unable to gain access to it), for following his publication of Hanmer nearly twenty years would pass before Ware finally saw Howth's work in 1652, by then in the possession of Carew's son, Thomas Stafford.

Once Ware gained access to Howth's compilation he gathered extensive notes from it.[30] As with Hanmer, he was particularly interested in Howth's sections on de Courcy.[31] His late access to *The Book of Howth* meant, of course, that Ware had not utilised it in his earlier works, in particular his 1639 *De Scriptoribus Hiberniae*. Howth does appear there, though obliquely, by way of Ware's inclusion of Primate Dowdall among his catalogue of authors, where he is identified as translator of the Latin 'Life of John de Courcy', a reference that seems to have been original to Howth and probably obtained by Ware via Hanmer.[32] In spite of the extensive excerpts and notes Ware gathered from Howth, once he had seen the original he made little use of it in later works, utilising it only minimally as one of the sources for his presentation of the reign of Henry VII in his 1664 work *Rerum Hibernicarum Annales*.[33] The paucity of Ware's subsequent use of *The Book of Howth* may have resulted from his perusal of the original which led him to the conclusion that it was 'very false in many particulars'.[34] There is no evidence that Ware sought thereafter to obtain a copy of *The Book of Howth* for his collection, perhaps disappointed in its contents once he had seen them, and his contribution to the history of

The Book of Howth would rely not on the manner in which he used it, but rather on his publication of Hanmer's *Chronicle of Ireland*, the principal conduit through which future historians and antiquarians would have access to Howth's text in print to any substantial degree until its 1871 publication.[35]

It was, in fact, Ware's advertisement of Howth's work via his publication of Hanmer that would bring Richard Cox, lord chancellor of Ireland, to consult *The Book of Howth* for his 1689–90 work, *Hibernia Anglicana*.[36] Cox, who was appointed to a series of offices from Recorder of Kinsale to lord chancellor of Ireland, would also, as Ware had done, seek out the original in London. Cox utilised the original in Lambeth, perhaps the first to do so as Ware had seen it while still in Stafford's possession.[37] Though Cox relied heavily on *The Book of Howth* for the medieval period, incorporating both his entries from and additions to *Pembridge's Annals*, it was of more critical use to Cox as he assessed the history of failed conquest.[38] Like Davies, Cox found in Howth's text information to substantiate the causes of this failure, though he did not, as Davies had done, attribute it to Old English factionalism. Cox, for instance, utilised *The Book of Howth* for information to demonstrate the late medieval Gaelic resurgence, reproducing Howth's list of 'payments to the wild Irish' under the year 1460 to illustrate the manner in which the Irish gained strength over their conquerors by 'usurping' land.[39]

Even though Cox had access to Howth's original, Hanmer's passages on the Anglo-Norman conquest taken from Howth surfaced here again. As with others before him, Cox recounted the role of Tristram Amorey St Lawrence, citing Hanmer as his source, though this was clearly information Hanmer had taken from Howth.[40] Hanmer would provide the conduit for Howth's version of the Anglo-Norman conquest yet again in Thomas Leland's 1773 *The History of Ireland from the Invasion of Henry II*.[41] Like Cox, Leland cited Howth directly, but he also incorporated Hanmer's version of de Courcy's role in the conquest, including passages on Tristram Amorey St Lawrence that Hanmer had copied from Howth.[42]

Following Leland *The Book of Howth* lay dormant for nearly a century.[43] Finally consulted again in 1861, it was dismissed as 'a compilation of Anglo-Irish fables, invented to flatter and amuse the inhabitants of the Pale', by J.T. Gilbert, though he suggested that its publication 'would throw much light' on the 'manners, customs, and language' of the Pale.[44] *The Book of Howth* would finally achieve publication in its own right, rather than in passages via Hanmer, ten years later – 300 years after its compilation – when Carew's papers were calendared. The former existence of Howth's work in manuscript only, and the paucity of copies or extracts, had necessarily limited its use. However, even its publication, although it made *The Book of Howth* available to a wider reading audience, ultimately did little to advance scholarly use of Howth's work. Douglas Hyde consulted it for his *Literary History of Ireland*, perhaps anticipating the contribution it might make to the Gaelic Literary Revival misled by the calendar editors' persistent reference to Howth and his work as 'Irish'. Hyde's hopes were disappointed; in the end he found only its references to Irish prophecies relevant.[45]

Richard Bagwell and J.H. Round would be the only two historians to make extensive use of *The Book of Howth* subsequent to its publication. There were significant differences in the ways in which they approached *The Book of Howth*, however. The calendar editors had offered little to explicate the text, and Round soon took up this task, publishing a series of three brief articles in 1883. His essays challenged many of the calendar editors' introductory comments and attempted to initiate debate on Howth's use of *The English Conquest of Ireland*.[46] Though this suggested the grander scale on which Howth's work merited examination, Round's essays had failed to generate critical interest in *The Book of Howth* even by the time he returned to its assessment nearly twenty years later in 1899.[47]

Despite Round's critical assessment and his note of caution regarding reliance on the calendar edition of *The Book of Howth*, Bagwell used the calendared edition exclusively for his three-volume *Ireland under the Tudors* (1885–90), stating that as it was edited 'on so full a plan it has not been thought necessary to consult the manuscripts'.[48] Though Bagwell was sceptical of Howth's information, as were others before him, noting that the 'details in the *Book of Howth* may not be all correct', he added that 'there is nothing antecedently improbable' and used it anyway.[49] Here he referred specifically to the speech purportedly given by Gormanston at the Battle of Knockdoe, very likely a fabrication on Howth's part in the service of the collection's larger defence of the Old English. In spite of his own caveat, Bagwell seems to have had little reservation about relying on Howth for information, citing him elsewhere for accounts of the Lambert Simnel affair and of the administrations of Surrey, Grey and Bellingham as viceroys.[50] This use of Howth again failed to accommodate Howth's context or purpose and bore some its most significant ramifications, as Bagwell replicated

Howth's assessments of the administrations of Surrey and Bellingham, assessments that had been fundamentally influenced by Howth's developing opposition to the policies of Sidney at the time those entries were made.

St John D. Seymour's early twentieth-century study of Howth's manuscript replicated Gilbert's and Round's earlier suggestions of this work's significance, describing it as 'the most valuable and interesting of the works that remain from this period'.[51] However, his assessment did not follow through the assertion. Seymour failed to notice that many of Howth's passages were in fact excerpted from sources such as Lydgate's *Fall of Princes*, and his description of one of Howth's Latin couplets as 'an early instance of those "book rhymes" so dear to schoolboys' or his characterisation of Howth's manuscript as 'told in a delightful manner . . . full of humorous . . . and quaint and striking passages' did little to develop the critical consideration called for by Round.[52]

Far from humorous or delightful, Howth's history of the conquest was created within the context of and in response to the deteriorating position of the Old English and reflects – quite darkly in some of its passages – Howth's anxiety. In the service of this rhetorical purpose Howth had modified, embellished and probably even fabricated events on occasion. With the rare exception of Davies, historians from Hanmer to Bagwell who turned to Howth's text to extract information perceived these 'inaccuracies' only vaguely, if at all, and failed to consider them within the work's larger purpose. Reproduced time and again and often out of context, these passages did perhaps acquire a 'quaint' quality, but they also became part of the repeated history of conquest for centuries. More significantly, they also contributed to the scepticism with which Howth's work has traditionally been regarded by undermining estimation of the text's value as documentation of the Old English community in a critical period of transition.

6. Conclusion:
Tudor Imperialism and
Old English Displacement

Through the archival evidence we catch only intermittent glimpses of what seem to be pendulum swings in Howth's political position. An early supporter of Sussex, Howth reappears with clarity in documentary records only much later in 1577–8 as one of the leading figures in the movement against Sidney's cess, with little explanation for this apparent reversal other than the standard assessment of this oppositional movement as a self-serving attempt to limit Sidney's ability to exploit local economies in support of his military policies under cover of prerogative power.[1] Following the highly dramatised domestic abuse case against Howth in 1579, he reappears as a member of the Court of Castle Chamber in the early 1580s, only to re-emerge in opposition to Perrot in the parliament of 1585–6. The silences in the archival records, however, are more than compensated for by Howth's collection. *The Book of Howth* reveals that Howth's opposition to Sidney's policies in the late 1570s was neither sudden nor entirely self-serving. Rather, it was the culmination of dissent that had been provoked a decade earlier by the contentious events surrounding the early sessions of the parliament of 1569–71, events that also provoked more widespread opposition within the Old English community. Here Chapter Three's demonstration that *The Book of Howth* was constructed in stages between 1569 and 1579 is critical to the collection's analysis and value. The items Howth entered can be grouped together by the date of their entry, his concerns at each stage identified, and these concerns then placed within specific historical contexts. Thus we learn not only that in 1569 Howth belatedly joined an oppositional Old English movement that had first emerged under Sussex, we can also track the evolution of Howth's opposition from that point to the period of the cess controversy of 1577–8. At each stage we can identify the policies that most concerned him, his perception of their detrimental effect on the security of his community and the entire conquest, and comprehend more clearly that his role in the cess controversy exposed long-standing issues extending beyond the constitutionality of the cess.

The overriding issue of concern to Howth as reflected in his compilation was the displacement of the Old English community by New English arrivals. Displacement was a term Howth used, in fact, in a passage of original composition in which he asked the reader to draw comparison between Sidney's and King John's treatment of the established colonial community. Note here again Howth's use of the rhetoric of 'evil counsel' and good counsel, or wisdom, defined as experience:

> This young prince, King Henry's son, by reason of the evil counsel
> of his new and roistering soldiers, all good orders were altered;
> amongst which he that were placed by reason of the great travail
> which he and his did by winning in the conquest were now
> displaced and with others their places exchanged. (f. 53v)

Howth used his compilation to argue that recurring dispute between the established and newly arriving colonial communities, with its consequent displacement of the established colonial community, had been a factor in the history of failed conquest ever since. The 1569 Act for the Attainder of Shane O'Neill justified Old English displacement by laying the blame for failed conquest at the feet of the Old English. Howth's collection sought to counter the attainder's historical presentation of Old English incompetence and failure by illustrating a continuum of loyalty and success that stretched from the twelfth century to the present, thus challenging the grounds on which New English supremacy based itself. In utilising this strategy, Howth participated in the trend practised by contemporaries such as Edmund Campion, John Hooker and Richard Stanihurst, no less than the author of Shane O'Neill's attainder, to use events of the past selectively and rhetorically, albeit in altered form, either to justify or reject strategies of conquest. Howth repeatedly compared successful episodes of conquest achieved by the Old English to periods when this was reversed with damaging ramifications by newly arriving colonials who had been able to supersede the Old English in military and conciliar positions.

It has been argued that the role of displacement as a cause of Old English opposition 'can be easily overstated', as Old English appointment to administrative offices did not drop significantly from 1556 to 1580.[2] Administrative displacement was gradual and minimal, and Howth's compilation does not reflect a specific concern with the loss of bureaucratic office. However, Howth's compilation clearly registers concern with displacement from positions of influence, and influential positions such as lord justice, lord chancellor, vice-treasurer and marshal of the field were given increasingly to New Englishmen after 1556.[3] What the loss of these positions meant was the loss of the ability to determine, implement and control the conquest. It meant also the loss of Old English voice and influence on the Irish privy council, an institution whose responsibilities increased over the period in question and through which new institutions such as provincial presidencies could be implemented outside parliamentary legislation.[4] The cess controversy offers a case in point, as Ellis has noted, when the few dissenting voices on the Irish council 'underlined the local community's declining influence with the Dublin administration'.[5] Thus, when neither parliament nor great councils were called, the Old English aristocracy at large had no access to a forum through which to effect counsel. And, as Chapter Four illustrated, Howth was particularly concerned that Old English displacement meant the loss of the Old English aristocracy's ability to press their counsel, a position Howth expanded upon in particular as he outlined his rejection of Sidney's attempted abolition of coign and livery (ff. 129r–130r). The abolition of coign and livery harboured more comprehensive ramifications to which Howth was sensitive. If implemented, the centralisation of power under the Dublin administration, not unlike the tendency towards centralisation evident elsewhere in Europe, would dismantle the traditional military structure administered by the Old English and the local social and economic institutions on which that structure was based. It would undermine the entire fabric on which Old English aristocratic identity and security were founded.

The issue of displacement was thus of primary concern to Howth as he began to compile in 1569, and it was the representation of its justification under Sidney in particular that compelled Howth to opposition. Old English displacement had begun earlier under Sussex, yet Howth did not object to Sussex's policies at the time, and in fact served as his spokesman at court against opponents. Nor did he raise the subject of displacement under Sussex in passages on his administration in *The Book of Howth*, though these passages were composed well after Sussex's departure and at a time when Howth was concerned with precisely this issue. Brady's suggestion that Sidney's policies were essentially continuations of Sussex's forces us then to consider why Howth was not moved to object to the process of displacement that began to intensify under Sussex but was clearly concerned with this process under Sidney.[6] Here Howth's collection offers insight not only into the factors that bred Old English opposition, but into debates concerning the nature, course and impact of reform government. Howth's political position on reform government clearly shifted between the administrations of Sussex and Sidney, and this transitional period is at the centre of Canny's and Brady's divergent assessments of the course and impact of conquest in the early Elizabethan period.[7]

While Sidney's policies might not have been original – and Sussex's policies had engendered opposition not unlike that against Sidney, particularly regarding the cess – there were radically new elements in their implementation, one of which, as Canny has argued, was 'attitudes towards the Irish'.[8] Also new was increased concern with Old English identity. Sidney was highly attuned to distinctions between the Old and New English communities. In *Two Bokes of the Histories of Ireland*, for example, Campion devoted an entire chapter to categorisation of the Old English aristocracy by the degree to which each family had adopted Gaelic practice, identifying some as 'not very Irish', others as 'now degenerate and become mere Irish', and yet others as 'now very wild Irish'.[9] Campion states specifically that he had acquired this list from Sidney, and as Howth copied this chapter into his own collection he would have been alerted to Sidney's attention to the issue of cultural identity among the Old English. Sidney's awareness that division between the Old and New English communities was at issue is also betrayed by his concern to create unity of purpose between them in his speech before the closing parliamentary session of 1571, as recorded by Campion.[10] This was a rhetorical strategy on Sidney's part in defence of his attempt to press legislation on that parliament which resulted only in aggravating the conflict between the two communities. Old English opposition to the wines bill, as noted in Chapter Four, led John Hooker to bombastically compare his Old English opponents to the 'unthankful Israelites' and 'ungrateful Athenians'.[11]

As with the presentation of Old English failure to accomplish successful conquest in O'Neill's attainder, such representations of the Old English could also be used to justify their displacement. Edmund Tremayne suggested that 'the best and most safest way to govern this land without corruption or doubt is to send good men, new and new, out of England to rule as is aforesaid in every good office'.[12] Without mentioning the Old English specifically, the necessity of their displacement is as implicit here as in O'Neill's attainder. Tremayne's proposal may well have originated with Sidney for, contrary to assumptions that Sidney adopted many of Tremayne's proposals, Canny argues that Tremayne served rather as Sidney's mouthpiece, much as Campion did.[13] Furthermore, we know from elsewhere that not only was Sidney well aware of the issue of displacement, he was well aware of the resentment it created in the Old English. In the midst of the first round of the cess controversy in 1577 Sidney wrote to Elizabeth denigrating the agents sent by the cess opponents to London, stating that one of them, Barnaby Scurlocke, had 'never ceased to impugn English government' ever since 'in the time of my Lord of Sussex's government he was displaced'.[14]

Canny has identified other reform practices, institutions and attitudes that contributed to the new nature of intensified conquest under Sidney, including attempted plantation, an increasing concern with religious reform and, as already mentioned, provincial presidencies, that together created 'trauma' for the Old English in the period 1565–76.[15] This was precisely the period when Howth was compelled to begin *The Book of Howth*, a text reflective of his own anxiety. However, Howth makes only passing reference to many of the factors Canny identified as critical to Old English security. Rather, his anxiety stemmed from what he perceived to be the displacement of his community in favour of the New English. The degree of displacement conveyed in Howth's compilation, in tandem with the specific factors he identified as causal, describes an aristocracy in the throes of debilitation. What Howth describes is an aristocracy in crisis.

Lawrence Stone's analysis of a general crisis and decline in the Tudor–Stuart aristocracy has received much criticism.[16] However, the points of Stone's thesis that have been challenged as well as refined suggest its potential merit when applied to the deteriorating position of the Old English aristocracy as portrayed by Howth. Most recently, for example, G.W. Bernard has argued against Stone's presentation of the Tudor aristocracy's lost role as counsellors.[17] Howth's compilation conveys a distinct concern that leading members of the Old English nobility were no longer able to fulfil this role. Similarly, Bernard challenges the accuracy of portrayals of the Tudor nobility's declining military role, noting that this would only have been the case had England created a 'standing army staffed by professional officers', something that, he notes, was never even attempted.[18] Once again, of course, Bernard's criticism underscores a vital consideration in the decline of the Old English aristocracy: a standing army staffed largely by New English professional officers was created in Ireland to the detriment of the Old English nobility's dominance of its influential positions. This standing army was a manifestation of the linked processes of Old English displacement at the hands of the New English and centralisation of the military under Sidney, something again poignantly reflected in Sidney's attempted abolition of coign and livery, to which Howth so ardently objected. Sidney in fact belaboured the need for a standing army in Ireland in his closing speech before the Dublin parliament in 1571, as well as belabouring Old English opposition to it.[19]

The trend towards centralisation forced transition on the nobility across Europe in the sixteenth century.[20] Given the common concern of centralising governments to regulate administrative, economic and military systems while controlling religious conformity and loyalty in the midst of change that could be rapid and, importantly, imposed by a government's prerogative powers, as was attempted with increasing intensity in Ireland under Sidney, it is not surprising that the Old English aristocracy resisted this trend, as did many of their counterparts elsewhere in Europe. In sixteenth-century Ireland this process was complicated by the additional factor of intensified conquest and the influx of a competing colonial community that proved itself more amenable to the elements of centralisation and reform deemed necessary by the viceroy's attempt to secure control.

The Book of Howth can no longer be dismissed as an incoherent collection. It reveals substantial information of importance to Howth's personal experience, not least the factors that triggered his evolving opposition. It also clarifies why he ultimately chose reconciliation with the Dublin authorities in the early 1580s just as some of his peers, Baltinglass for instance, engaged in more intensive opposition. Howth was not and had not ever been disloyal to the crown. Rather he opposed its policies and sought to regain influence from which position he could affect policy. The position he at long last accomplished in the Dublin administration in the early 1580s was precisely that for which his compilation had lobbied.

The Book of Howth also helps to compensate for the paucity of information regarding the position of the lords in the parliamentary sessions of 1569–71 by revealing the degree to which Howth participated in the opposition known to have been generated in the commons by this parliament's legislation. Similarly, it indicates the need for reconsideration of the cess controversy of 1577–8 as more than a reflection of aristocratic economic self-interest. Howth's collection thus helps to answer many of the questions raised in recent decades concerning Elizabethan conquest, including principally the

Old English community's reception of its implementation and effect. Howth's collection also suggests that these questions might be better answered by taking into consideration larger European patterns as opposed to their consideration within the confines of colonial control as exercised by England in Ireland, for those aspects of reformed conquest that Howth specifically opposed and that most affected him were measures that illustrate the degree to which the Dublin administration participated in the much larger European-wide movement towards centralisation as it adapted that process to facilitate England's conquest of Ireland. Howth's compilation also conveys the degree to which cultural imperialism played a role in the deterioration of the Old English community. This was a situation that would only intensify for Howth's successors. Before the privy council in London in 1599, Howth's grandson, Christopher St Lawrence, would exclaim: 'I am sorry that when I am in England I should be esteemed an Irish man, and in Ireland, an English man; I have spent my blood, engaged and endangered my life often to do her majesty service and do beseech to have it so regarded.'[21] His grandfather would have endorsed every aspect of this statement: its presentation of the ambiguous cultural identity of the Old English, their loyalty and sacrifice in England's service, and their plea for recognition and reward.

Appendix A:
Lands held by Christopher St Lawrence, 7th Baron of Howth

County of Dublin

Parish of Baldongan. 380 acres*
Parish of Baldoyle
     Stapolin
Parish of Ballymadun
     Boraneston. 1 manor, 2 messuages; 70 acres
Parish of Balscaddan. 2 messuages; 14 acres
Parish of Clondalkin. 1 manor, 1 messuage; 10 acres
Parish of Coolock. 1 messuage
     Raheny. 60 acres
Parish of Finglas
     Skyfuble. 1 messuage; 53 acres
Parish of Kilbarrocke. 6 messuages; 180 acres
Parish of Killester. 3 messuages; 74 acres
Parish of Hollywood
     Kittanstowne/Kitteston/Kyltagheston. 100 acres*
Parish of Howth
     Howth manor
     Townlands, Island of Howth. 350 acres
Parish of Lusk
     Colcot/Colecot/Little Coalecott. 40 acres
     Effelston. 2 messuages; 131 acres
     Great Tyrrelston. 140 acres
     Hedgestown/Hogiston
     Jordanston. 160 acres*
     Kenure. 1 messuage; 3 acres
     Obriston/Oberstown/O Breston. 20 acres
     Rathmooney/Ramouney. 200 acres*
     Rogerston. 10 messuages; 120 acres
     Rowans (Much, Middle and Little Roan). 100 acres
     Scallardeston. 30 acres
     Toman/Twomond. 100 acres*
     Whiteston. 2 messuages; 95 acres and 1 watermill
Parish of Parnelston. 5 messuages; 51 acres
Parish of Swords. 1 manor
Parish of Ward. 300 acres
     Spreckleston. Sallonston (aka Athfallan)

Parish of Westpalstown
        Caylaghton
                Total in County Dublin: 2,781 acres

County of Louth
Drogheda. Rent of 40s. from 7 shops; business unknown
Darieston. 3 messuages; 62 acres

County of Meath
Parish of Donomore. 235 acres*
Parish of Donshaughlin. 435 acres*
Parish of Emlough. 350 acres*
Parish of Killberry. 290 acres*
Parish of Kilpatrick. 160 acres*
Town of Navan. 3 stangs, 14 tenements; 3 acres*
Lismullen. 1 manor house
                Total in County Meath: 1,473 acres

* Though these lands have been identified as holdings of the 7th baron, no specific acreage has been found for his tenure; acreage amounts for these holdings are as given in the 1654 survey.
    Total identifiable holdings: 4,316 acres; 5 manors
    Approximate worth: £130 per annum

Appendix B:
Stages of
Manuscript Construction

DATE OF ENTRY	FOLIOS	HAND*	CONTENTS
Phase One			
1569–71	1 r–v	VII	description of Ireland
	2r–5v	VII	excerpts from the *Polychronicon*
	6r–59v	VII⁺	copy of *The English Conquest of Ireland*
	60r–61r	VII	Kildare, Desmond, Ormond genealogies and obituaries
	61v–101v	VII	excerpts from *Pembridge's Annals* and a chronicle maintained by John Plunkett
	104r–120r	VII	excerpts from Walter Hussey's chronicle covering selected events of 1485–1554
	149r–151r	XII	excerpt from Finglas's 'Breviate'
	155r–158v	XIII	knights' fees owed under Edward II
	159r–160r	VII	Lydgate excerpt on Knights Templar
	160r–167v	VII	annalistic entries from Hall, Fabyan and the *Polychronicon*
	168r–173r	VII	Life of Muhammad from *Polychronicon*
	176r–v	VII	political prophecies
1571	120v–127v	IX	entries of original composition covering 1554–66
	146v–147r	IX	list of giants
	160r, 161r, 162v	IX	brief entries on King Arthur
1571–2	A1r–A13r	III	Fionn mac Cumhaill and the Fianna
	102r–103(i)v	III	Suleiman and the Siege of Rhodes
	127v–133r	III	entries of original composition covering 1566–72
	154v	III	Siege of Rouen
	173v–174v	III	list of Irish and English captains

* Roman numerals as assigned to each hand by the calendar editors are used here; however, corrections have been made to the specific folios contributed by each hand; see *Calendar of Carew Manuscripts*, vol. V, p. xiii.

+ Hand VIII alternates very briefly with Hand VII on ff. 14v–17r, 66v, 69v, 84r, 87v and 88r.

| 1572–3 | A13v–A19v, 58v, 103(i)v, 113v, 133r, 152v–154v, 175r–v | IV | excerpts from Campion |

Phase Two

1573–6	133v–134r	X	plantation in Ulster
1577	134v–135v	Howth	commentary on cess and copy of 1577 submission statement
1578	136r	Howth	arrest of Kildare, Desmond, Clanrickard
	136v	XI	1578 submission statement
1579	137r	Howth	brief note on appointment of Drury, cess, murder of Henry Davells
	160v	Howth	brief entry on Pope Joan

Additional entries made by Howth of imprecise date.

Date unknown	A1r–v	Fianna, Zenobia, Methe, O'Neill and O'Donnell kings
1572?	A20r–A22v	Battle of Clontarf
1572 or before	151r–152v	list of rebellions in England
1572 or after	132v–133r	provincial presidencies, unnatural events, Desmond Rebellion
1579?	177r–v	note on Irish cities, creation of knights, biographical information on Walter Hussey, Latin couplet

Folios 137v–146r, 147v and 148 are blank.

Appendix C:
Select emendations to the
Calendar of the Carew Manuscripts
edition of *The Book of Howth*

The calendared edition of Howth's collection contains a variety of errors that compromise the clarity of the text. A selection of these errors has been grouped into two categories below. The third section below contains marginalia that were lost when the folios in Howth's manuscript were cut for binding, reconstructed here from recently identified copies of Howth's work. Readings clarified by reference either to these copies or to the source from which Howth copied are noted as such.

I. *Mistranscriptions*

Calendar, p. 10
'and so one after other did come that the giant and he bound them both and after did agree with them that they should be put at liberty' should read 'and so one after other did come but the giant he bound them both and after did agree with them that they should be put at liberty' (f. A9 and see Lambeth MS 248)

Calendar, p. 19
'septs, Irish of name, planted in these quarters, they reckon the Byrnes, Tolles, Conanaghtes which is the one of McMorowes, O'Mores, O'Conors, O'Demseys, O'Dune' should read 'septs Irish of name planted in these quarters they reckon the Byrnes, Tooles, Cavanaghs which is the ne [sic for nation] of McMorowes, O'Mores, O'Connors, O'Dempseys, O'Dune' (f. A15r and see Campion, p. 7)

Calendar, p. 19
'a noble river which Camerans called Denelifinus Ptoleme ly biu mu' should read 'a noble river which Camerans called Denelifius Ptoleme ly bin um' (f. A15v and see Campion, p. 7)

Calendar, pp. 20–1
'Under Dublin whereto I mounto, 3,– Unild, Glandelaghe, the bishoprics of Elphine, Kyldar, . . .' The editors suggest an alternate reading of 'Under Dublin I-moverto 3 Unild, Glandelaghe', etc.; however, it should read 'Under Dublin whereto Innocentius 3 united Glendalough, the bishoprics of Elphin, Kildare,' etc. (f. A16v and see Campion, p. 10)

Calendar, p. 22
'McMoryshe alias FytzGerrald Baron of Kerry, now L.Courcey, not very Irish, of kin to Sir John Courcey' should read:

McMaurice alias Fitzgerald Baron of Kerry now
Lord Courcey not very Irishe of kin to Sir John Courcey

(The editors have run together into one paragraph what the Howth scribe
entered as two separate entries for McMaurice and Lord Courcey. Either text
was lost when this folio was cut for binding or Howth's scribe altered the
description of McMaurice as he copied from Campion where this entry reads
'McMaurice alias Fitzgerald Baron of Kerry now mere Irish'; f. A17v and see
Campion, p. 13.)

Calendar, p. 23
'Plunket, Baron of Lowth, to Sir Olifer Plunket and his heirs males . . . this is the
2 brother of Beovley O'Neyll, Baron of Donganon' should read

> Plunkett, Baron of Lowth, to Sir Oliver Plunkett and his
> heirs males . . . this is the 2 brother of Beouley (Beaulieu)
> O'Neill, Baron of Dungannon

(Here again the editors combined two separate entries on the Baron of Lowth
and the Baron of Dungannon, implying incorrectly that they were brothers; f.
A18r and see Campion, pp. 13–14. Howth added the biographical information
regarding his father-in-law, John Plunket of Beaulieu, to his copy of Campion's
entry on Lowth.)

Calendar, p. 23
'These are the savages: – Jordans, FytzSymondes, Chamberlains, Russells . . .'
should read 'These are the Savages, Jordans, Fitzsimons, Chamberlains, Russells'
etc. (f. A18r and see Campion, p. 14)

Calendar, p. 71
'in the manner of England; that privilege forth with another that rather was
purchased of the Pope, a dream that was before. Alexander he sent over into
England . . .' should read 'in the manner of England that privilege forthwith
another that rather was purchased of the Pope Adrian that was before Alexander
he sent over in to England.' (In addition to mistranscribing 'Pope Adrian' as the
'pope a dream' the editors' punctuation has also garbled the passage's meaning;
it is Adrian's papal notice that is sent to England, not Alexander who sends to
England; f. 27r.)

Calendar, p. 80
'and he never sent till that he had taken of him the castle of Wicklow' should read
'and he never stint till that he had taken of him the castle of Wicklow' (f. 33r)

Calendar, p. 80
'all it was in spring felony; and the cheer that he ever gave after was much to be
doubted' should read 'all it was in spying, felony, and the cheer that he ever
gave after was much to be doubted' (f. 33v. This passage also probably contains
a scribal error; the passage in *The English Conquest of Ireland* reads 'all it was in
spying, felony, and treachery, and the cheer that he ever gave after was much to
be doubted'.)

II. *Marginalia and interlining*

Howth frequently appended marginalia and interlining to supplement the information contained within text entered earlier by his scribes. The calendar editors transcribed the additions below (as well as others) as integral to passages they were intended to complement. This editorial practice not only compromises the continuity of the narrative, it also conceals Howth's interest in that particular passage and is compounded by the editors' failure to identify the additional hand as Howth's.

Calendar, p. 101
At the completion of the passage from *The English Conquest of Ireland* outlining England's right to Ireland on the bottom of f. 48v the scribe moved to the top of f. 49r to begin the next passage's commentary on Giraldus Cambrensis. Howth later augmented this passage by appending a note on the surrender of Irish kings to Henry VIII in the available space at the foot of f. 48v, revealing his concern with England's right to Ireland.

Calendar, pp. 115–16
In this case again the scribe concluded a passage on John de Courcy copied from *The English Conquest of Ireland* on f. 58v and moved to the top of f. 59r to begin the next passage on Hugh de Lacey. As above, Howth later utilised the blank folio space at the foot of f. 58v to append passages on the conquest of Ulster, Elizabeth's inherited title to Ulster, and the submission of Irish kings, again revealing his interest in England's right to Ireland.

Calendar, pp. 146 and 150
Among many others, on these pages the editors noted only that marginalia had been added by another hand but did not identify the hand as Howth's. In each of these cases Howth provided supplemental information on the Burkes relevant to the descent of the title to Ulster. (ff. 80v and 84r)

III. *Reconstructed marginalia missing or incomplete in the* Calendar

Calendar, p. 120
'Margaret that married the Earl of Glamorgan, Joan that married Thomas Earl of Kildare, Catherine that married the Earl of Londry, Margaret that married the Earl of Desmond, Eleanor married lo' (f. 61v; reconstructed from Lambeth MS 248; the closing lines remain obscured by the Lambeth binding)

Calendar, p. 122
'They used shoes to the knees, cleft afore, and laced with thongs of leather, their hosen to the knee or ham. It was a shame to be called an Englishman but Normans or Frenchman' (f. 62v; reconstructed from Lambeth MS 248)

Calendar, p. 146
'The Earl of Desmond, the Earl of Kildare, with a chosen number of gentlemen as Verdons, Petites, Tutes, Nugents, Howths, Plunketts, Talbots, Barnwalls, Tyrells, and diverse others served valiant at the winning of Calais' (f. 81r; reconstructed from Lambeth MS 248)

Calendar, p. 154

'There was 3 also of the Irish that did commit that murder which they say was of the Howths but it was untrue as it appeareth after in the chronicles' (f. 86v; reconstructed from Lambeth MS 248)

Calendar, p. 248

'The time of Lent was begun by Excombertus a Saxon king in Kent AD 635 and Cadwall king of Britain in Fabian the fifth part ff. 135' (f. 168r; reconstructed from Lambeth MS 248)

Calendar, p. 22

'St Lawrence, Baron of Howth, which came before the conquest in company with Sir John Courcey, Earl and President of Ulster with a .... ut ait Galfredus Rodebuc St Laurens fuit viri strenui atque fortes et robustissimi in bello' (f. A17v and see Trinity College MS 593; this passage has been too heavily lined through to permit full reconstruction.)

Bibliography

Primary Sources

Bodleian Library, Oxford

Carte MSS
    55–8: Papers of Sir William Fitzwilliam
Laud MSS
    526: Papers of Sir George Carew
    610: Papers of Sir George Carew
    611: Papers of Sir George Carew
    612: Papers of Sir George Carew
    613: Papers of Sir George Carew
    614: Papers of Sir George Carew
Rawlinson MSS
    B 487: Miscellaneous fragments relating to Ireland
    B 488: Annals of Tigernach and other fragments

British Library

Additional MSS
    4791: Papers of Sir James Ware
    4796: Papers of Sir James Ware
    4813: Papers of Sir James Ware (*Annals of Ireland, 1558–91*)
    4821: Papers of Sir James Ware
    4822: Papers of Sir James Ware
    19837–42: Entry-book of Recognizances in the Court of Chancery in Ireland 1570–1634
    40674: Annals of Ireland compiled by Philip Flatsbury
    47172: Entry-book of the Court of Castle Chamber in Dublin
    48015: (Yelverton 16) Papers relating to Ireland 1538–*c*.1600
Cottonian MSS
    Domitian xviii: Miscellaneous papers relating to Ireland
Harleian MSS
    35: Miscellaneous tracts
    177: Latin abridgement of *Expugnatio Hibernica*
    2408: Brief chronicle of Ireland to 1546
Lansdowne MSS
    418: Papers of Sir James Ware

Farmleigh House, Dublin

MS IV E.6: Edmund Campion's *Two Bokes of the Histories of Ireland*
MS IV C.26: Edmund Campion's *Two Bokes of the Histories of Ireland*

Lambeth Palace Library

MS 248: Irish historical tracts
MS 264: Brut Chronicle
Carew MSS
    597: Pelham letter book, 1578–9
    598: *The English Conquest of Ireland*
    600: Miscellaneous Irish papers
    608: Miscellaneous Irish papers
    621: Miscellaneous Irish papers
    623: *The Book of Howth*
    628: Tables of council books, 1543–1605
    635: Irish genealogies
    636: Catalogue of Carew's papers

National Library of Ireland

MS 9039: Inspeximus of reversal of attainder of Richard Bermingham
    exemplified by request of Christopher St Lawrence, Lord of Howth
Genealogical Office, MS 64: Funeral entries
Genealogical Office, MS 805: Howth Family Tree, 1189–1542
Ainsworth Report 140: St Lawrence Family Papers

Public Record Office, London

SP 63: State Papers, Ireland

Trinity College, Dublin

MS 539: Miscellaneous Irish papers
MS 581: Miscellaneous Irish papers
MS 583: *Pembridge's Annals*
MS 584: Miscellaneous Irish papers including extracts from
    The Book of Howth
MS 591: Miscellaneous Irish papers
MS 592: *The English Conquest of Ireland*
MS 593: *The English Conquest of Ireland* and extracts from
    The Book of Howth
MS 656: Miscellaneous Irish papers
MS 663: Records of Elizabethan heraldry
MS 664: Notebook of Sir James Ware
MS 842: Patrick Finglas, 'Breviate of the Getting of Ireland'
MS 852: Records from Court of Castle Chamber

Guides and Bibliographies

Abbot, T.K., *Catalogue of the Manuscripts in the Library of Trinity College, Dublin* (Dublin: Hodges, Figgis & Co., 1900)

Donovan, Brian C. and David Edwards, *British Sources for Irish History 1485–1641: A Guide to Manuscripts in Local, Regional and Specialised Repositories in England, Scotland and Wales* (Dublin: Irish Manuscripts Commission, 1997)

Edwards, R.W. Dudley and Mary O'Dowd, *Sources for Early Modern Irish History, 1534–1641* (Cambridge University Press, 1985)

Hayes, R.J., *Manuscript Sources for the History of Irish Civilization*, 11 vols (Boston: G.K. Hall, 1965)

James, M.R., *A Descriptive Catalogue of the Manuscripts in the Library of Lambeth Palace* (Cambridge University Press, 1930)

Matthew, H.C.G. and Brian Harrison (eds), *Oxford Dictionary of National Biography*, 61 vols (Oxford University Press, 2004)

Todd, Henry J., *Catalogue of the Archiepiscopal Manuscripts in the Library of Lambeth Palace* (London, 1812)

Printed Primary Sources

Acts of the Privy Council of England, 1542–1631, J.R. Dasent et al. (eds), 46 vols (London, 1890–1964)

Calendar of the Carew Manuscripts Preserved in the Archiepiscopal Library at Lambeth, 1515–1624, J.S. Brewer and William Bullen (eds), 6 vols (London, 1867–73)

'A Calendar of the Contents of the Red Book of the Exchequer', James Frederick Ferguson (ed.), *Proceedings and Transactions of the Kilkenny and Southeast of Ireland Archaeological Society*, vol. 3 (1854–5), pp. 35–66

Calendar of Inquisitions Formerly in the Office of the Chief Remembrancer of the Exchequer Prepared from the manuscripts of the Irish Record Commission, Margaret C. Griffith (ed.) (Dublin: Irish Manuscripts Commission, 1991)

'Calendar of the Irish Council Book: 1 March 1581 to 1 July 1586, made by John P. Prendergast between 1867 and 1869', David B. Quinn (ed.), *Analecta Hibernica*, vol. 24 (1967), pp. 91–180

Calendar of the Manuscripts of the Marquis of Salisbury, Preserved at Hatfield House, Hertfordshire, 24 vols (London: Historical Manuscripts Commission, 1883–1976)

Calendar of Patent and Close Rolls of Chancery in Ireland, J. Morrin (ed.), 3 vols (Dublin, 1861–3)

Calendar of State Papers, Ireland. Tudor Period 1571–1575, Mary O'Dowd (ed.) (Dublin: Irish Manuscripts Commission, 2000)

Calendar of the State Papers Relating to Ireland of the Reigns of Henry VIII, Edward VI, Mary, and Elizabeth I, 1509–1603, H.C. Hamilton, E.G. Atkinson and R.P. Mahaffy (eds), 11 vols (London, 1860–1912)

Census of Ireland, circa 1659: With Supplementary Material from the Poll Money Ordinances (1660–1661), Seamus Pender (ed.) (Dublin: Irish Manuscripts Commission, 1939)

Chartularies of St Mary's Abbey, Dublin with the Register of its House at Dunbrody, and Annals of Ireland, J.T. Gilbert (ed.), 2 vols (London, 1884)

Civil Survey AD 1654–1656, Robert C. Simington (ed.), vol. VII: County of Dublin (Dublin: Irish Manuscripts Commission, 1945)

Crown Surveys of Lands 1540–41 with the Kildare Rental Begun in 1518, Gearoid MacNiocaill (ed.) (Dublin: Irish Manuscripts Commission, 1992)

Dublin City Franchise Roll, 1468–1512, Colm Lennon and James Murray (eds) (Dublin Corporation, 1998)

Extent of Irish Monastic Possessions, 1540–41, from Manuscripts in the Public Record Office, N.B. White (ed.) (Dublin: Irish Manuscripts Commission, 1943)

Facsimiles of National Manuscripts of Ireland, J.T. Gilbert (ed.), 4 vols (Dublin, 1874–84)

Fitzwilliam Accounts, 1560–1565, A.K. Longfield (ed.) (Dublin, 1960)

Hooker, John, 'John Hooker's Diary, or Journal, January 17 to February 23, 1568–69' in C.L. Falkiner (ed.), *Proceedings of the Royal Irish Academy*, vol. 25 C (1905), pp. 563–6

Inquisitionum in Officio Rotulorum Cancellariae Hiberniae Asservatarum repertorium, J. Hardiman (ed.), 2 vols (Dublin, 1826–9)

'The Irish Abridgement of the Expugnatio Hibernica', Whitley Stokes (ed.), *English Historical Review*, vol. 20 (1905), pp. 77–115

Irish Fiants of the Tudor Sovereigns during the Reigns of Henry VIII, Edward VI, Philip & Mary, and Elizabeth I, K.W. Nicholls (ed.), 4 vols (Dublin: Eamonn de Burca, 1994)

Irish Monastic and Episcopal Deeds, AD 1200–1600, N.B. White (ed.) (Dublin: Irish Manuscripts Commission, 1936)

Letters and Memorials of State, Arthur Collins (ed.), 2 vols (London, 1746)

Lyrics of the Red Book of Ossory, Richard Leighton Greene (ed.) (Oxford: Blackwell, 1974)

The Manuscripts of Charles Haliday, esq., of Dublin. Acts of the Privy Council in Ireland, 1556–71, in *Fifteenth Report of the Royal Commission on Historical Manuscripts* (London: HM Stationery Office, 1897)

Records of the Honorable Society of Lincoln's Inn. The Black Books. 5 vols (London: Lincoln's Inn, 1897–1968)

'The Red Book of the Diocese of Ossory', in *Tenth Report of the Royal Commission on Historical Manuscripts* (London: HM Stationery Office, 1885)

The Red Book of the Earls of Kildare, Gearoid MacNiocaill (ed.) (Dublin: Irish Manuscripts Commission, 1964)

The Red Book of Ormond, Newport B. White (ed.) (Dublin: Irish Manuscripts Commission, 1932)

Registers of Christ Church Cathedral, Dublin, Raymond Refausse and Colm Lennon (eds) (Dublin: Four Courts Press, 1998)

Report on the Manuscripts of the Earl of Egmont, 2 vols (London: Historical Manuscripts Commission, 1905)

Report on the Manuscripts of Lord De L'Isle and Dudley Preserved at Penshurst Place, 6 vols (London: Historical Manuscripts Commission, 1925–66)

Sidney State Papers, 1565–70, Tomas O Laidhin (ed.) (Dublin: Irish Manuscripts Commission, 1962)

State Papers, Henry VIII, 11 vols (London, 1830–52)

The Statutes at Large, Passed in the Parliaments Held in Ireland, 1310–1800, 20 vols (Dublin, 1786–1801)

Walsingham Letter-Book or Register of Ireland, May 1578 to December 1579, J. Hogan and N. McNeill O'Farrell (eds) (Dublin: Irish Manuscripts Commission 1959)

Contemporary Writings

Annala Rioghacta Eireann (Annals of the Four Masters), John O'Donovan (ed./trans.), 7 vols (2nd edn, Dublin, 1856)

Annales Hiberniae (Grace's Annals), Richard Butler (ed.) (Dublin, 1843)

Annalium Hiberniae Chronicon (The Annals of Ireland by Friar John Clyn and Thady Dowling), Richard Butler (ed.) (Dublin, 1849)

Beacon, Richard, *Solon, his Follie*, Clare Carroll and Vincent P. Carey (eds) (Binghamton, NY: Medieval and Renaissance Texts & Studies, 1996)

Camden, William, *Britannia*, Richard Gough (ed.), 4 vols (2nd edn, London, 1806 reprint)

Campion, Edmund, *Two Bokes of the Histories of Ireland (1571)*, A.F. Vossen (ed.) (Assen: Van Gorcum, 1963)

Cath Finntragha, Cecile O'Rahilly (ed.) (Dublin Institute for Advanced Studies, 1975)

Chaucer, Geoffrey, 'The Miller's Tale' in *Norton Anthology of English Literature*, M.H. Abrams (ed.) vol. I (6th edn, New York: W.W. Norton, 1993), pp. 101–17

Cox, Richard, *Hibernia Anglicana: or, The History of Ireland, from the Conquest thereof by the English, to this Present Time*, 2 vols (London, 1689–90)

Davies, John, *A Discovery of the True Causes why Ireland was Never Entirely Subdued and brought under Obedience of the Crown of England until the Beginning of His Majesty's Happy Reign (1612)*, James P. Myers (ed.) (Washington, DC: Catholic University of America Press, 1988)

Derricke, John, *The Image of Irelande with a Discoverie of Woodkarne (1581)* (Delmar, NY: Scholars' Facsimiles & Reprints, 1998).

Duanaire Finn, 57 vols (London: Irish Texts Society, 1899–1994), vol. VII, ed. and trans. Eoin MacNeill, 1904, vol. XXVIII, ed. and trans. Gerard Murphy, 1933

English Conquest of Ireland: A Parallel Text from MS Trinity College Dublin, E.2.31, about 1425 AD and MS Rawlinson, B. 490, Bodleian Library, about 1440 AD, Frederick J. Furnivall (ed.) (London: Early English Texts Society, 1896)

Fabyan, Robert, *The New Chronicles of England and France* (London, 1811, reprint of 1516 edn)

Finglas, Patrick, 'Breviate of the Getting of Ireland and the Decay of the Same' in *Hibernica, or some ancient pieces relating to Ireland*, Walter Harris (ed.), 2 vols (Dublin, 1770), vol. 1, pp. 79–103

Gerrard, William, 'Sir William Gerrard's Notes of his Report on Ireland, 1577–78', C. McNeill (ed.), *Analecta Hibernica*, vol. 2 (1931), pp. 95–201

Giraldus Cambrensis, *Expugnatio Hibernica (The Conquest of Ireland)*, A.B. Scott and F.X. Martin (eds/trans) (Dublin: Royal Irish Academy, 1978)

——/Gerald of Wales, *The History and Topography of Ireland*, John J. O'Meara (trans.) (rev. edn, Harmondsworth: Penguin Books, 1982)

Hall, Edward, *Hall's Chronicle, Containing the History of England during the Reign of Henry the IV . . . to the Reign of Henry VIII* (London, 1809 reprint)

Hanmer, Meredith, *The Chronicle of Ireland*, in *Ancient Irish Histories: The Works of Spenser, Campion, Hanmer, and Marleburrough*, vol. II, James Ware (ed.) (New York: Kennikat Press, 1970 reprint)

Herbert, William, *Croftus Sive de Hibernia Liber*, Arthur Keaveney and John A. Madden (eds) (Dublin: Irish Manuscripts Commission, 1992)

Higden, Ranulf, *Polychronicon Ranulphi Higden Monachi Cestrensis; Together with the English Translations of John Trevisa and of an Unknown Writer of the Fifteenth Century*, Joseph Rawson Lumby (ed.), 9 vols (London, 1865–6 reprint)

Holinshed, Raphael, *Chronicles of England, Scotland and Ireland*, Henry Ellis (ed.), 6 vols (London, 1807–8 reprint)

Keating, Geoffrey, *Foras Feasa ar Eirinn* (*The History of Ireland*), David Comyn and Patrick S. Dinneen (eds/trans), 4 vols (London: Irish Texts Society, 1902–14)

Leland, Thomas, *The History of Ireland from the Invasion of Henry II*, 3 vols (London, 1773)

Lydgate, John, *Here Begynneth the Boke of Iohan Bochas, Discryuing the Fall of Princes, Princesses, and Other Nobles: Translated into Englysshe by Iohn Lydgate Monke of Bury, Begynnyng at Adam and Eue, and Endyng with Kyng Iohan of Fraunce, Taken Prisoner at Poyters by Prince Edwarde* (London, 1527), STC 3176

——*Fall of Princes*, Henry Bergin (ed.), 4 vols (Washington, DC: Carnegie Institution of Washington, 1923–7)

Lynch, John, *Cambrensis Eversus*, Matthew Kelly (ed./trans.), 3 vols (Dublin, 1851)

Malory, Sir Thomas, *Le Morte D'Arthur: Caxton's Malory*, James W. Spisak, William Matthews and Bert Dillon (eds), 2 vols (Berkeley and Los Angeles: University of California Press, 1983)

O'Grady, Standish, *Silva Gadelica*, 2 vols (London, 1892)

Sidney, Sir Henry, *A Viceroy's Vindication? Sir Henry Sidney's Memoir of Service in Ireland, 1556–78*, Ciaran Brady (ed.) (Cork University Press, 2002)

Song of Dermot and the Earl, Goddard H. Orpen (ed.) (Oxford: Clarendon Press, 1892)

Spenser, Edmund, *A View of the Present State of Ireland*, W.L. Renwick (ed.) (Oxford: Clarendon Press, 1970)

——*View of the State of Ireland*, Andrew Hadfield and Willy Maley (eds) (Oxford: Blackwell, 1997)

Stow, John, *A Summary of the Chronicles of England* (London, 1575), STC 23325

Tales of the Elders of Ireland: Acallam na Senorach, Ann Dooley and Harry Roe (eds/trans) (Oxford University Press, 1999)

Talland Etair (*The Siege of Howth*), Whitley Stokes (ed.), *Revue Celtique*, vol. 8 (1887), pp. 47–63

Transactions of the Ossianic Society, 6 vols (Dublin, 1854–61)

Walshe, Edward, 'Conjectures Concerning the State of Ireland (1552)', D.B. Quinn (ed.), *Irish Historical Studies*, vol. 5 (1946–7), pp. 303–33

Ware, James, *Rerum Hibernicarum Annales, Regnantibus Henrico VII, Henrico VIII, Edwardo VI & Maria* (Dublin, 1664)

—— *De Scriptoribus Hiberniae. The Whole Works of Sir James Ware*, Walter Harris (ed.), 2 vols (Dublin, 1764)

—— (ed.), *Ancient Irish Histories: the works of Spenser, Campion, Hanmer, and Marleburrough* (Dublin, 1633)

White, Rowland, 'Discors Touching the Reformation of the Realm of Ireland', Nicholas Canny (ed.), *Irish Historical Studies*, vol. 20 (1976–7), pp. 439–63

—— 'Dysorders of the Irisshery, 1571', Nicholas Canny (ed.), *Studia Hibernica*, vol. 19 (1979), pp. 147–60

SECONDARY SOURCES

Asch, Ronald G., *Nobilities in Transition 1550–1700: Courtiers and Rebels in Britain and Europe* (London: Arnold, 2003)

Ashton, Robert, 'The Aristocracy in Transition', *Economic History Review*, vol. 22 (1969), pp. 308–22

Aylmer, G.E., review of Lawrence Stone, *The Crisis of the Aristocracy 1558–1641*, in *Past and Present*, vol. 32 (1965), pp. 113–25

Bagwell, Richard, *Ireland under the Tudors*, 3 vols (London: Holland Press, 1963 reprint)

Baker, J.H., *The Common Law Tradition: lawyers, books and the law* (London: Hambledon Press, 2000)

Ball, Francis Elrington, *History of County Dublin. Part V. Howth and its Owners* (Dublin: Royal Society of Antiquaries of Ireland, 1917)

Barry, John, 'Derricke and Stanihurst: a dialogue', in Jason Harris and Keith Sidwell (eds), *Making Ireland Roman: Irish Neo-Latin Writers and the Republic of Letters* (Cork University Press, 2009), pp. 36–47.

Bell, Ilona, 'Elizabeth I – Always Her Own Free Woman', in Carole Levin and Patricia A. Sullivan (eds), *Political Rhetoric, Power and Renaissance Women* (Albany, NY: State University of New York Press, 1995), pp. 57–82

—— '"Souereaigne Lord of lordly Lady of this land": Elizabeth, Stubbs, and the *Gaping Gvlf*', in Julia M. Walker (ed.), *Dissing Elizabeth: Negative Representations of Gloriana* (Durham and London: Duke Universitiy Press, 1998), pp. 99–117

Belloc, Elizabeth, 'Howth Castle', *Irish Monthly*, vol. 80 (1952), pp. 326–9

Bernard, G.W., *Power and Politics in Tudor England* (Aldershot: Ashgate, 2000)

Blanks, David R., 'Western Views of Islam in the Premodern Period: A Brief History of Past Approaches', in David R. Blanks and Michael Frassetto (eds), *Western Views of Islam in Medieval and Early Modern Europe* (New York: St Martin's Press, 1999), pp. 1–9

Boran, Elizabethanne, 'Ussher and the Collection of Manuscripts in Early Modern Europe', in Jason Harris and Keith Sidwell (eds), *Making Ireland Roman: Irish Neo-Latin Writers and the Republic of Letters* (Cork University Press, 2009), pp. 176–94

Bottigheimer, Karl, 'The Failure of the Reformation in Ireland: *une question bien posée*', *Journal of Ecclesiastical History*, vol. 36 (1985), pp. 196–207

Bradshaw, Brendan, 'The Opposition to the Ecclesiastical Legislation in the Irish

Reformation Parliament', *Irish Historical Studies*, vol. 26 (1969), pp. 285–303

——'The Beginnings of Modern Ireland', in Brian Farrell (ed.), *The Irish Parliamentary Tradition* (Dublin: Gill & Macmillan, 1973), pp. 68–87

——*The Dissolution of the Religious Orders in Ireland under Henry VIII* (Cambridge University Press, 1974)

——'Cromwellian Reform and the Origins of the Kildare Rebellion, 1533–34', *Transactions of the Royal Historical Society*, 5th ser., vol. 27 (1977), pp. 69–93

——'Sword, Word and Strategy in the Reformation in Ireland', *Historical Journal*, vol. 21 (1978), pp. 475–502

——*The Irish Constitutional Revolution of the Sixteenth Century* (Cambridge University Press, 1979)

——'Nationalism and Historical Scholarship in Modern Ireland', *Irish Historical Studies*, vol. 26 (1989), pp. 329–51

——'The English Reformation and Identity Formation in Ireland and Wales', in Brendan Bradshaw and Peter Roberts (eds), *British Consciousness and Identity: the making of Britain, 1533–1707* (Cambridge University Press, 1998)

——,Andrew Hadfield and Willy Maley (eds), *Representing Ireland: Literature and the Origins of Conflict, 1534–1660* (Cambridge University Press, 1993)

Brady, Ciaran, 'Faction and the Origins of the Desmond Rebellion of 1579', *Irish Historical Studies*, vol. 22 (1981), pp. 289–312

——'The Killing of Shane O'Neill: some new evidence', *The Irish Sword*, vol. 15 (1982), pp. 116–23

——'Conservative Subversives: the community of the Pale and the Dublin administration, 1556–1586', in Patrick J. Corish (ed.), *Radicals, Rebels & Establishments* (Belfast: Appletree Press, 1985), pp. 11–32

——'Court, Castle and Country: the Framework of Government in Tudor Ireland', in Ciaran Brady and Raymond Gillespie (eds), *Natives and Newcomers: the Making of Irish Colonial Society, 1541–1641* (Dublin: Irish Academic Press, 1986), pp. 22–49

——'The Road to the View: On the Decline of Reform Thought in Tudor Ireland', in Patricia Coughlan (ed.), *Spenser and Ireland: An Interdisciplinary Perspective* (Cork University Press, 1989), pp. 25–45

——*The Chief Governors: the rise and fall of reform government in Tudor Ireland, 1536–1588* (Cambridge University Press, 1994)

——'The Captains' Games: army and society in Elizabethan Ireland', in Thomas Bartlett and Keith Jeffery (eds), *A Military History of Ireland* (Cambridge University Press, 1996), pp. 136–59

——'England's Defence and Ireland's Reform: The Dilemma of the Irish Viceroys, 1541–1641', in Brendan Bradshaw and John Morrill (eds), *The British Problem, c.1534–1707: State Formation in the Atlantic Archipelago* (New York: St Martin's Press, 1996), pp. 89–117

——*Shane O'Neill* (Dundalk, 1996)

——'Shane O'Neill Departs from the Court of Elizabeth: Irish, English, Scottish Perspectives and the Paralysis of Policy, July 1559 to April 1562', in S.J. Connolly (ed.), *Kingdoms United? Great Britain and Ireland since 1500, Integration and Diversity* (Dublin: Four Courts Press, 1999), pp. 13–28

——'The Attainder of Shane O'Neill, Sir Henry Sidney and the Problems of Tudor State-building in Ireland', in Ciaran Brady and Jane Ohlmeyer (eds), *British Interventions in Early Modern Ireland* (Cambridge University Press, 2005), pp. 28–48

——and Raymond Gillespie (eds), *Natives and Newcomers: the making of Irish Colonial society, 1541–1641* (Dublin: Irish Academic Press, 1986)

Brammall, Kathryn M., 'Monstrous Metamorphosis: Nature, Morality, and the Rhetoric of Monstrosity in Tudor England', *Sixteenth Century Journal*, vol. 27 (1996), pp. 3–21

Brennan, Michael, *The Sidneys of Penshurst and the Monarchy, 1500–1700* (Aldershot: Ashgate, 2006)

Brundage, James A., 'Domestic Violence in Classical Canon Law', in Richard W. Kaeuper (ed.), *Violence in Medieval Society* (Woodbridge: Boydell Press, 2000), pp. 183–95

Butlin, R.A., 'Land and People, *c*.1600', in T.W. Moody, F.X. Martin and F.J. Byrne (eds), *New History of Ireland*, III: *Early Modern Ireland, 1534–1691* (Oxford: Clarendon Press, 1976), pp. 142–67

Canny, Nicholas, *The Formation of the Old English Elite in Ireland* (Dublin: National University of Ireland, 1975)

——*The Elizabethan Conquest of Ireland: a pattern etablished 1565–76* (New York: Harper & Row, 1976)

——'Why the Reformation Failed in Ireland: *une question mal posée*', *Journal of Ecclesiastical History*, vol. 30 (1979), pp. 423–50

——'Identity Formation in Ireland: the emergence of the Anglo-Irish', in Nicholas Canny and Anthony Pagden (eds), *Colonial Identity in the Atlantic World 1500–1800* (Princeton University Press, 1987), pp. 159–212

——*Kingdom and Colony: Ireland in the Atlantic world, 1560–1800* (Baltimore: Johns Hopkins Press, 1988)

——'Irish, Scottish and Welsh Responses to Centralisation, *c*.1530–*c*.1640: a comparative perspective', in Alexander Grant and Keith J. Stringer (eds), *Uniting the Kingdom? The Making of British History* (London: Routledge, 1995), pp. 147–69

——'Revising the Revisionist', *Irish Historical Studies*, vol. 30 (1996), pp. 242–54

——*Making Ireland British 1580–1650* (Oxford University Press, 2001)

Cardini, Franco, *Europe and Islam*, Caroline Beamish (trans.) (Oxford: Blackwell, 2001)

Carey, Vincent P., 'John Derricke's *Image of Irelande*, Sir Henry Sidney, and the Massacre at Mullaghmast, 1578', *Irish Historical Studies*, vol. 31 (1999), pp. 305–27

——'"Neither Good English nor Good Irish": bi-lingualism and identity formation in sixteenth-century Ireland', in Hiram Morgan (ed.), *Political Ideology in Ireland, 1541–1641* (Dublin: Four Courts Press, 1999), pp. 45–61

——*Surviving the Tudors: The 'Wizard' Earl of Kildare and English rule in Ireland, 1537–1586* (Dublin: Four Courts Press, 2002)

——'A "dubious loyalty": Richard Stanihurst, the "wizard" earl of Kildare, and English-Irish identity', in Vincent P. Carey and Ute Lotz-Heumann (eds), *Taking Sides? Colonial and Confessional Mentalités in Early Modern Ireland* (Dublin: Four Courts Press, 2003), pp. 61–77

Carney, James, 'Literature in Irish, 1169–1534', in Art Cosgrove (ed.), *New History of Ireland, II: Medieval Ireland, 1169–1534* (Oxford: Clarendon Press, 1987), pp. 688–707

Carpenter, Andrew, *Verse in English from Tudor and Stuart Ireland* (Cork University Press, 2003)

Carroll, Clare, *Circe's Cup: Cultural Transformations in Early Modern Ireland* (University of Notre Dame Press, 2001)

Childs, Wendy, and Timothy O'Neill, 'Overseas Trade', in Art Cosgrove (ed.), *New History of Ireland, II: Medieval Ireland, 1169–1534* (Oxford: Clarendon Press, 1987), pp. 492–524

Clark, Mary, Yvonne Desmond and Nodlaig P. Hardiman (eds), *Sir John T. Gilbert 1829–1898: Historian, Archivist and Librarian* (Dublin: Four Courts Press, 1999)

Clarke, Aidan, *The Old English in Ireland, 1625–1642* (London: MacGibbon and Kee, 1966)

Coburn Walsh, Helen, 'The Rebellion of William Nugent, 1581', in R.V. Comerford et al. (eds), *Religion, Conflict and Coexistence in Ireland* (Dublin: Gill & Macmillan, 1990), pp. 26–52

Conrad, F.W., 'The Problem of Counsel Reconsidered: the case of Sir Thomas Elyot' in Paul A. Fideler and T.F. Mayer (eds), *Political Thought and the Tudor Commonwealth* (London: Routledge, 1992), pp. 75–107.

Cooper, J.P., *Land, Men and Beliefs: Studies in Early-Modern History* (London: Hambledon Press, 1983)

Coote, Leslie, *Prophecy and Public Affairs in Later Medieval England* (Woodbridge: Boydell & Brewer, 2000)

Cosgrove, Art, 'Anglo-Ireland and the Yorkist Cause, 1447–60', in Art Cosgrove (ed.), *New History of Ireland, II: Medieval Ireland, 1169–1534* (Oxford: Clarendon Press, 1987), pp. 557–68

Crane, Mary Thomas, *Framing Authority: sayings, self, and society in sixteenth-century England* (Princeton University Press, 1993)

Crawford, Jon G., *Anglicizing the Government of Ireland: The Irish Privy Council and the expansion of Tudor rule, 1556–1578* (Dublin: Irish Academic Press, 1993)

Crick, Julia, 'The Art of the Unprinted: transcription and English antiquity in the age of print', in Julia Crick and Alexandra Walsham (eds), *The Uses of Script and Print, 1300–1700* (Cambridge University Press, 2004), pp. 116–34

Cunningham, Bernadette, and Raymond Gillespie, *Stories from Gaelic Ireland: Microhistories from the sixteenth-century Irish annals* (Dublin: Four Courts Press, 2003)

Curtis, Edmund, *History of Ireland* (3rd edn, London: Methuen, 1937)

D'Alton, John, *History of the County of Dublin* (Dublin, 1838)

——*History of Drogheda*, 2 vols (Dublin, 1844)

Daniel, Norman, *Islam and the West: The Making of an Image* (rev. edn, Oxford: Oneworld Publications, 1993)

De Blacam, Aodh, *Gaelic Literature Surveyed* (2nd rev. edn, Dublin: Talbot Press, 1933)

Dillon, Myles, *Early Irish Literature* (University of Chicago Press, 1948)

Dix, E.R.M., *Printing in Dublin Prior to 1601*, (2nd edn, Dublin, 1932)

Dolan, Frances E., 'Household Chastisements: gender, authority, and domestic violence', in Patricia Fumerton and Simon Hunt (eds), *Renaissance Culture and the Everyday* (Philadelphia: University of Pennsylania Press, 1999), pp. 204–28

Down, Kevin, 'Colonial Society and Economy in the High Middle Ages', in Art Cosgrove (ed.), *New History of Ireland*, II: *Medieval Ireland, 1169–1534* (Oxford: Clarendon Press, 1987), pp. 439–91

Duffy, Sean, 'The First Ulster Plantation: John de Courcy and the men of Cumbria', in T.B. Barry, Robin Frame and Katharine Simms (eds), *Colony and Frontier in Medieval Ireland: Essays Presented to J.F. Lydon* (London: Hambledon Press, 1995), pp. 1–27

Dwyer Amussen, Susan, 'Being Stirred to Much Unquietness: violence and domestic violence in early modern England', *Journal of Women's History*, vol. 6 (1994), pp. 70–89

Edwards, David, 'The Butler Revolt of 1569', *Irish Historical Studies*, vol. 28 (1993), pp. 228–55

——'Beyond Reform: martial law and the Tudor reconquest of Ireland', *History Ireland*, vol. 5 (1997), pp. 16–21

——*The Ormond Lordship in County Kilkenny, 1515–1642: The Rise and Fall of Butler Feudal Power* (Dublin: Four Courts Press, 2003)

——(ed.), *Regions and Rulers in Ireland, 1100–1650* (Dublin: Four Courts Press, 2004)

Edwards, R. Dudley, *Church and State in Tudor Ireland: A history of penal laws against Irish Catholics 1534–1603* (London: Longman, Green, 1935)

——and T.W. Moody, 'The History of Poynings' Law, Part I, 1494–1615', *Irish Historical Studies*, vol. 2 (1941), pp. 415–24

Ellis, Steven G., 'Taxation and Defence in Late Medieval Ireland: the Survival of Scutage', *Journal of the Royal Society of Antiquaries of Ireland*, vol. 107 (1977), pp. 5–28

——'Historiographical Debate: representations of the past in Ireland: whose past and whose present?', *Irish Historical Studies*, vol. 27 (1991), pp. 289–308

——*Tudor Frontiers and Noble Power: the making of the British state* (Oxford: Clarendon Press, 1995)

——'A Crisis of the Aristocracy? Frontiers and noble power in the early Tudor State', in John Guy (ed.), *The Tudor Monarchy* (London: Arnold, 1997), pp. 330–39

——*Ireland in the Age of the Tudors, 1447–1603: English expansion and the end of Gaelic rule* (New York: Longman, 1998)

——'More Irish than the Irish themselves?: the "Anglo-Irish" in Tudor Ireland', *History Ireland*, vol. 7, i (1999), pp. 22–6

——'An English Gentleman and his Community: Sir William Darcy of Platten', in Vincent P. Carey and Ute Lotz-Heumann (eds), *Taking Sides? Colonial and Confessional Mentalités in Early Modern Ireland* (Dublin: Four Courts Press, 2003), pp. 19–41

Elton, W.R., *Shakespeare's 'Troilus and Cressida' and the Inns of Court Revels* (Aldershot: Ashgate, 2000)

Esposito, Mario, 'The English Conquest of Ireland', *Notes and Queries*, 12th ser., vol. 3 (1917), pp. 495–6

Falkiner, C.L., 'The Parliament of Ireland under the Tudor Sovereigns: with some notices of the speakers of the Irish House of Commons', *Proceedings of the Royal Irish Academy*, vol. 25 C (1905), pp. 508–41 and 553–66

Falls, Cyril, *Elizabeth's Irish Wars* (London: Methuen, 1950)

Ferguson, Arthur B., *Clio Unbound: Perception of the social and cultural past in Renaissance England* (Durham, NC: Duke University Press, 1979)

Fisher, R.M., 'Reform, Repression and Unrest at the Inns of Court, 1518–1558', *Historical Journal*, vol. 20 (1977), pp. 783–801

——'Privy Council Coercion and Religious Conformity at the Inns of Court, 1569–1584', *Recusant History*, vol. 15 (1981), pp. 305–24

Fitzgerald, Lord Walter, 'Notes on the St Lawrences, Lords of Howth', *Journal of the Royal Society of Antiquaries of Ireland*, vol. 37 (1907), pp. 349–59

Fitzsimons, Fiona, 'Wolsey, the Native Affinities, and the Failure of Reform in Henrician Ireland', in David Edwards (ed.), *Regions and Rulers in Ireland, 1100–1650* (Dublin: Four Courts Press, 2004), pp. 78–121

Fletcher, Alan J., *Drama, Performance, and Polity in Pre-Cromwellian Ireland* (University of Toronto Press, 2000)

Fletcher, Anthony, *Tudor Rebellions* (3rd edn, New York: Longman, 1983)

——*Gender, Sex and Subordination in England 1500–1800* (New Haven: Yale University Press, 1995)

Flower, Robin, 'Manuscripts of Irish Interest in the British Museum', *Analecta Hibernica*, vol. 2 (1931), pp. 292–340

Fox, Alistair, 'Prophecies and Politics in the Reign of Henry VIII', in Alistair Fox and John Guy (eds), *Reassessing the Henrician Age: Humanism, Politics and Reform 1500–1550* (Oxford: Basil Blackwell, 1986), pp. 77–94

Gilbert, J.T., 'The Historic Literature of Ireland', in *The Celtic Records and Historic Literature of Ireland* (Dublin, 1861), pp. 409–65

——*History of the Viceroys of Ireland* (Dublin, 1865)

Gillespie, Ray, *Reading Ireland: print, reading and social change in early modern Ireland* (Manchester University Press, 2005)

——and Andrew Hadfield (eds), *The Oxford History of the Irish Book*, vol. III (Oxford University Press, 2006)

Gransden, Antonia, *Legends, Traditions and History in Medieval England* (London and Rio Grande: Hambledon Press, 1992)

Guy, John, *Tudor England* (Oxford University Press, 1988)

——'The Rhetoric of Counsel in Early Modern England', in Dale Hoak (ed.), *Tudor Political Culture* (Cambridge University Press, 1995), pp. 292–310

Hadfield, Andrew, 'Briton and Scythian: Tudor representations of Irish origins', *Irish Historical Studies*, vol. 28 (1993), pp. 390–408

——'English Colonialism and National Identity in Early Modern Ireland', *Eire-Ireland*, vol. 28 (1993), pp. 69–86

——'Tacitus and the Reform of Ireland', in Jennifer Richards (ed.), *Early Modern Civil Discourses* (Basingstoke: Palgrave Macmillan, 2003), pp. 118–19

——'Historical Writing, 1550–1660', in Raymond Gillespie and Andrew Hadfield (eds), *The Oxford History of the Irish Book*, vol. III (Oxford University Press, 2006), pp. 250–63.

Hanawalt, Barbara A., 'Violence in the Domestic Milieu of Late Medieval England', in Richard W. Kaeuper (ed.), *Violence in Medieval Society* (Woodbridge: Boydell Press, 2000), pp. 197–214

Harris Sacks, David, 'The Countervailing of Benefits: monopoly, liberty, and benevolence in Elizabethan England', in Dale Hoak (ed.), *Tudor Political Culture* (Cambridge University Press, 1995), pp. 272–91

Hayes-McCoy, G.A., 'Conciliation, Coercion, and the Protestant Reformation, 1547–71', in T.W. Moody, F.X. Martin and F.J. Byrne (eds), *New History of Ireland*, III: *Early Modern Ireland, 1534–1691* (Oxford: Clarendon Press, 1976), pp. 69–93

Heal, Felicity, 'Appropriating History: Catholic and Protestant Polemics and the National Past', in *The Uses of History in Early Modern England*, quote at p. 105.

Herrup, Cynthia, *A House in Gross Disorder: sex, law, and the 2nd earl of Castlehaven* (Oxford University Press, 1999)

Hines, John, *The Fabliau in English* (New York: Longman, 1993)

Hogan, James, 'Shane O'Neill Comes to the Court of Elizabeth', in Seamus Pender (ed.), *Essays and Studies Presented to Professor Tadhg Ua Donnchadha* (Cork University Press, 1947), pp. 154–70

Horner, Olga, 'Christmas at the Inns of Court', in Meg Twycross (ed.), *Festive Drama, Papers from the Sixth Triennial Colloquium of the International Society for the Study of Medieval Theatre* (Cambridge, England: D.S. Brewer, 1996), pp. 41–53

Hughes, James L.J. (ed.), *Patentee Officers in Ireland 1173–1826* (Dublin: Irish Manuscripts Commission, 1960)

Hyde, Douglas, *A Literary History of Ireland* (London, 1899)

Ivic, Christopher, 'Incorporating Ireland: cultural conflict in Holinshed's Irish Chronicles', *Journal of Medieval and Early Modern Studies*, vol. 29 (1999), pp. 473–98

James, Mervyn, *Society, Politics and Culture: studies in early modern England* (Cambridge University Press, 1986)

James, M.R., 'The Carew Manuscripts', *English Historical Review*, vol. 42 (1927), pp. 261–7

Jansen Jaech, Sharon L., 'English Political Prophecy and the Dating of MS Rawlinson C.813', *Manuscripta*, vol. 25 (1981), pp. 141–50

——'British Library MS Sloane 2578 and Popular Unrest in England, 1554–56' *Manuscripta*, vol. 29 (1985), pp. 30–41

——'Prophecy, Propaganda, and Henry VIII: Arthurian Tradition in the Sixteenth Century', in Valerie M. Lagorio and Mildred Leake Day (eds), *King Arthur through the Ages*, vol. I (New York: Garland Publishing, 1990), pp. 275–91

——*Political Protest and Prophecy under Henry VIII* (Woodbridge: Boydell & Brewer, 1991)

Jefferies, Henry, 'The Irish Parliament of 1560: the Anglican reforms authorised', *Irish Historical Studies*, vol. 26 (1988), pp. 128–41

——'The Early Tudor Reformations in the Irish Pale', *Journal of Ecclesiastical History*, vol. 52 (2001), pp. 34–62

Jones, Michael, *Gentry and Lesser Nobility in Late Medieval Europe* (New York: St Martin's Press, 1986)

Jones, Norman, *The Birth of the Elizabethan Age: England in the 1560s* (Oxford: Blackwell, 1993)

——'Parliament and the Political Society of Elizabethan England', in Dale Hoak (ed.), *Tudor Political Culture* (Cambridge University Press, 1995), pp. 226–42

Kenny, Colum, *King's Inn and the Kingdom of Ireland: The Irish 'Inn of Court' 1541–1800* (Dublin: Irish Academic Press, 1992)

——*Kilmainham: The story of a settlement older than Dublin* (Dublin: Four Courts Press, 1995)

Kewes, Paulina, 'History and its Uses', in Paulina Kewes (ed.), *The Uses of History in Early Modern England* (San Marino, CA: Huntington Library, 2006), pp. 1–30

Knott, Eleanor, and Gerard Murphy, *Early Irish Literature* (London: Routledge & Kegan Paul, 1966)

Lagorio, Valerie M., and Mildred Leake Day (eds), *King Arthur through the Ages* (New York: Garland Publishing, 1990)

Leerssen, Joep, *Mere Irish and Fíor-Ghael: studies in the idea of Irish nationality, its development and literary expression prior to the nineteenth century* (Cork University Press, 1996)

Lennon, Colm, 'Richard Stanihurst (1547–1618) and Old English Identity', *Irish Historical Studies*, vol. 21 (1978), pp. 121–43

——'Reform Ideas and Cultural Resources in the Inner Pale in the Mid-sixteenth Century', *Stair*, vol. 2 (1979), pp. 3–10

——*Richard Stanihurst, the Dubliner* (Dublin: Irish Academic Press, 1981)

——'The Counter-Reformation in Ireland, 1542–1641', in Ciaran Brady and Raymond Gillespie (eds), *Natives and Newcomers: the making of Irish colonial society, 1534–1641* (Dublin: Irish Academic Press, 1986), pp. 75–92

——*Lords of Dublin in the Age of Reformation* (Dublin: Irish Academic Press, 1989)

——'The Chantries in the Irish Reformation: the case of St Anne's Guild, Dublin, 1550–1630', in R.V. Comerford et al. (eds), *Religion, Conflict and Coexistence in Ireland* (Dublin: Gill & Macmillan, 1990), pp. 6–25

——*Sixteenth-Century Ireland: The Incomplete Conquest* (Dublin: Gill & Macmillan, 1994)

——'Edmund Campion's *Histories of Ireland* and Reform in Tudor Ireland', in Thomas M. McCoog, SJ (ed.), *The Reckoned Expense: Edmund Campion and the Early English Jesuits* (Woodbridge: Boydell Press, 1996), pp. 67–83

——'Political Thought of Irish Counter-Reformation Churchmen: the testimony of the "Analecta" of Bishop David Rothe', in Hiram Morgan (ed.), *Political Ideology in Ireland 1541–1641* (Dublin: Four Courts Press, 1999), pp. 181–202

——'Mass in the Manor House: the Counter-Reformation in Dublin, 1560–1630', in James Kelly and Daire Keogh (eds), *History of the Catholic Diocese of Dublin* (Dublin: Four Courts Press, 2000), pp. 112–26

——'Taking Sides: the emergence of Irish Catholic ideology', in Vincent P. Carey and Ute Lotz-Heumann (eds), *Taking Sides? Colonial and Confessional Mentalités in Early Modern Ireland* (Dublin: Four Courts Press, 2003), pp. 78–93

Levin, Carole, '"We shall never have a merry world while the Queene lyveth": Gender, Monarchy, and the Power of Seditious Words', in Julia M. Walker (ed.), *Dissing Elizabeth: Negative Representations of Gloriana* (Durham and London: Duke University Press, 1998), pp. 77–95

Levy, F.J., *Tudor Historical Thought* (San Marino, CA: Huntington Library, 1967)

Lodge, John, *The Peerage of Ireland*, 7 vols (Dublin, 1789)

Lotz-Heumann, Ute, 'Confessionalisation in Ireland: periodisation and character, 1534–1649', in Alan Ford and John McCafferty (eds), *The Origins of Sectarianism in Early Modern Ireland* (Cambridge University Press, 2005), pp. 24–53

Lydon, James, 'Ireland and the English Crown, 1171–1541', *Irish Historical Studies*, vol. 29 (1995), pp. 281–94

McBrierty, Vincent. J., *The Howth Peninsula: its history, lore & legend* (North Dublin Round Table, 1981)

McCabe, Richard A., 'Making History: Holinshed's Irish *Chronicles*, 1577 and 1587', in David J. Baker and Willy Maley (eds), *British Identities and English Renaissance Literature* (Cambridge University Press, 2002), pp. 51–67

McCavitt, John, 'The Flight of the Earls, 1607', *Irish Historical Studies*, vol. 29 (1994), pp. 159–73

McGlynn, Margaret, *The Royal Prerogative and the Learning of the Inns of Court* (Cambridge University Press, 2003)

McGowan-Doyle, Valerie, '"Spent blood": Christopher St Lawrence and Pale loyalism', in Hiram Morgan (ed.), *The Battle of Kinsale* (Bray: Wordwell Press, 2004), pp. 179–191

——'Fall of Princes: Lydgate, Sir Henry Sidney and Tudor conquest in *The Book of Howth*', in Thomas Herron and Michael Potterton (eds), *Ireland in the Renaissance* (Dublin: Four Courts Press, 2007), pp. 74–87

McKisack, May, *Medieval History in the Tudor Age* (Oxford: Clarendon Press, 1971)

Maginn, Christopher, 'The Baltinglass Rebellion, 1580: English dissent or a Gaelic uprising?', *Historical Journal*, vol. 47 (2004), pp. 205–32

Marotti, Arthur F., *Manuscript, Print and the English Renaissance Lyric* (Ithaca, NY: Cornell University Press, 1995)

Martin, F.X., 'Diarmait MacMurchada and the Coming of the Anglo-Normans' in Art Cosgrove (ed.), *New History of Ireland, II: Medieval Ireland, 1169–1534* (Oxford: Clarendon Press, 1987), pp. 43–66

Matar, Nabil, *Islam in Britain, 1558–1685* (Cambridge University Press, 1998)

——*Turks, Moors, and Englishmen in the Age of Discovery* (New York: Columbia University Press, 1999)

Matheson, Lister M., 'King Arthur and the Medieval English Chronicles', in Valerie M. Lagorio and Mildred Leake Day (eds), *King Arthur through the Ages*, vol. I (New York: Garland Publishing, 1990), pp. 248–74

Metzger, Marcia Lee, 'Controversy and Correctness: English Chronicles and the Chroniclers, 1553–1568', *Sixteenth Century Journal*, vol. 27 (1996), pp. 437–51

Meyerson, Mark, Daniel Thiery and Oren Falk (eds), *'A Great Effusion of Blood'? Interpreting Medieval Violence* (University of Toronto Press, 2004)

Morgan, Hiram, 'The Colonial Venture of Sir Thomas Smith in Ulster, 1571–75', *Historical Journal*, vol. 28 (1985), pp. 261–78

——'The End of Gaelic Ulster: a thematic interpretation of events between 1534 and 1610', *Irish Historical Studies*, vol. 26 (1988), pp. 8–32

——'The Fall of Sir John Perrot', in John Guy (ed.), *The Reign of Elizabeth I: Court and Culture in the Last Decade* (Cambridge University Press, 1995), pp. 109–25

——'British Policies before the British State', in Brendan Bradshaw and John Morrill (eds), *The British Problem, c.1534–1707: state formation in the Atlantic archipelago* (New York: St Martin's Press, 1996), pp. 66–88

——'Beyond Spenser? A historiographical introduction to the study of political ideas in early modern Ireland', in Hiram Morgan (ed.), *Political Ideology in Ireland, 1541–1641* (Dublin: Four Courts Press, 1999), pp. 9–21

——'Giraldus Cambrensis and the Tudor Conquest of Ireland', in Hiram Morgan (ed.), *Political Ideology in Ireland, 1541–1641* (Dublin: Four Courts Press, 1999), pp. 22–44

——'Overmighty Officers: the Irish lord deputyship in the early modern British State', *History Ireland*, vol. 7 (1999), pp. 17–21

——(ed.), *Political Ideology in Ireland, 1541–1641* (Dublin: Four Courts Press, 1999)

Moroney, Maryclaire, 'Apocalypse, Ethnography, and Empire in John Derricke's *Image of Irelande* (1581) and Spenser's *View of the Present State of Ireland* (1596)', *English Literary Renaissance*, vol. 29 (1999), pp. 355–74

——'Recent Studies in Tudor and Jacobean Literature about Ireland', *English Literary Renaissance*, vol. 31 (2001), pp. 131–67

Mortimer, Nigel, *John Lydgate's* Fall of Princes*: narrative tragedy in its literary and political contexts* (Oxford University Press, 2005)

Moss, Ann, *Printed Commonplace-Books and the Structuring of Renaissance Thought* (Oxford: Clarendon Press, 1996)

Murphy, Andrew, 'Reviewing the Paradigm: A New Look at Early Modern Ireland', *Eire-Ireland*, vol. 31 (1996), pp. 13–40

——'Revising Criticism: Ireland and the British model', in David J. Baker and Willy Maley (eds), *British Identities and English Renaissance Literature* (Cambridge University Press, 2002), pp. 24–33

Murphy, Gerard, 'The Ossianic Lore and romantic Tales of Medieval Ireland', in Eleanor Knott and Gerard Murphy (eds), *Early Irish Literature* (London: Routledge & Kegan Paul, 1966), pp. 145–93

Murray, James, 'Archbishop Alen, Tudor Reform and the Kildare Rebellion', *Proceedings of the Royal Irish Academy*, vol. 89 C (1989), pp. 1–16

New History of Ireland, II: *Medieval Ireland, 1169–1534*, Art Cosgrove (ed.) (Oxford: Clarendon Press, 1987) III: *Early Modern Ireland, 1534–1691*, T.W. Moody, F.X. Martin and F.J. Byrne (eds) (Oxford: Clarendon Press, 1976)

Nicholls, Kenneth W., *Gaelic and Gaelicised Ireland in the Middle Ages* (Dublin: Gill & Macmillan, 1972)

——*Land, Law and Society in Sixteenth Century Ireland* (Dublin: National University of Ireland, 1976)

——'Worlds Apart? The Ellis Two-Nation Theory on Late Medieval Ireland', *History Ireland*, vol. 7, ii (1999), pp. 22–6

Nicolson, William, *The English, Scotch and Irish Historical Libraries* (London, 1776)

Nutt, Alfred, *Ossian and the Ossianic Literature* (2nd edn, London, 1910)

O'Byrne, Emmett, *War, Politics, and the Irish of Leinster, 1156–1606* (Dublin: Four Courts Press, 2003)

Ó Catháin, Diarmaid, 'Some Reflexes of Latin Learning and of the Renaissance in Ireland c.1450–c.1600', in Jason Harris and Keith Sidwell (eds), *Making*

Ireland Roman: Irish Neo-Latin Writers and the Republic of Letters (Cork University Press, 2009), pp. 14–35

O'Curry, Eugene, *Lectures on the Manuscript Materials of Ancient Irish History* (Dublin, 1878)

O'Neill, Timothy, *Merchants and Mariners in Medieval Ireland* (Bury St Edmunds Press, 1987)

O'Sullivan, William, 'Ussher as a Collector of Manuscripts', *Hermathena*, vol. 88 (1956), pp. 34–58

——'The Eighteenth Century Rebinding of the Manuscripts', *Long Room*, vol. 1 (1970), pp. 19–28

Palmer, William, 'Gender, Violence, and Rebellion in Tudor and Early Stuart Ireland', *Sixteenth Century Journal*, vol. 23 (1992), pp. 699–712

——'That "Insolent Liberty": honor, rites of power, and persuasion in sixteenth-century Ireland', *Renaissance Quarterly*, vol. 46 (1993), pp. 308–27

Parker, David R., *The Commonplace Book in Tudor London* (Lanham, MD: University Press of America, 1998)

Parmiter, Geoffrey de C., *Elizabethan Popish Recusancy in the Inns of Court* (London: Bulletin of the Institute of Historical Research, 1976)

Patterson, Annabel, *Reading Holinshed's Chronicles* (University of Chicago Press, 1994)

——'Foul, his Wife, the mayor, and Foul's Mare: the power of anecdote in Tudor historiography', in Donald R. Kelley and David Harris Sacks (eds), *The Historical Imagination in Early Modern Britain* (Cambridge University Press, 1997), pp. 159–78

Pawlisch, Hans S., *Sir John Davies and the Conquest of Ireland* (Cambridge University Press, 1985)

Pennington, D.H., review of Lawrence Stone, *The Crisis of the Aristocracy 1558–1641*, *English Historical Review*, vol. 81 (1966), pp. 562–5

Petti, Anthony G., *English Literary Hands from Chaucer to Dryden* (Cambridge University Press, 1977)

Phillips, Helen, *An Introduction to the Canterbury Tales: Reading, Fiction, Context* (New York: St Martin's Press, 2000)

Prest, W.R., *The Inns of Court, 1590–1640* (Totowa, NJ: Rowman and Littlefield, 1972)

Quinn, D.B., 'The Early Interpretation of Poynings' Law, 1494–1534', *Irish Historical Studies*, vol. 2 (1941), pp. 241–54

——'Parliaments and Great Councils in Ireland, 1461–1586', *Irish Historical Studies*, vol. 3 (1943), pp. 60–77

——*The Elizabethans and the Irish* (Ithaca, NY: Cornell University Press, 1966)

——'Aristocratic Autonomy, 1460–94', in Art Cosgrove (ed.), *New History of Ireland*, II: *Medieval Ireland, 1169–1534* (Oxford: Clarendon Press, 1987), pp. 591–618.

——and K.W.Nicholls, 'Ireland in 1534', in T.W. Moody, F.X. Martin and F.J. Byrne (eds), *New History of Ireland*, III: Early Modern Ireland, 1534–1691, (Oxford: Clarendon Press, 1976)

Rambo, Elizabeth, *Colonial Ireland in Medieval English Literature* (Selinsgrove, PA: Susquehanna University Press, 1994)

Robbins, Rossell Hope, *Secular Lyrics of the xivth and xvth Centuries* (Oxford: Clarendon Press, 1952)

Round, J.H., 'The Book of Howth: Part I', *The Antiquary*, vol. 7 (1883), pp. 196–9
——'The Book of Howth: Part II', *The Antiquary*, vol. 8 (1883), pp. 21–4
——'The Book of Howth: Part III', *The Antiquary*, vol. 8 (1883), pp. 116–18
——'The Conquest of Ireland', in *Commune of London and Other Studies* (London, 1899), pp. 137–70
Rustici, Craig M., *The Afterlife of Pope Joan: Deploying the Popess Legend in Early Modern England* (Ann Arbor, MI: University of Michigan Press, 2006)
Scattergood, John, *Manuscripts and Ghosts: Essays on the Transmission of Medieval and Early Renaissance Literature* (Dublin: Four Courts Press, 2006)
Scherb, Victor I., 'Assimilating Giants: The Appropriation of Gog and Magog in Medieval and Early Modern England', *Journal of Medieval and Early Modern Studies*, vol. 32 (2002), pp. 59–84
Schwoebel, Robert, *The Shadow of the Crescent: the renaissance image of the Turk* (Nieuwkoop: B. de Graaf, 1967)
Seymour, St John D., *Anglo-Irish Literature 1200–1582* (Cambridge University Press, 1929)
Sharpe, J.A., 'Domestic Homicide in Early Modern England', *Historical Journal*, vol. 24 (1981), pp. 29–48
Silke, John J., 'Irish Scholarship and the Renaissance, 1580–1673', *Studies in the Renaissance*, vol. 20 (1973), pp. 169–206
Simms, Katharine, 'The MacMahon Pedigree: a medieval forgery', in David Edwards (ed.), *Regions and Rulers in Ireland, 1100–1650* (Dublin: Four Courts Press, 2004), pp. 27–36
Smith, J. Huband, *A Day at Howth* (Dublin, 1857)
Smith, Norman R., 'Portentous Births and the Monstrous Imagination in Renaissance Culture', in Timothy S. Jones and David A. Sprunger (eds), *Marvels, Monsters, and Miracles: studies in the medieval and early modern imaginations* (Kalamazoo, MI: Medieval Institute Publications, 2002), pp. 267–83
Smyth, William J., *Map-making, Landscapes and Memory: a geography of colonial and early modern Ireland c.1530–1750* (Cork University Press, 2006)
Stephens, Walter, *Giants in those Days: folklore, ancient history and nationalism* (Lincoln, NE: University of Nebraska Press, 1989)
Stone, Lawrence, *The Crisis of the Aristocracy 1558–1641* (Oxford: Clarendon Press, 1965)
Tait, Clodagh, David Edwards and Pádraig Lenihan (eds), *Age of Atrocity: Violence and political conflict in early modern Ireland* (Dublin: Four Courts Press, 2007)
Taylor, John, *The Universal Chronicle of Ranulf Higden* (Oxford: Clarendon Press, 1966)
Taylor, Rupert, *The Political Prophecy in England* (New York: AMS Press, 1967)
Tenison, E.M., *Elizabethan England*, 12 vols (Glasgow University Press, 1932–60)
Thomas, Keith, *Religion and the Decline of Magic* (New York: Macmillan, 1971)
Thorp, Malcolm R., 'Catholic Conspiracy in Early Elizabethan Foreign Policy', *Sixteenth Century Journal*, vol. 15 (1984), pp. 431–48

Treadwell, Victor, 'The Irish Parliament of 1569–71', *Proceedings of the Royal Irish Academy*, vol. 65 C (1966), pp. 55–89

——'Sir John Perrot and the Irish Parliament of 1585–86', *Proceedings of the Royal Irish Academy*, vol. 86 C (1985), pp. 259–308

Vitkus, Daniel J., 'Early Modern Orientalism: Representations of Islam in Sixteenth- and Seventeenth-Century Europe', in David R. Blanks and Michael Frassetto (eds), *Western Views of Islam in Medieval and Early Modern Europe* (New York: St Martin's Press, 1999), pp. 207–30

Walker, Julia M (ed.), *Dissing Elizabeth: Negative Representations of Gloriana* (Durham and London: Duke University Press, 1998)

Watt, J.A., 'The Anglo-Irish Colony under Strain, 1327–99', in Art Cosgrove (ed.), *New History of Ireland*, II: *Medieval Ireland, 1169–1534* (Oxford: Clarendon Press, 1987), pp. 352–96

Wood, Herbert, 'The Court of Castle Chamber or Star Chamber in Ireland', *Proceedings of the Royal Irish Academy*, vol. 32 C (1914), pp. 152–70

Woolf, D.R., 'Of Danes and Giants: Popular Beliefs about the Past in Early Modern England', *Dalhousie Review*, vol. 71 (1991), pp. 166–209

——*Reading History in Early Modern England* (Cambridge University Press, 2000)

——*The Social Circulation of the Past: English Historical Culture 1500–1730* (Oxford University Press, 2003)

——'From Hystories to the Historical: Five Transitions in Thinking about the Past, 1500–1700', in Paulina Kewes (ed.), *The Uses of History in Early Modern England* (San Marino, CA: Huntington Library, 2006), pp. 46–7.

Woolf, Stuart, 'The Aristocracy in Transition: A Continental Comparison', *Economic History Review*, vol. 23 (1970), pp. 520–31

Unpublished Theses and Other Works

Dorsett, Jason, 'Sir George Carew: the study and conquest of Ireland' (DPhil thesis, Oriel College, Oxford, 2000)

Gaisford-St Lawrence, Stephen, 'The Lords of Howth 1177–1909' (privately compiled family history, 1956)

McGowan-Doyle, Valerie, '"Ancient English Gentlemen"? The Old English Communities of Tudor Ireland in Edmund Campion's *Two Bokes of the Histories of Ireland*' (MA thesis, John Carroll University, 1999)

McNally, David, 'Sir John Plunket of Donsoghley Castle' (MA, NUI Maynooth, 2001)

Murray, James, 'The Tudor Diocese of Dublin: episcopal government, ecclesiastical politics and the enforcement of the Reformation, *c.*1534–1590' (PhD thesis, Trinity College, Dublin, 1997)

Power, Gerald, 'The Nobility of the English Pale in Tudor Ireland, 1496–1566' (PhD thesis, NUI Galway, 2008)

Notes and References

INTRODUCTION

1 Howth's manuscript is now bound as Lambeth Palace Library MS 623. Its only publication is as calendared in J.S. Brewer and William Bullen (eds), *Calendar of the Carew Manuscripts Preserved in the Archiepiscopal Library at Lambeth, 1515–1624*, 6 vols (London, 1867–73), vol. v, pp. 1–260. References to Howth's original are hereafter cited by folio number as *The Book of Howth*. References to the calendar edition are cited as *Calendar of Carew MSS*, vol. v.

2 Ciaran Brady, 'Conservative Subversives: the community of the Pale and the Dublin administration, 1556–1586', in Patrick J. Corish (ed.), *Radicals, Rebels & Establishments* (Belfast: Appletree Press, 1985), pp. 11–32; Nicholas Canny, *The Formation of the Old English Elite in Ireland*, (Dublin: National University of Ireland, 1975) and *The Elizabethan Conquest of Ireland: A Pattern Established 1565–76* (New York: Harper & Row, 1976); Vincent P. Carey, *Surviving the Tudors: The 'Wizard' Earl of Kildare and English Rule in Ireland, 1537–1586* (Dublin: Four Courts Press, 2002), 'A "dubious loyalty": Richard Stanihurst, the "wizard" earl of Kildare, and English-Irish identity', in Vincent P. Carey and Ute Lotz-Heumann (eds), *Taking Sides? Colonial and Confessional Mentalités in Early Modern Ireland* (Dublin: Four Courts Press, 2003), pp. 61–77 and '"Neither Good English nor Good Irish": bi-lingualism and identity formation in sixteenth-century Ireland', in Hiram Morgan (ed.), *Political Ideology in Ireland, 1541–1641* (Dublin: Four Courts Press, 1999), pp. 45–61; David Edwards, *The Ormond Lordship in County Kilkenny 1515–1642* (Dublin: Four Courts Press, 2003) and 'The Butler Revolt of 1569', *Irish Historical Studies*, vol. 28 (1993), pp. 228–55. For a selection of Colm Lennon's works see *Richard Stanihurst, the Dubliner* (Dublin: Irish Academic Press, 1981); 'Richard Stanihurst (1547–1618) and Old English Identity', *Irish Historical Studies*, vol. 21 (1978), pp. 121–43; *Lords of Dublin in the Age of Reformation* (Dublin: Irish Academic Press, 1989), 'Mass in the Manor House: the counter-reformation in Ireland, 1560–1630', in James Kelly and Daire Keogh (eds), *History of the Catholic Diocese of Dublin* (Dublin: Four Courts Press, 2000), pp. 112–26; 'Taking Sides: the emergence of Irish Catholic ideology', in *Taking Sides? Colonial and Confessional Mentalités in Early Modern Ireland*, pp. 78–93. See also Helen Coburn Walsh, 'The Rebellion of William Nugent, 1581', in R.V. Comerford et al. (eds), *Religion, Conflict and Coexistence in Ireland* (Dublin: Gill & Macmillan, 1990), pp. 26–52 and Christopher Maginn, 'The Baltinglass Rebellion, 1580: English Dissent or a Gaelic Uprising?', *Historical Journal*, vol. 47 (2004), pp. 205–32.

CHAPTER ONE: CONTEXTS

1   Clodagh Tait, David Edwards and Pádraig Lenihan (eds), *Age of Atrocity: violence and political conflict in early modern Ireland* (Dublin: Four Courts Press, 2007), see esp. editors' introduction, pp. 9–10; Canny, *Elizabethan Conquest*; Canny, 'Revising the Revisionist', *Irish Historical Studies*, vol. 30 (1996), pp. 242–54; Ciaran Brady, *The Chief Governors: the rise and fall of reform government in Tudor Ireland, 1536–1588* (Cambridge University Press, 1994).

2   Brady, 'Conservative Subversives', p. 11; see also *Chief Governors*, p. 209. Few comprehensive studies of the Old English in this period exist; however, see Canny, *The Formation of the Old English Elite* and Lennon, *Lords of Dublin in the Age of Reformation*. For a selection of studies of individuals within this community, see Lennon, *Richard Stanihurst, the Dubliner*; Carey, *Surviving the Tudors*; Edwards, *The Ormond Lordship*. For a recent, detailed study of the Old English in the early Tudor period, see Gerald Power, 'The nobility of the English Pale in Tudor Ireland, 1496–1566' (unpublished PhD, NUI Galway, 2008).

3   Brendan Bradshaw, *The Irish Constitutional Revolution of the Sixteenth Century* (Cambridge University Press, 1979), Chapter Six, esp. pp. 166–7 and 'Cromwellian Reform and the Origins of the Kildare Rebellion, 1533–34', *Transactions of the Royal Historical Society*, 5th ser., vol. 27 (1977), pp. 69–93.

4   On St Leger and the Old English, see Power, esp. pp. 67–72.

5   Canny, *Elizabethan Conquest*, pp. 35–6.

6   Ibid., p. 36 and *The Formation of the Old English Elite*, pp. 6, 15. On the Laois–Offaly plantation see also Brady, *Chief Governors*, pp. 94–6.

7   For a study of the office of viceroy, see Brady, *Chief Governors*; for the privy council see Jon G. Crawford, *Anglicizing the Government of Ireland: The Irish Privy Council and the Expansion of Tudor Rule, 1556–1578* (Dublin: Irish Academic Press, 1993); for provincial presidencies and plantations see Canny, *Elizabethan Conquest*.

8   Brady, *Chief Governors*, pp. 89–91, 102–3.

9   The impact of Sidney's terms as lord deputy, and Old English responses to them, are discussed in greater detail in Chapters Two and Five.

10 Brady, *Chief Governors*, p. 12. See also Maginn, 'The Baltinglass Rebellion'; Coburn Walsh, 'The Rebellion of William Nugent'; Victor Treadwell, 'Sir John Perrot and the Irish Parliament of 1585–86', *Proceedings of the Royal Irish Academy*, vol. 86 C (1985), pp. 259–308.

11 *Calendar of the State Papers Relating to Ireland . . . 1509–1603*, 11 vols (London: 1860–1912), vol. IX (1600), pp. 286, 431 and vol. X (1600–1), p. 117. See also Valerie McGowan-Doyle, '"Spent blood": Christopher St Lawrence and Pale loyalism', in *The Battle of Kinsale*, ed. Hiram Morgan (Bray: Wordwell Press, 2004), pp. 179–91.

12 For a selection of Lennon's work, see 'Mass in the Manor House'; 'The Counter-Reformation in Ireland, 1542–1641', in Ciaran Brady and Raymond Gillespie (eds), *Natives and Newcomers: the making of Irish colonial society, 1534–1641* (Dublin: Irish Academic Press, 1986), pp. 75–92; 'The Chantries in the Irish Reformation: the case of St Anne's Guild, Dublin, 1550–1630', in R.V. Comerford et al. (eds), *Religion, Conflict and Coexistence in Ireland* (Dublin: Gill & Macmillan, 1990), pp. 6–25; 'Political Thought of Irish Counter-Reformation

Churchmen: The Testimony of the "Analecta" of Bishop David Rothe', in Hiram Morgan (ed.), *Political Ideology in Ireland 1541–1641* (Dublin: Four Courts Press, 1999), pp. 181–202; and 'Taking Sides: the emergence of Irish Catholic ideology'.

13   Ronald G. Asch, *Nobilities in Transition 1550–1700: Courtiers and Rebels in Britain and Europe* (London: Arnold, 2003), pp. 103–12; Maginn, 'The Baltinglass Rebellion'.

14   For Kildare see Carey, *Surviving the Tudors*; for Ormond see Edwards, *The Ormond Lordship.*

15   Notable exceptions dating to the period of Howth's compilation are the works of Rowland White and Richard Stanihurst. For White see Nicholas Canny, 'Rowland White's "Discors Touching Ireland", *c.*1569', *Irish Historical Studies*, vol. 20 (1976–7), pp. 439–63 and 'Rowland White's "Dysorders of the Irisshery", 1571', *Studia Hibernica*, vol. 19 (1979), pp. 147–60. For Stanihurst, see *De Rebus in Hibernia Gestis* (Antwerp, 1584) and Description of Ireland in H. Ellis (ed.), *Holinshed's Chronicles of England, Scotland and Ireland*, 6 vols (London, 1807–8), vol. 6, pp. 1–69.

16   D.R. Woolf, *Reading History in Early Modern England* (Cambridge University Press, 2000) and *The Social Circulation of the Past: English Historical Culture, 1500–1730* (Oxford University Press, 2003). For studies of manuscript use in the early age of print and commonplace books, see Julia Crick and Alexandra Walsham (eds), *The Uses of Script and Print, 1300–1700* (Cambridge University Press, 2004) and Mary Thomas Crane, *Framing Authority: sayings, self, and society in sixteenth-century England* (Princeton University Press, 1993).

17   D.R. Woolf, 'From Hystories to the Historical: Five Transitions in Thinking about the Past, 1500–1700', in Paulina Kewes (ed.), *The Uses of History in Early Modern England* (San Marino, CA: Huntington Library, 2006), pp. 46–7.

18   Selected general studies include: F.J. Levy, *Tudor Historical Thought* (San Marino, CA: Huntington Library, 1967); D.R. Woolf, *Reading History in Early Modern England* and *The Social Circulation of the Past.* For a selection of studies on a range of more specific topics see the essays in Kewes, *The Uses of History in Early Modern England.*

19   Woolf, *Reading History in Early Modern England*, pp. 26–36.

20   Paulina Kewes, 'History and its Uses', in *The Uses of History in Early Modern England*, p. 16.

21   Woolf, 'From Hystories to the Historical', pp. 45–6.

22   Felicity Heal, 'Appropriating History: Catholic and Protestant Polemics and the National Past', in *The Uses of History in Early Modern England*, quote at p. 105.

23   Andrew Hadfield addresses this in several studies; see in particular 'Briton and Scythian: Tudor representations of Irish origins', *Irish Historical Studies*, vol. 28 (1993), pp. 395–6.

24   Attention has been given to this subject in numerous locations; see in particular Hiram Morgan, 'Giraldus Cambrensis and the Tudor Conquest of Ireland', in Hiram Morgan (ed.), *Political Ideology in Ireland 1541–1641* (Dublin: Four Courts Press, 1999), pp. 22–44.

25   Andrew Hadfield, *Literature, Travel, and Colonial Writing in the English Renaissance, 1545–1625* (Oxford University Press, 1998) as cited in Hadfield, 'Tacitus and the Reform of Ireland', in Jennifer Richards (ed.), *Early Modern Civil Discourses* (Basingstoke: Palgrave Macmillan, 2003), pp. 118–19.

26 William Herbert, *Croftus Sive de Hibernia Liber*, Arthur Keaveney and John A. Madden (eds) (Dublin: Irish Manuscripts Commission, 1992), p. 53.

27 *State Papers, Henry VIII*, 11 vols (London, 1830–52), vol. II, pp. 1–31; *Calendar of Carew MSS, 1515–74*, pp. 1–8. Patrick Finglas, 'Breviate of the Getting of Ireland and the Decay of the Same' in *Hibernica, or some ancient pieces relating to Ireland*, Walter Harris (ed.), 2 vols (Dublin, 1770), vol. I, pp. 79–103. All future references are to this edtiion unless otherwise noted. For a fuller discussion of Darcy and this text, see Bradshaw, *Irish Constitutional Revolution*, pp. 37–9 and Steven Ellis, 'An English Gentleman and his Community: Sir William Darcy of Platten', in *Taking Sides? Colonial and Confessional Mentalités in Early Modern Ireland*, pp. 19–41. For a discussion of Finglas' text, see Bradshaw, *Irish Constitutional Revolution*, pp. 39–48. For an opposing interpretation of these early reform texts, see Fiona Fitzsimons, 'Wolsey, the Native Affinities, and the Failure of Reform in Henrician Ireland', in David Edwards (ed.), *Regions and Rulers in Ireland, 1100–1650* (Dublin: Four Courts Press, 2004), pp. 78–121.

28 Bradshaw, *Irish Constitutional Revolution*, pp. 37–41.

29 Harris (ed.), *Hibernica*, pp. 83, 87.

30 Bradshaw, *Irish Constitutional Revolution*, p. 95.

31 Ibid., pp. 98–100.

32 *The Statutes at Large passed in the parliaments held in Ireland, 1310–1800*, 20 vols (Dublin: 1786–1801), vol. I, pp. 322–38. See also Ciaran Brady, 'The Attainder of Shane O'Neill, Sir Henry Sidney and the Problems of Tudor State-Building in Ireland', in Ciaran Brady and Jane Ohlmeyer (eds), *British Interventions in Early Modern Ireland* (Cambridge University Press, 2005), pp. 28–48. O'Neill's attainder is discussed at greater length in Chapter Four.

33 Canny, 'Rowland White's "Discors Touching Ireland"', p. 450.

34 Canny, 'Rowland White's "Dysorders of the Irisshery"', pp. 147–60. This argument is dependent on Canny's dating of White's treatises.

35 Edmund Campion, *Two Bokes of the Histories of Ireland (1571)*, A.F. Vossen (ed.) (Assen: Van Gorcum, 1963); Colm Lennon, 'Edmund Campion's *Histories of Ireland* and Reform in Tudor Ireland', in Thomas M. McCoog, SJ (ed.), *The Reckoned Expense: Edmund Campion and the Early English Jesuits* (Woodbridge: Boydell Press, 1996), pp. 67–83. See also Valerie McGowan-Doyle, '"Ancient English Gentlemen"? The Old English Communities of Tudor Ireland in Edmund Campion's *Two Bokes of the Histories of Ireland*' (unpublished MA thesis, John Carroll University, 1999). See Chapter Four below for extended discussion of Howth's use of Campion's text.

36 Campion, pp. 10–14.

37 Ibid., pp. 7, 151.

38 Christopher Ivic, 'Incorporating Ireland: Cultural Conflict in Holinshed's Irish *Chronicles*', *Journal of Medieval and Early Modern Studies*, vol. 29 (1999), pp. 473–98; Richard A. McCabe, 'Making History: Holinshed's Irish *Chronicles*, 1577 and 1587', in David J. Baker and Willy Maley (eds), *British Identities and English Renaissance Literature* (Cambridge University Press, 2002), pp. 51–67.

39 On Stanihurst, see Lennon, *Richard Stanihurst, the Dubliner*; Carey, 'A "dubious loyalty": Richard Stanihurst, the "wizard" earl of Kildare, and English-Irish identity'. For a discussion of Stanihurst's later text, *De Rebus in Hibernia Gestis*, see

John Barry, 'Derricke and Stanihurst: a dialogue', in Jason Harris and Keith Sidwell (eds), *Making Ireland Roman: Irish Neo-Latin Writers and the Republic of Letters* (Cork University Press, 2009), pp. 36–47.

40 Hooker's role in this case is discussed in greater detail in Chapter Four.

41 Ciaran Brady, *Chief Governors*, pp. 148–58. The cess controversy is discussed in greater detail in Chapter Two.

42 'Sir William Gerrard's notes of his Report on Ireland, 1577–78', C. McNeill (ed.), *Analecta Hibernica*, vol. 2 (1931), pp. 95–201; for this reference see p. 96.

43 John Derricke, *The Image of Irelande with a Discoverie of Woodkarne (1581)* (Delmar, NY, 1998). Maryclaire Moroney, 'Apocalypse, Ethnography, and Empire in John Derricke's *Image of Irelande (1581)* and Spenser's *View of the Present State of Ireland (1596)*', *English Literary Renaissance*, vol. 29 (1999), pp. 355–74, quotation on p. 368. Vincent Carey, 'John Derricke's *Image of Irelande*, Sir Henry Sidney, and the Massacre at Mullaghmast, 1578', *Irish Historical Studies*, vol. 31 (1999), pp. 305–27.

44 Moroney, p. 368.

45 Edmund Spenser, *View of the State of Ireland*, Andrew Hadfield and Willy Maley (ed.) (Oxford: Blackwell, 1997), p. 175.

CHAPTER TWO: CHRISTOPHER ST LAWRENCE

1 On Gaelicisation for the Nugents and the Fitzgeralds see Carey, *Surviving the Tudors* and '"Neither Good English nor Good Irish: bi-lingualism and identity formation in sixteenth-century Ireland'. On other aspects of interaction between Anglo-Irish and Irish families, see Emmett O'Byrne, *War, Politics and the Irish of Leinster, 1156–1606* (Dublin: Four Courts Press, 2003), pp. 79–80. For a discussion of the Pale, or the maghery (land of peace) as opposed to the marches, see Ellis, 'An English Gentleman and his Community, pp. 22–5.

2 For varying analyses of the degree of Gaelicisation see Canny, *Elizabethan Conquest*, pp. 17, 26–7 and *The Formation of the Old English Elite*, pp. 3–4; Colm Lennon, *Sixteenth-Century Ireland: The Incomplete Conquest* (Dublin: Gill & Macmillan, 1994), pp. 10–11, 43; Steven G. Ellis, *Ireland in the Age of the Tudors, 1447–1603* (New York: Longman, 1998), pp. 31, 47–8. For the 7th Baron's familiarity with pre-Norman Irish history and lore, see Chapter Four. On fosterage and intermarriage between the Irish and Anglo-Irish, see Lennon, *Sixteenth-Century Ireland*, pp. 75–6; Canny, *The Formation of the Old English Elite*, pp. 9–10; Edwards, *The Ormond Lordship*, pp. 212, 221. These practices were more common the further removed a family was from the inner Pale. See Carey, *Surviving the Tudors*, pp. 108, 121. O'Byrne cites numerous examples; see, for example, pp. 97, 104.

3 Francis Elrington Ball, *History of County Dublin. Part v. Howth and its Owners* (Dublin: Royal Society of Antiquaries of Ireland, 1917), p. 71; E.M. Tenison, *Elizabethan England*, 12 vols (Glasgow University Press, 1932–60), vol. XI, pp. 38–40. There is some difficulty in dating the renovations precisely. One of several building tablets bears the date 1564, but is no longer in its original location. There have been many renovations to the castle over the succeeding centuries that inhibit precise dating, though the main hall in Elizabethan style was clearly added by the 7th Baron. See also Alan J. Fletcher, *Drama, Performance, and Polity in Pre-Cromwellian Ireland* (University of Toronto

Press, 2000), pp. 149, 231, 253, 256, 388 and Andrew Carpenter, *Verse in English from Tudor and Stuart Ireland* (Cork University Press, 2003), p. 19.

4 Lennon, *Lords of Dublin*, pp. 82–4 and *Sixteenth-Century Ireland*, p. 25; Canny, *Elizabethan Conquest of Ireland*, p. 19. There is no evidence that the St Lawrences ever contracted a marriage with an Irish family.

5 Lennon, *Lords of Dublin*, p. 21; Canny, *The Formation of the Old English Elite*, pp. 2, 5.

6 There are no extant Howth family papers from which to draw more detailed conclusions regarding their income. Ellis estimates their worth as £100; see Ellis, *Ireland in the Age of the Tudors*, p. 34. It was probably higher based on their landholdings; see Appendix A. William Smyth estimates that by the time of the 1641 Civil Survey the reporting of landholding was underestimated in the range of 30 per cent. By that time the Howths were the second largest landowners in the Pale; see William J. Smyth, *Map-making, Landscapes and Memory: a geography of colonial and early modern Ireland c.1530–1750* (Cork University Press, 2006), p. 235. On their income from rent and mills, see J. Morrin (ed.), *Calendar of Patent and Close rolls of Chancery in Ireland*, 3 vols (Dublin, 1861–3), vol. I, p. 76 and vol. II, p. 100.

7 The marriages of the 2nd, 4th and 5th barons in particular added substantially to the family's holdings; Margaret C. Griffith (ed.), *Calendar of Inquisitions Formerly in the Office of the Chief Remembrancer of the Exchequer* (Dublin: Irish Manuscripts Commission, 1991), pp. 168–70.

8 Their holdings would increase dramatically in the seventeenth century in reward for the 9th Baron's role in the Nine Years War and his conversion to Protestantism. In 1641 the 11th Baron claimed to have lost rents of £1,245 on lands in Tyrone and Monaghan alone; John Lodge, *The Peerage of Ireland*, 7 vols (Dublin, 1789), vol. III, p. 201.

9 Lennon, *Lords of Dublin*, p. 22; *Calendar of State Papers, Ireland*, vol. II, p. 195. On Irish shipping see Timothy O'Neill, *Merchants and Mariners in Medieval Ireland* (Bury St Edmunds Press, 1987); Wendy Childs and Timothy O'Neill, 'Overseas Trade', in Art Cosgrove (ed.), *New History of Ireland*, II (Oxford: Clarendon Press, 1987), pp. 492–524.

10 John D'Alton, *History of Drogheda*, 2 vols (Dublin, 1844), vol. II, p. 122.

11 Port officials were appointed to collect customs and also to attempt to curb piracy, a problem for Howth as well as elsewhere. On piracy, see O'Neill, *Merchants and Mariners*, pp. 119–29 and *Calendar of State Papers, Ireland*, vol. I (1509–73), p. 86. For other references to ships utilising Howth as a port see *Calendar of State Papers, Ireland*, vol. I (1509–73), p. 325 and vol. II (1574–85), p. 195.

12 For a discussion of Drogheda's prominence and the areas it served, see Lennon, *Lords of Dublin*, pp. 21–2. See also D.B. Quinn and K.W. Nicholls, 'Ireland in 1534', in T.W. Moody, F.X. Martin and F.J. Byrne (eds), *New History of Ireland*, III (Oxford: Clarendon Press, 1976), p. 5. Even by the late fifteenth century Howth had been of enough significance that one Dublin merchant, Bartholomew Rosynell, included it on a list of Irish ports for English merchants, indicating the sailing time between various Irish and English ports, and something of its traffic is also suggested by the entrance of the Black Death into Ireland through Howth; O'Neill, *Merchants and Mariners*, p. 118; Kevin Down, 'Colonial Society

and Economy in the High Middle Ages', in *New History of Ireland*, II, p. 449; D'Alton, *History of Drogheda*, vol. II, pp. 88.

13 O'Neill, *Merchants and Mariners*, pp. 112, 116.

14 *Calendar of State Papers, Ireland*, vol. XI (1601–3), p. 317; R.A. Butlin, 'Land and People, *c.*1600', in *New History of Ireland*, III, p. 164; O'Neill, *Merchants and Mariners*, pp. 31–2; Lord Walter Fitzgerald, 'Notes on the St Lawrences, Lords of Howth', *Journal of the Royal Society of Antiquaries of Ireland*, vol. 37 (1907), p. 352; Ball, p. 49; Robert C. Simington (ed.), *The Civil Survey, AD 1654–1656* (Dublin: Irish Manuscripts Commission, 1945), vol. VII, p. 169.

15 Ball, p. 44; *Calendar of Patent and Close Rolls, Ireland*, vol. II, p. 29. Other officials who passed through Howth included Bellingham, Croft, Sussex, Fitzwilliam and Gerrard as well as the entourage that accompanied Shane O'Neill to London in 1562; K.W. Nicholls (ed.), *Irish Fiants of the Tudor Sovereigns during the Reigns of Henry VIII, Edward VI, Philip & Mary, and Elizabeth I* 4 vols (Dublin: Eamonn de Burca, 1994), vol. I, nos 426, 1162; *Calendar of Patent and Close Rolls, Ireland*, vol. I, p. 189; *Calendar of Carew MSS*, vol. I, p. 278; *Calendar of Carew MSS*, vol. II, p. 157; James Hogan, 'Shane O'Neill comes to the court of Elizabeth', in Seamus Pender (ed.), *Essays and Studies Presented to Professor Tadgh Ua Donnchadha* (Cork University Press, 1947), p. 165. See also Fitzwilliam to Burghley, 26 Oct. 1572 (written from Howth), State Papers, Ireland (Public Record Office, London), 63/38/24. Hereafter, this series of State Papers, Ireland, is referred to in abbreviated form as SP 63.

16 See Ellis, *Ireland in the Age of the Tudors*, pp. 51–6 and 59–61; Art Cosgrove, 'Anglo-Ireland and the Yorkist Cause, 1447–60', in *New History of Ireland*, II, pp. 564–5; D.B. Quinn, 'Aristocratic Autonomy, 1460–94', in *New History of Ireland*, II, p. 597.

17 Ball, pp. 49–52; Colm Lennon and James Murray (eds), *Dublin City Franchise Roll, 1468–1512* (Dublin Corporation, 1998), p. 35.

18 Bodleian Laud MS 614, f. 327; Lodge, p. 198. On the Knights of St George, see Ellis, *Ireland in the Age of the Tudors*, pp. 72–4 and Quinn, 'Aristocratic Autonomy', pp. 603–4.

19 *Irish Fiants of the Tudor Sovereigns*, vol. I, nos 44, 49, 78; *Calendar of Patent and Close Rolls, Ireland*, vol. I, pp. 77, 149–51, 306.

20 Ellis, *Ireland in the Age of the Tudors*, p. 82. See also Quinn, 'Aristocratic Autonomy', p. 607; Carey, *Surviving the Tudors*, Chapter One; James L.J. Hughes (ed.), *Patentee Officers in Ireland 1173–1826* (Dublin: Irish Manuscripts Commission, 1960), p. 68.

21 Ellis, *Ireland in the Age of the Tudors*, p. 82.

22 *The Book of Howth*, f. 114v. Lodge identifies Nicholas as a devoted Lancastrian; p. 189. His behaviour in this case cannot be reduced so simply. If it was Nicholas, in fact, who alerted Henry VII – and this information is contained only in *The Book of Howth* – it may have been as much to thwart Kildare as to display Lancastrian affiliations. Whether accurate or fabrication, one must bear in mind the rationale behind this episode in *The Book of Howth* as a rhetorically charged illustration of historical Howth loyalty (see Chapter Four). It has the concomitant advantage of illustrating the difficult political contexts into which the Old English had been placed specifically because of Kildare factionalism.

23 See Steven G. Ellis, *Tudor Frontiers and Noble Power: the making of the British state* (Oxford: Clarendon Press, 1995) for a study of the relationship between Kildare and the crown.

24 *Calendar of Carew MSS*, vol. I, p. 27.

25 See, *inter alia*, *Calendar of Patent and Close Rolls, Ireland*, vol. I, pp. 305–6, 346–7, 430; *The Manuscripts of Charles Haliday, Esq., of Dublin. Acts of the Privy Council in Ireland, 1556–71*, in *Fifteenth Report of the Royal Commission on Historical Manuscripts* (London: HM Stationery Office, 1897), pp. 82, 91, 137–9; *Irish Fiants of the Tudor Sovereigns*, vol. II, nos 2445, 3601, 4462, 4515.

26 Though no record of the date of his birth is extant, I estimate it to have been in 1510. Two deeds reference the death of the 4th Baron, but conflictingly record its date as 20 April 1542 and 20 April 1543; *Calendar of Inquisitions, Ireland*, pp. 125, 169. However, both of these documents state that his eldest son's age was 34 at the time of his father's death, thus he would have been born in either 1508 or 1509. As the third son, Christopher's birth was probably not before 1510.

27 *The Records of the Honorable Society of Lincoln's Inn. The Black Books. Volume 1 from AD 1422 to AD 1586* (London: Lincoln's Inn, 1897), p. 55. Many students remained in residence for extended periods of time, as Howth did, with no intention of completing legal instruction, sometimes rarely participating in the formal exercises at all, though ostensibly their residency would have provided them with enough legal instruction to manage aristocratic estates. See *Acts of the Privy Council of England*, ed. J.R. Dasent, 46 vols (London, 1890–1964), 1571–5, p. 248, 31 May 1574; it was not until this Act that students were forbidden to remain in residence longer than three years unless participating in the legal exercises. See also J.H. Baker, *The Common Law Tradition: lawyers, books and the law* (London: Hambledon Press, 2000). Lincoln's Inn records do not indicate that Howth's attendance culminated in being called to the bar.

28 Bradshaw, *Irish Constitutional Revolution*, pp. 140–6.

29 Ibid., esp. Chapters Four and Six; Canny, *Elizabethan Conquest*, pp. 31–2.

30 On the declining position of the Pale aristocracy under Grey, see Power, pp. 44–56; for an alternative view see Brady, *Chief Governors*, Chapter One.

31 On improved conditions for the Old English under St Leger, see Power, p. 73.

32 Margaret McGlynn, *The Royal Prerogative and the Learning of the Inns of Court* (Cambridge University Press, 2003), p. 25. Staunford later sent a copy of this work to Nicholas Nugent; see Ray Gillespie, *Reading Ireland: print, reading and social change in early modern Ireland* (Manchester University Press, 2005), p. 13.

33 For Staunton's use of Fortescue and Bracton, see McGlynn, p. 9. For Howth's references to all three, see *The Book of Howth*, f. 134v. Sir Henry Bracton (*c.*1210–68), dean of Exeter cathedral and justice of King's Bench under Henry III, was long recognised for his extensive work on English legal history and common law. Sir John Fortescue (*c.*1394–*c.*1476), lord chief justice, wrote extensively on absolute vs. constitutional monarchy. The works of both remained key sources in the Tudor period.

34 McGlynn, p. 15.

35 Richard Stanihurst's well-known reference to the way in which his accent was perceived by English students at Oxford may have been an experience Howth shared. On Stanihurst, language and identity, see Lennon, *Richard Stanihurst, the Dubliner*, Chapter Seven.

36 *Lincoln's Inn Black Books*, pp. 28, 75.

37 Ibid., p. 8.

38 Ibid., p. 169.

39 Ibid., p. 261. Howth's brother, Richard, was elected escheator of Lincoln's Inn at this session.

40 Ibid., p. 315.

41 Ibid., p. 205. Some students from Ireland had been at Dove House since at least 1522 when inn receipts indicate payment for Nicholas Barnewall's residency.

42 There is no record of Howth in Lincoln's Inn documents following their June 1554 mandate that he adhere to sumptuary codes by shaving his beard or face expulsion, though whether he left because of this mandate is unknown; ibid., p. 310. Recalcitrant behaviour among legal students was a feature of the 1550s. Similar mandates were frequently issued to students for failure to adhere to sumptuary codes, part of a larger movement to enforce conformity in dress, behaviour and religion; see R.M. Fisher, 'Reform, Repression and Unrest at the Inns of Court, 1518–1558', *Historical Journal*, vol. 20 (1977), pp. 783–801. By May 1555 Howth was residing at The Ward, the traditional residence of the Howth heir, from where he was commissioned keeper of the peace for County Dublin; *Calendar of Patent and Close Rolls, Ireland*, vol. I, p. 350. The birth of his eldest son Nicholas that same year also suggests that he had returned from London soon after the June 1554 Lincoln's Inn mandate; *Calendar of Inquisitions, Ireland*, p. 302.

43 Brady, *Chief Governors*, pp. 76, 81–5; Canny, *Elizabethan Conquest*, pp. 35–9; Power, pp. 67–73.

44 See Sidney's records as vice-treasurer noting payment for 'chief officers with English captains and their bands' for the period 13 April 1556 to 14 October 1558; *Report on the Manuscripts of Lord De L'Isle and Dudley Preserved at Penshurst Place*, 6 vols (London: Historical Manuscripts Commission, 1925–66), vol. I, pp. 365–6. The index to these edited papers indicates that the 7th Baron received the pay, though the text states only 'Lord of Howth'. Richard was still the 6th Baron in 1556. He received £164 for the period ending 25 June 1556. This conveys his relatively low position of command; compare to George Stanley who received £2,662 as Marshal of the Field, William Fitzwilliam who received £35, and Nicholas Bagenall who received £560. Only Robert St Leger, who was paid £67, received less than Howth. 'My lord of Howth' is also specifically mentioned in a diary of Sussex's 1556 journey; see *Calendar of Carew MSS, 1515–74*, p. 261 and TCD MS 581, ff. 97–9.

45 Ellis, *Ireland in the Age of the Tudors*, pp. 272–3; *Book of Howth*, f. 121r; *Calendar of Carew MSS, 1515–74*, p. 261; Power, p. 108.

46 Brady, *Chief Governors*, p. 83; *De L'Isle and Dudley* MSS, vol. I, p. 366; *The Book of Howth*, f. 123r. The 6th Baron routinely accompanied governors on raids against Shane O'Neill from 1550 to 1556; 1557 seems to have been the first occasion on which he was not included among positions of military leadership.

47 *Haliday MSS*, pp. 70–1, 80–5, 88–94, 137–9, 161–7; *Irish Fiants of the Tudor Sovereigns*, vol. II, nos 542, 2117, 2444, 2445, 3182, 3601, 3657, 4148, 4462, 4515, 5134, 5342, 5353.

48 Records in the *Haliday MSS* do not indicate any sessions attended by the 6th Baron.

49 For his attendance at the 11 December 1558 session, see *Calendar of Patent and Close Rolls, Ireland, Elizabeth*, vol. I, nos 1, 2. For his attendance at a selection of other sessions see *Haliday MSS*, pp. 70–1, 101–3, 113–14, 125–6, 134–5, 154, 222–3, 239–40, 249; Lambeth Palace Library, MS 608, f. 38.

50 For conflicting interpretations of this parliament and its passage of the Elizabethan reforms, see Henry Jefferies, 'The Irish Parliament of 1560', *Irish Historical Studies*, vol. 26 (1988), pp. 128–41; R. Dudley Edwards, *Church and State in Tudor Ireland* (London: Longman, Green, 1935), pp. 170–91; Brendan Bradshaw, 'The Beginnings of Modern Ireland', in Brian Farrell (ed.), *The Irish Parliamentary Tradition* (Dublin: Gill & Macmillan, 1973), pp. 80–1.

51 *Haliday* MSS, pp. 88–94. Howth had likely also already established a more personal relationship with Sussex, serving as host to him at Howth Castle on the occasion of his departure for London in December 1558 via Howth; *Calendar of Carew MSS, 1515–74*, p. 278.

52 See, for example, the council session of 29 October 1560, *Haliday MSS*, pp. 112–13.

53 Instructions to the Earl of Sussex on his return to Ireland, 24 May 1561, SP 63/3/78.

54 Queen to the nobility and Council of Ireland, 21 May 1561, SP 63/3/68; *Irish Fiants of the Tudor Sovereigns*, vol. II, no. 379.

55 Lord Lieutenant and Council to Queen, 16 July 1561, SP 63/4/22. Kildare is traditionally credited for the negotiations with O'Neill, though Sussex asserts an instrumental role for Howth; on Kildare's role in negotiating with O'Neill, see Carey, *Surviving the Tudors*, pp. 114–20. Howth may have been caught as a pawn in Sussex's attempt to discredit Kildare. See also Ciaran Brady, 'Shane O'Neill Departs from the Court of Elizabeth: Irish, English, Scottish Perspectives and the Paralysis of Policy, July 1559 to April 1562', in S.J. Connolly (ed.), *Kingdoms United? Great Britain and Ireland since 1500: Integration and Diversity* (Dublin: Four Courts Press, 1999), pp. 13–28.

56 Crawford, *Anglicizing the Government of Ireland*, pp. 296–7; Power, pp. 116–24.

57 Lord Lieutenant and Council to Privy Council, 3 Dec. 1562, SP 63/7/51; Lord Lieutenant Sussex to Privy Council, 1 Mar. 1563, SP 63/8/12; Lord Lieutenant and Council to Queen, 16 Mar. 1563, SP 63/8/20.

58 *The Book of Howth*, f. 124v.

59 Ibid.

60 Lord Lieutenant Sussex to Privy Council, 1 Mar. 1563, SP 63/8/12; Lord Lieutenant and Council to Queen, 16 Mar. 1563, SP 63/8/20; Lord Lieutenant and Council to Queen, 31 Mar. 1563, SP 63/8/24; Lord Lieutenant and Council to Privy Council, 20 May 1563, SP 63/8/47; Crawford, p. 297.

61 *Calendar of Carew MSS, 1515–74*, p. 349; Brady, *Chief Governors*, p. 105; Crawford, p. 297.

62 *Haliday MSS*, pp. 134–5.

63 Ibid., pp. 135–6.

64 On Arnold's administration, see Lennon, *Sixteenth-Century Ireland*, p. 182; Brady, *Chief Governors*, p. 109; Power, pp. 125–8.

65 Fitzwilliam to Cecil, 22 Oct. 1565, SP 63/15/14.

66 Sidney and Irish Council to Elizabeth, 22 Nov. 1566, SP 63/19/55.

67 *Haliday MSS*, pp. 239–49; *Book of Howth*, ff. 130v–131r.

68   *Book of Howth*, ff. 130v–131r.

69   Ibid., f. 130v.

70   Ibid., ff. 130v–131r.

71   *Irish Fiants of the Tudor Sovereigns*, vol. II, no. 2445; *Calendar of Carew MSS, 1575–88*, p. 148; *Haliday MSS*, pp. 137–42, 161–7; *Calendar of State Papers, Ireland, 1509–73*, p. 319; Sidney and Irish Council to Elizabeth, 22 Nov. 1566, SP 63/19/55.

72   Brady, *Chief Governors*, pp. 140–43, *passim*; Crawford, pp. 348–9; Ellis, *Ireland in the Age of the Tudors*, pp. 304–5.

73   *Calendar of Carew MSS, 1575–88*, p. 57.

74   Viscount Baltinglass and other barons and gentlemen to the Queen, 10 Jan. 1577, SP 63/57/1; Sidney to Elizabeth, 18 May 1577, SP 63/58/29; Questions to be resolved by Barnaby Scurlocke, Richard Netterville and Henry Burnell sent hither by the lords of the pale to seek redress for the burden of the cess, 14 May 1577, SP 63/58/23. A copy of this last item is also bound with other items in TCD MS 581.

75   Viscount Baltinglass and other barons and gentlemen to the Queen, 10 Jan. 1577, SP 63/57/1; Viscount Baltinglass and others to the Privy Council, 10 Jan. 1577, SP 63/57/1.iv; Petition of the inhabitants of the English Pale to the Lord Deputy and Council, 10 Jan. 1577, SP 63/57/1.i.

76   Lord Deputy to Privy Council, 11 Jan. 1577, SP 63/57/1.v.

77   Lord Deputy to Privy Council, 11 Jan. 1577, SP 63/57/1.v; Sidney to Elizabeth, 20 May 1577, SP 63/58/29.

78   Queen to the Lord Deputy and Council, 14 May 1577, SP 63/58/20.

79   Queen to the Lord Deputy and Council, 14 May 1577, SP 63/58/20; Privy Council to Lord Deputy, 14 May 1577, SP 63/58/21.

80   Sidney to Elizabeth, 20 May 1577, SP 63/58/29.

81   For details of this council session see Nicholas White's report to Burghley, *Calendar of the Manuscripts of the Marquis of Salisbury, Preserved at Hatfield House, Hertfordshire* (*Salisbury MSS*), 24 vols (London: Historical Manuscripts Commission, 1883–1976), vol. II, pp. 154–5. White reported to Burghley that the cess opponents were asked to leave while council debated their imprisonment. However, a later submission statement prepared by Sidney and offered to the opponents for their signature notes they left the council session of their own accord; see Submission by the Lord Deputy offered to the lords of the Pale, 20 June 1577, SP 63/58/51. This episode was not recorded in Sidney's version of events sent to Elizabeth; see Lord Deputy and Council to the Queen, 20 June 1577, SP 63/58/49. Sidney also wrote to Walsingham concerning Nicholas White, one of the few members of the Irish council to oppose their incarceration, stating 'there was not a worse man of this country birth than Nicholas White'; Sidney to Walsingham, 20 June 1577, SP 63/58/50. Allegations were later levied against White as an accomplice; Allegations against Nicholas White, Dec. 1577, SP 63/59/64, 65, 66.

82   Lord Deputy and Council to the Queen, 20 June 1577, SP 63/58/49; *Salisbury MSS*, vol. II, pp. 154–5. For Elizabeth's letter see Queen to the Lord Deputy and Council, 14 May 1577, SP 63/58/20. Canny remarked that without Elizabeth's eventual intervention, the Pale opposition would have 'risen in arms against the "tyranny" of the lord deputy' at this point; *Elizabethan Conquest*, p. 152. Though

the Baltinglass Revolt and Nugent Conspiracy might suggests such a conclusion in hindsight, neither the archival record nor *The Book of Howth* suggest that the cess opponents considered such an aggressive response at this point. They were far more concerned to convince Elizabeth and the Dublin administration of their loyalty and to have their grievances addressed.

83   Submission of the lords and gentlemen to the Lord Deputy and Council offered by the lords of the Pale to Sidney, 20 June 1577, SP 63/58/53, 54. An additional submission statement catalogued with these under 20 June 1577 as SP 63/58/51 has been calendared incorrectly; it should be calendared with documents concerning the February 1578 imprisonment. SP 63/58/51 (and its copy, 63/58/52) is the submission offered to the lords by Sidney on 1 February 1578 that only Richard Missett, Christopher Fleming, Nicholas Taaffe and Barnaby Scurlocke signed; see Sidney to Elizabeth, 19 Feb. 1578, SP 63/60/12.

84   Richard Netterville to Howth, 18 May 1577, SP 63/58/26; Arthur Collins (ed.), *Letters and Memorials of State*, 2 vols (London, 1746), vol. I, p. 197.

85   Submission of the lords and gentlemen to the Lord Deputy and Council, 20 June 1577, SP 63/58/54 (SP 63/58/55 is a copy of 63/58/54).

86   For the assertion that Talbot was serving as messenger between those imprisoned in the Fleet and those in Dublin Castle, see 'Sir William Gerrard's Notes', p. 107.

87   See, for instance, John Netterville's testimony; Examinations of John Netterville, William Talbot and others, 1 July 1577, SP 63/58/59. He indicates receipt of a letter from his brother, Richard Netterville, then in Fleet prison, notifying him that neither 'the cause or the main of [their] message as they thought was misliked'.

88   Examinations of John Netterville, William Talbot and others, 1 July 1577, SP 63/58/59.

89   Questions ministered to the lords and gentlemen now committed, 20 Feb. 1578, SP 63/60/16. As with other documents concerning the cess controversy, this undated item has probably been miscalendared as well. These questions of interrogation seem to belong to the period of the 1577 incarceration. Note Sidney's specific reference to two rounds of interrogation in his 20 June 1577 letter to Elizabeth; *Letters and Memorials of State*, vol. I, p. 197. It is possible that this interrogation preceded the examination regarding Talbot. There are no references to interrogations in the documentation extant for the 1578 period of imprisonment. Note also that Missett's interrogation is included here; he recanted in 1578 and was not imprisoned at that time.

90   Questions ministered to the lords and gentlemen now committed, 20 Feb. 1578, SP 63/60/16.

91   Declaration of the Lord of Delvin, the Lord of Howth and others, 20 Feb. 1578, SP 63/60/17; The declaration of Christopher Lord of Howth, 20 Feb. 1578, SP 63/60/19.

92   See *Haliday MSS*, p. 286. The calendar of the council book records their submission and release, but with no date. They were still imprisoned on 6 July 1577; see Thomas, James and Lavalen Nugent to Lord Deputy, 6 July 1577, SP 63/58/63 and Petition of Baron Delvin and others to the Lord Chancellor, 6 July 1577, SP 63/58/63.iv. A series of documents on the cess drawn up later that month indicates their subsequent release; see Griefs, remedies, proposals, notes touching cess, July 1577, SP63/58/74–83; *Calendar of Carew MSS, 1575–88*, pp.

106–9. For Elizabeth's letters see ibid., pp. 66, 68. Submission of the lords and gentlemen to the Lord Deputy and Council, 20 June 1577, SP 63/58/54, 55.

93 Notes of the griefs of the English Pale, July 1577, SP 63/58/74; Griefs of the Pale, July 1577, SP 63/58/75; Remedies to ease the griefs conceived of the cess, July 1577, SP 63/58/76; A way to ease the griefs of the cess, July 1577, SP 63/58/77; A remedy for the griefs made by the cess, July 1577, SP 63/58/78; Considerations for the cess of the Deputy's household, July 1577, SP 63/58/79; Notes on victualling needs for 1,000 soldiers, July 1577, SP 63/58/80; Notes on levying beeves for 1,000 soldiers, July 1577, SP 63/58/81; Cess of grain and beeves on the English Pale and Irishry with consent of the nobility, July 1577, SP 63/58/82; Notes touching cess, July 1577, SP 63/58/83; *Calendar of Carew MSS, 1575–88*, pp. 106–9, 119–20.

94 Lambeth Palace Library, MS 628, f. 362v. For an expanded discussion of Gerrard's role, see Crawford, pp. 400–1 and 'Sir William Gerrard's Notes'.

95 Elizabeth to Sidney, 31 Oct. 1577, SP 63/59/33.

96 *Calendar of Carew MSS, 1575–88*, p. 125.

97 Sidney to Elizabeth, 19 Feb. 1578, SP 63/60/12. For the prepared statement accepted by Missett, Fleming, Scurlocke and Taaffe, see Submission by the Lord Deputy offered to the lords of the Pale, (miscalendared) 20 June 1577, SP 63/58/51, 52. For the statement offered by the cess opponents that Sidney refused, see First submission delivered by the lords, knights, and gentlemen to the Lord Deputy and Council, 1 Feb. 1578, SP 63/60/7 (and a copy enclosed with Sidney's letter to Elizabeth calendared as SP 63/60/12.i). For their fines, see *Report on the Manuscripts of the Earl of Egmont* (*Egmont MSS*), 2 vols (London: Historical Manuscripts Commission, 1905), vol. I, p. 8.

98 Sidney to Elizabeth, 19 Feb. 1578, SP 63/60/12.

99 Crawford, p. 402.

100 Sidney to Elizabeth, 30 April 1578, SP 63/60/47; Sidney to Privy Council, 30 April 1578, SP 63/60/48.

101 Last submission of the lords and gentlemen of the Pale, 28 June 1578, SP 63/61/12; The reckoning of the lords, knights, esquires and gentlemen discharged, 30 June 1578, SP 63/61/25. An undated submission statement catalogued as the next item (SP 63/61/26) has been calendared incorrectly; it belongs to the June 1577 period of imprisonment. Compare to Submission of the lords and gentlemen to the Lord Deputy and Council, 20 June 1577, SP 63/58/55 and note the reference both make to having been imprisoned for ten days. Other documents containing this reference also contain Richard Missett's signature; he was not imprisoned a second time in 1578. See also a denied request for release on 29 April 1578, *De L'Isle and Dudley MSS*, vol. II, p. 81.

102 This presentation of the final stage of the cess dispute is taken from Crawford, pp. 402–4.

103 *Haliday MSS*, p. 287.

104 TCD MS 852, f. 94; BL Add. MS 47172, ff. 39–40; *Egmont MSS*, vol. II, p. 11.

105 TCD MS 852, f. 94.

106 Crawford, pp. 230–1.

107 TCD MS 852, f. 94; this documents the fine as £20 (£10 in lieu of each ear being nailed). *Egmont MSS*, p. 11 indicates a fine of £40.

108 There are no studies of domestic violence for Tudor Ireland. For studies of

domestic violence in early modern England, see Francis E. Dolan, 'Household Chastisements: gender, authority, and domestic violence', in Patricia Fumerton and Simon Hunt (eds) *Renaissance Culture and the Everyday* (Philadelphia: University of Pennsylvania Press, 1999), pp. 204–28; Susan Dwyer Amussen, '"Being stirred to much unquietness": violence and domestic violence in Early Modern England', *Journal of Women's History*, vol. 6 (1994), pp. 70–89; James A. Brundage, 'Domestic Violence in Classical Canon Law', in Richard W. Kaeuper (ed.), *Violence in Medieval Society* (Woodbridge: Boydell Press, 2000), pp. 183–95; J.A. Sharpe, 'Domestic Homicide in Early Modern England', *Historical Journal*, vol. 24 (1981), pp. 29–48.

109 See Cynthia Herrup, *A House in Gross Disorder: Sex, Law, and the 2nd Earl of Castlehaven* (Oxford University Press, 1999), p. 74. Herrup demonstrates that character denigration and establishing a history of immorality were also central elements in the Castlehaven trial.

110 Sally rods from the Irish *saileach* (willow) used to discipline children or servants.

111 See Anthony Fletcher, *Gender, Sex &and Subordination in England 1500–1800* (New Haven: Yale University Press, 1995), pp. 214–15. Fletcher cites a case in which a servant had also been stripped before being beaten.

112 TCD MS 852, f. 85; BL Add. MS 47172, f. 42.

113 *Egmont MSS*, pp. 12, 15. The Court of Castle Chamber did not have the power to apply the death sentence, only to impose fines or terms of imprisonment, though they occasionally made use of the pillory as they did in Tyrrell's perjury case; Crawford, pp. 230–1. The precise dates of Howth's imprisonment and release are unknown. As he was imprisoned for nineteen weeks and other evidence indicates he had been released by mid-October at the latest (*Fiants Ireland, Elizabeth*, vol. II, no. 3601; *Calendar of Carew MSS, 1575–88*, p. 157), he was possibly arrested in late May, coinciding with Tyrrell's trial, while cess negotiations were still under way.

114 Dwyer Amussen, p. 72; Dolan, pp. 212–13; Fletcher, p. 192. See also Fletcher, Chapters Ten and Eleven, *passim*.

115 BL Add. MS 47172, f. 41.

116 Herrup, p. 127.

117 Herrup, pp. 36–7.

118 BL Add. MS 47172, ff. 41–2.

119 *Irish Fiants of the Tudor Sovereigns*, vol. II, no. 3558. The proceedings for the dissolution were heard on 26 June 1579, between Tyrrell's trial on 22 May and Howth's on 8 July. The marriage had been arranged in 1569 when both Patrick Barnewall and Mary St Lawrence were still children. The other marriage contracted between the Howths and Barnewalls, that of Nicholas, Howth's eldest son, to Margaret Barnewall, had ended with Margaret's death in 1575.

120 *Walsingham Letter-Book or Register of Ireland, May 1578 to December 1579*, J. Hogan and N. McNeill O'Farrell (eds) (Dublin: Irish Manuscripts Commission 1959), p. 130; *Irish Fiants of the Tudor Sovereigns*, vol. II, no. 3601. For later appointments, see ibid., nos 3657, 4148, 4515. On martial law, see David Edwards, 'Beyond Reform: martial law and the Tudor reconquest of Ireland', *History Ireland*, vol. 5 (1997), pp. 16–21.

121 For Gerrard's recantation of support for Sidney, see Ellis, *Ireland in the Age of the Tudors*, pp. 308–9.

122 Lambeth Palace Library, MS 597, Pelham letter book, f. 263v.

123 *Egmont MSS*, p. 15; BL Add. MS 47172, ff. 59–61.

124 Brady, *Chief Governors*, p. 210; Ellis, *Ireland in the Age of the Tudors*, p. 314; Maginn, 'The Baltinglass Rebellion'; Coburn Walsh, 'The Rebellion of William Nugent'.

125 Crawford, pp. 223–4 n. 196.

126 See BL Add. MS 47172, ff. 65v–74r and *Egmont MSS*, pp. 16–17. Leaves are missing from Court of Castle Chamber records for this period; Howth's tenure may have begun earlier.

127 Treadwell, 'Sir John Perrot and the Irish Parliament of 1585–86', p. 265.

128 For a discussion of Perrot's deputyship and its difficulties see Ellis, *Ireland in the Age of the Tudors*, pp. 318–22; Brady, *Chief Governors*, pp. 293–6; Lennon, *Sixteenth-Century Ireland*, pp. 205–7. On Perrot see also Hiram Morgan, 'The fall of Sir John Perrot', in John Guy (ed.), *The Reign of Elizabeth i: Court and Culture in the Last Decade* (Cambridge University Press, 1995), pp. 109–25. Treadwell argues that New English recalcitrance was as significant to Perrot's failures as the Old English.

129 Perrot to Walsingham, 25 Jan. 1586, SP 63/122/42.

130 Treadwell, 'Sir John Perrot and the Irish Parliament of 1585–86', p. 292.

131 Perrot to Walsingham, 25 Jan. 1586, SP 63/122/42. Howth sought to mend his relationship with Perrot by sending him a gift of a goshawk; John Garland to Sir John Perrot, 12 Sept. 1589, SP 63/146/40.

132 Louth to Burghley, 4 Feb. 1586, SP 63/122/62; Louth to Walsingham, 4 Feb. 1586, SP 63/122/63.

133 Nicholas Canny, *Making Ireland British 1580–1650* (Oxford University Press, 2001), p. 60.

134 Treadwell, 'Sir John Perrot and the Irish Parliament of 1585–86', pp. 274, 278.

135 Ibid., p. 295.

136 *Irish Fiants of the Tudor Sovereigns*, vol. iii, nos 5134, 5342, 5353.

137 See McGowan-Doyle, '"Spent blood"', pp. 179–91.

138 Lord Deputy and Council to Privy Council, 18 Feb. 1578, SP 63/60/12. Sidney also drew an analogy between the cess opponents and witchcraft; see *Annals of Ireland, 1558–91*, BL Add. MS 4813, f. 108v. This writer refers frequently to the Irish Council Book, here citing from f. 178.

139 N.B. White (ed.), *Extent of Irish Monastic Possessions* (Dublin: Irish Manuscripts Commission, 1943), p. 33.

140 Colm Lennon, 'The Chantries in the Irish Reformation', and 'Mass in the manor House', p. 116.

141 For Christopher Barnewall's Catholic sympathies, see Lennon, *Lords of Dublin*, pp. 142–3. It was Barnewall who harboured Campion in the spring of 1571 prior to his departure.

142 Lennon, *Lords of Dublin*, pp. 143, 214 and 'The Counter-Reformation in Ireland, 1542–1641'. Howth's first wife died shortly after his 1579 release from prison, of unknown causes.

143 Ball, p. 79.

144 Lennon, 'Mass in the Manor House', p. 113.

145 'Visitation of Dublin, 1630', *Archivium Hibernicum*, vol. 8 (1941), pp. 62–3.

146 *Calendar of State Papers, Ireland, 1600*, p. 236.

147   'Sir William Gerrard's Notes', pp. 95–6.

148   Bradshaw notes that Old English attempts to maintain an influential position with English administrations often meant that they 'incurred the disfavour of Kildare, without acquiring any close association with the Butlers'. See *Irish Constitutional Revolution*, pp. 79–80.

CHAPTER THREE: COMPILING OPPOSITION

1   The use of vellum rather than paper was probably a matter of availability and economics, as paper was scarce and expensive in Ireland at the time; Gillespie, *Reading Ireland*, p. 57.

2   This folio was added by a later scribe who required additional space for his entry on Suleiman; see below.

3   The text resumes on f. 146v. Folio 137 was originally left blank also by Hand VII, but Howth later appended a brief entry at the top of f. 137r noting Drury's appointment as lord justice. On the scribal practice of leaving blank space for future entry, see John Scattergood, 'Humanism in Ireland in the Sixteenth Century: the evidence of Dublin, Trinity College Library MS 160', in *Manuscripts and Ghosts: essays on the transmission of medieval and early renaissance literature* (Dublin: Four Courts Press, 2006), p. 280.

4   There is evidence these folios were cut for binding. The first folio contained a header that has been rendered illegible by cutting. It, as well as others in this set, may have once contained foliation.

5   The manuscript has suffered several rebindings, at least one of which caused this disturbance to Howth's papers. It was not part of the compilation when James Ware consulted it in 1652. See Chapter Five.

6   *Calendar of Carew MSS*, vol. V, pp. 60, 195; in the case of the former the addition had been made by Howth.

7   Hand VIII makes several brief appearances on these folios (ff. 14v–17r, 66v, 87v–88r). His hand occurs always in the midst of Hand VII's text, suggesting that his role was only temporary as he filled in during brief absences of Hand VII. Howth also took up this work occasionally during some of Hand VII's brief absences.

8   Two of the documents in the miscellaneous collection may represent items already in Howth's possession that were incorporated into the manuscript rather than copied into it (ff. 149–51 and 155–8), perhaps by Hand VII as he created the miscellaneous collection's foundational layer. This is suggested by his foliation on these documents and their placement to precede his miscellaneous entries. Each of these two documents is in a hand that occurs nowhere else in the manuscript, Hands XII and XIII respectively, and each is also reflective of earlier styles, Hand XII in early/mid-Tudor facile secretary and Hand XIII in the older *Anglicana formata*.

9   The calendar editors' identification of this hand on f. 133v is incorrect. These entries were made by Hands IV and X. All of Hand IX's additions to the miscellaneous collection utilised folio space left blank by Hand VII.

10   Folios A1–A23 were originally unnumbered, further evidence that foliation had occurred at an earlier stage of the manuscript's compilation.

11   J.H. Round, 'The Book of Howth: Part I', *The Antiquary*, vol. 7 (1883), pp. 196–9. Round was incorrect in identifying that section of the manuscript outlining the

Old English aristocracy as Howth's original composition. This section had in fact been copied from Edmund Campion's *Two Bokes of the Histories of Ireland* (see below).

12   A point also made by Round but inconclusively demonstrated by him; ibid., p. 196.

13   *Calendar of Carew MSS*, vol. v, p. xii.

14   Ibid.

15   For a selection of documents containing the 7th Baron's signature, see Submission of the lords and gentlemen to the Lord Deputy and Council, 20 June 1577, SP 63/58/54; First submission delivered by lords, knights, and gentlemen to the Lord Deputy and Council, 1 Feb. 1578, SP 63/60/7; Declaration of the Lord of Delvin, Lord of Howth, Lord of Trimleston et al., 20 Feb. 1578, SP 63/60/17; and his signature on the proceedings of 6 May 1586, Journal of the House of Lords in Ireland, J.T. Gilbert (ed.), *Facsimiles of National Manuscripts of Ireland*, 4 vols (Dublin, 1874–84), vol. iv, no. 21. See also the 7th Baron's letter to Fitzwilliam, Carte MS 55, f. 241.

16   No identity is known for any of Howth's scribes which might provide a further clue as to these initials.

17   Howth's hand does not occur on ff. A3–4, A6, A10–12, A16, A19, 153, 146–7 or 169–72. Several of Howth's entries are extensive; see, for example, ff. A20v–A22r, where he entered the final three folios of the passage on the Field of Clontarf.

18   *Calendar of Carew MSS*, vol. v, p. xiii. The extensive marginalia in the manuscript were entered primarily by Howth and Carew, with minimal marginalia by other hands. The calendar editors' general practice was to exclude Carew's marginalia; however, some of Carew's marginalia were included in the calendar edition though not always identified as such. The fact that much of the marginalia belonged to Howth was noted only obliquely in the calendar editors' introductory comment that 'the marginal notes are chiefly in this handwriting', i.e., the hand identified by them as Hand ii, here confirmed as Howth's.

19   See f. 61v. Howth's final addition to this folio, completed at the foot of the page, was cut off in binding and hence incomplete in the 1871 calendar edition. However, it can be reconstructed from the copy of this section now archived as Lambeth Palace Library MS 248. See Appendix C for corrections to the calendar edition.

20   The editors were inconsistent in their attempt to identify every hand change. For instance, on f. 62v, Howth appended a footnote to the bottom of the folio which Brewer and Bullen not only failed to identify, but incorporated as an entry in the midst of a list of chronicle entries with no indication that this was not its original location within the text. Editorial practices such as this are largely responsible for the impression the printed text gives of random collection activity.

21   See f. 110v; for other examples see ff. 17r, 111r, 117r.

22   There are no family papers or accounts from which to determine payments made to scribes or their identity.

23   Howth had been released by mid October; see Chapter Two.

24   Julia Crick, 'The Art of the Unprinted: transcription and English antiquity in the age of print', in Julia Crick and Alexandra Walsham (eds), *The Uses of Script and Print, 1300–1700* (Cambridge University Press, 2004), pp. 116–34.

25   A third variant of this document precedes these two on f. A23, probably an errant folio. It may have been bound into the manuscript in this location by a later owner for its relevance to the other two copies. When viewing *The Book of Howth* in 1652, Ware clearly noted that refoliation began after f. 22; see his notes, TCD MS 664, f. 192v. For the practice of rebinding similar items together, see Woolf, *The Social Circulation of the Past*, pp. 170–1 and Jason Dorsett, 'Sir George Carew: the study and conquest of Ireland' (unpublished DPhil thesis, Oriel College, Oxford, 2000), pp. 58–9.

26   Though reservations have been raised regarding characterisation of the Anglo-Norman arrival as a conquest, Howth referred to it as such, as did his contemporaries; see F.X. Martin, 'Diarmait MacMurchada and the Coming of the Anglo-Normans', in *New History of Ireland*, ii, pp. 43–66.

27   The additions occur on ff. 34–40, 42–4, 51–3, 55–9.

28   This collation is obscured by the calendar edition's replication of Carew's erroneous note attributing the entire section to Dowdall. Carew apparently misunderstood Howth's note regarding his source for the additional information, appending a note to the entry's start (f. 6r) stating that the entire entry had been taken from Dowdall, though Howth's note clearly indicates that was the source only for the additional information. See Round, 'The Book of Howth: Part i', p. 199 for early notice of the calendar edition's replication of Carew's error. Katharine Simms also notes Meredith Hanmer's reference to Dowdall's translation of a text acquired from O'Neill; however, Hanmer very likely acquired this reference from Howth; Katharine Simms, 'The MacMahon Pedigree: a medieval forgery', in David Edwards (ed.), *Regions and Rulers in Ireland, 1100–1650* (Dublin: Four Courts Press, 2004), p. 28. On Hanmer's use of Howth, see Chapter Five below. Carew's misreading may also be responsible for the similar misattribution in the Abbot catalogue of manuscripts in Trinity College Library, Dublin, where MS 592 is erroneously identified as 'perhaps a copy of Dowdall's translation of O'Neill's book'. TCD MS 592 is a copy of *The English Conquest of Ireland*. It contains none of the material additional to *The Book of Howth* that Howth claimed to have come from Dowdall's work.

29   Mario Esposito, 'The English Conquest of Ireland', *Notes and Queries*, 12th ser., vol. 3 (1917), pp. 495–6. The other extant versions of this document are: 1) BL Add. MS 40674; 2) Lambeth Palace Library MS 598 (in *Calendar of Carew MSS*, vol. v, pp. 261–317); 3) Bodleian Rawlinson B 490 (in F.J. Furnivall (ed.), *English Conquest of Ireland* (London: Early English Texts Society, 1896), 107, pp. 3–151); 4) TCD MS 593 (of which a brief excerpt was contained in Furnivall, pp. xiv–xvi); 5) TCD MS 592 (in Furnivall, pp. 2–150). Due either to Furnivall's error or typographical error, the press-mark of this last manuscript was identified as E.2.31 (now MS 575). It should read E.3.31 (now MS 592); see Esposito, p. 495 for notification of this error. For a more recent discussion of *The English Conquest of Ireland* see Morgan, 'Giraldus Cambrensis and the Tudor Conquest of Ireland', pp. 25–6.

30   Esposito, p. 496.

31   For example, where TCD MS 592 contains the passage 'Reymond hym dyght for to wende ynto England,' Howth's scribe copied 'Raymond him dight for to wend in to Ingland' (f. 30v), whereas Bodleian Rawlinson B 490, BL Add. MS 40674 and Lambeth Palace Library MS 598 all render the phrase 'Reymond made hym

redy to go into England' (with variations in spelling). The close approximation of language between Howth's copy and the other extant English versions seems to rule out the possibility that Howth's scribe was creating a new translation of the fourteenth-century Latin abridgement of the *Expugnatio Hibernica* (BL Harley MS 177), the document speculated by Robin Flower to have served as the basis for the fifteenth-century versions. See Robin Flower, 'Manuscripts of Irish Interest in the British Museum', *Analecta Hibernica*, vol. 2 (1931), p. 304.

32 For additional discussion of this aspect of Howth's inserted material, see J.H. Round, 'The Book of Howth: Part ii', *The Antiquary*, vol. 8 (1883), pp. 21–4 and 'The Book of Howth, Part iii', *The Antiquary*, vol. 8 (1883), pp. 116–18.

33 On Gaelic encroachment as reflected in Irish and Anglo-Norman annals in this period, see J.A. Watt, 'The Anglo-Irish Colony under Strain, 1327–99', in *New History of Ireland*, ii, p. 366.

34 See Hiram Morgan, 'British Policies before the British State', in Brendan Bradshaw and John Morrill (eds) *The British Problem, c.1534–1707: State Formation in the Atlantic Archipelago* (New York: St Martin's Press, 1996), pp. 66–88.

35 For the entry in *Pembridge's Annals*, see the passage as recorded in *Annales Hiberniae* (*Grace's Annals*), Richard Butler (ed.) (Dublin, 1843) and in BL Add. MS 40674 (Flatsbury's copy) or as in J.T. Gilbert (ed.), *The Chartularies of St Mary's Abbey, Dublin* (London, 1884), vol. ii, p. 370. For another passage added to *Pembridge's Annals* by Howth, see ff. 79r–80v. For this massacre see also Kenneth Nicholls, *Gaelic and Gaelicised Ireland in the Middle Ages* (Dublin: Gill & Macmillan, 1972), p. 81; on the Verdon family, see ibid., p. 153.

36 This footnote was appended by Howth to the bottom of f. 86v. Its text was damaged when the folio was cut for binding but can be reconstructed from the copy now bound as Lambeth Palace Library MS 248 (see Chapter Five). Brewer and Bullen calendared what remained of the footnote on p. 154, thereby separating it from the text it was intended to accompany and suggesting erroneously that the reference to murders committed by the Howths referred to William's and Walter's murders of the Gernons.

37 The copy of *Pembridge's Annals* now bound as TCD MS 583 may have once been in Howth's possession. It contains marginalia that appear to be in his hand, though it is annotated far less extensively than was his usual practice; see, for example, Howth's marginalia in Lambeth Palace Library MS 264 as well as throughout *The Book of Howth*.

38 Both of Carew's headers, as well as the break in the text artificially introduced by him, were replicated in the calendar edition. This also erroneously suggested that Howth's later note regarding Hussey as a source meant that Hussey's work began only where Carew entered the header on Knockdoe. Howth created this as a single entry.

39 On Surrey's deputyship, see Fitzsimons, 'Wolsey, the Native Affinities, and the Failure of Reform', pp. 78–121; Power, pp. 26–8.

40 For a more detailed discussion of St Leger's administration see Bradshaw, *Irish Constitutional Revolution*, pp. 196–221; Brady, *Chief Governors*, pp. 25–44; Power, pp. 56–72.

41 Though Campion's history would have been completed or near completion at this time, Howth does not seem to have gained access to it until the following year; see below.

42   Hand IX's only other contribution was a series of brief additions made to folio space left blank by Hand VII in the manuscript's miscellaneous collection; see ff. 160r, 161r, 162v.

43   Hand III made other significant contributions to *The Book of Howth*, notably many of the folios addressing the pre-conquest history of Ireland now bound at the manuscript's start; see below.

44   On Sussex's administration, see Brady, *Chief Governors*, Chapter Three; Power, Chapter Five.

45   On early plantation schemes in Ulster, see Lennon, *Sixteenth-Century Ireland*, pp. 276–81; Canny, *Elizabethan Conquest*, Chapter Four; Hiram Morgan, 'The Colonial Venture of Sir Thomas Smith in Ulster, 1571–75', *Historical Journal*, vol. 28 (1985), pp. 261–78. For Chatterton's grant, see Lord Deputy Fitzwilliam to Burghley, 26 Oct. 1572, SP 63/38/24 and Marshall Bagenal and the Dean of Armagh to the Lord Deputy, 7 Apr. 1573, SP 63/40/2i.

46   John Stow, *A Summary of the Chronicles of England* (London, 1575, STC 23325); Robert Fabyan, *The New Chronicles of England and France* (London, 1811, reprint of 1516 edn); Edward Hall, *Hall's Chronicle* (London, 1809, collation of 1548 and 1550 edns). For discussions of these works, see Levy, *Tudor Historical Thought* and Woolf, *Reading History in Early Modern England*. Howth also includes other references too vague to permit identification, such as 'an old book', 'another book' or 'the French chronicle'. He may be referring to any number of sources as the information copied in these cases appears in multiple locations.

47   Howth's suggestion that Fabyan recorded the date of the conquest as 1155 is inaccurate, however. Fabyan had only recorded that Henry II became king in 1155; see Fabyan, p. 272; *The Book of Howth*, f. 6r.

48   For Howth's references to Fabyan, see ff. A22v, 6r, 8v, 23r, 101v, 154v, 163r, 165r–v, 166r–v, 168r. For references to Hall, see ff. 102r–103iv, 112v, 113v, 154v, 177r. For references to the *Polychronicon*, see ff. A22v, 2r–5v, 55v, 163r–v, 164v, 168r–173r; Howth occasionally refers to this as 'Caxton' (f. 5v), as it was commonly known, revealing that he utilised Caxton's edition of this work (on this practice see Woolf, *Reading History in Early Modern England*, p. 16).

49   Fabyan relied on the *Polychronicon* for some of his information; see, for example, Fabyan, p. 3/.

50   Howth had earlier included a similar footnote listing lords in Ireland who participated in the Siege of Calais, though no source is cited there (f. 81v). This note was damaged when the folio was cut for binding but can be reconstructed from the copy in Lambeth Palace Library, MS 248; the concluding phrase should read 'served valiant at the wynninge of callice'. A document in Lambeth Palace Library MS 507 also addresses forces sent from Ireland to Calais, but as its list of names differs, it does not seem to have been the source from which Howth worked, or vice versa.

51   Canny, *Elizabethan Conquest*, p. 126. Sidney drew this comparison in 1566.

52   Howth also identified early medieval disunity among European rulers as the reason Irish kings were able to force tribute from Denmark, Cornwall, France and England (see f. A10r) and attributed Danish invasions of England to discord there (f. 162v).

53 It should be noted that this same scribe utilised blank folios following Hand VII's entry on the life of Muhammad to enter the companion lists of Irish and Gaelicised captains and loyal and disloyal counties in Ireland; see below. Based on the entries made by his scribe between mid 1571 and mid 1572, Howth seems to have been particularly interested in the detrimental effects of political division at that time.

54 See the *Polychronicon*, vol. VI, pp. 15–51. For a discussion of representations of Muhammad and Islam, see Nabil Matar, *Turks, Moors, and Englishmen in the Age of Discovery* (New York: Columbia University Press, 1999); Daniel J. Vitkus, 'Early Modern Orientalism: Representations of Islam in Sixteenth- and Seventeenth-Century Europe', in David R. Blanks and Michael Frassetto (eds), *Western Views of Islam in Medieval and Early Modern Europe* (New York: St Martin's Press, 1999), pp. 207–30; David R. Blanks, 'Western Views of Islam in the Premodern Period: A Brief History of Past Approaches', ibid., pp. 1–9; Robert Schwoebel, *The Shadow of the Crescent: The Renaissance Image of the Turk* (Nieuwkoop: B. de Graaf, 1967).

55 *Statutes at Large, Ireland*, vol. I, p. 327; Campion, p. 141; Ciaran Brady, *Shane O'Neill* (Dundalk: Dundalgan Historical Association of Ireland, 1996), p. 3.

56 It is also possible that Howth had been alerted to the value of drawing attention to Islamic expansion by Sidney's 1566 comparison of O'Neill to the Turks; see above, Canny, *Elizabethan Conquest*, p. 126.

57 See Hand X's other entry relating events of September 1573, f. 134r.

58 Compare ff. 152v–154v to Campion, pp. 78–81. Howth's copy is verbatim; however, its sections are out of order. The scribe apparently intended to enter the item on folios 153–4 which had been left blank by earlier scribes; he began it at the top of f. 153, but ran out of space and returned to the blank verso of f. 152 to enter the closing passages. It should be borne in mind that as Campion's holograph is no longer extant we cannot determine the precise degree to which Howth corrupted Campion's text as compared to the degree to which the extant copies of Campion represent later scribal corruption. This assessment is based on Vossen's 1963 edition.

59 The nature of Campion's first chapter is discussed in greater detail in McGowan-Doyle, '"Ancient English Gentlemen"? The Old English Communities of Tudor Ireland in Edmund Campion's *Two Bokes of the Histories of Ireland*', pp. 30–8.

60 Compare f. 16r to Campion, p. 8. The word 'thyng' in Howth's text is highly suspect. It appears to have been entered as 'incest', though either the scribe, or possibly Howth, later altered it to read 'thyng'. Campion incorrectly identified this as Lough Foyle, an error reproduced by Howth. See Giraldus Cambrensis/Gerald of Wales, *The History and Topography of Ireland*, John J. O'Meara (trans.) (Harmondsworth: Penguin Books, 1982), p. 64 and the corresponding note on p. 132.

61 Compare f. 16r to Campion, p. 9. Howth's text clearly reads 'citizan' and not a word that can be rendered as Scythian; it was also transcribed as 'citizen' by the calendar editors. For a discussion of Scythian lineage, see Hadfield, 'Briton and Scythian'. Given the importance of purported Scythian lineage to denigrations of the Irish, Howth may have here again, as with his omission of references to drinking blood, sought to diminish discussions of incivility and Old English degeneration.

62 Compare f. 16r to Campion, p. 9 for both omissions.

63 Compare f. 17v to Campion, pp. 12–13.

64 Compare f. 17v to Campion, p. 13. This passage was later struck out in Howth's manuscript though by whom or at what date is unknown. Much of it is illegible there, but can be partially reconstructed from the copy now bound as Lambeth Palace Library MS 248, f. 136.

65 Vossen, p. 58. Vossen did not consult all extant copies in creating his critical edition of 1963, for instance the copy now bound as the first item in Lambeth Palace Library, MS 248.

66 Compare f. 16v to Campion, p. 10.

67 Compare f. 17r to Campion, p. 10. For another of Campion's references to Sidney, see p. 7. For a discussion of Campion's text and Sidney, see Lennon, 'Edmund Campion's *Histories of Ireland* and Reform in Tudor Ireland'.

68 The reference to James Yonge's 'Precepts of Government' cited by Howth in this passage was copied verbatim from Campion; there is no evidence Howth saw Yonge's work.

69 The language of the text accompanying this and Howth's other references to this work (ff. 160r, 161r, 162v) suggest that he may have been using Caxton's edition of Thomas Malory's *Le Morte D'Arthur*, though if this was his source he did not copy as closely here as from other works; see James W. Spisak, William Matthews and Bert Dillon (eds), *Le Morte D'Arthur: Caxton's Malory*, 2 vols (Berkeley and Los Angeles: University of California Press, 1983), referred to hereafter as Malory. Compare f. 160r to vol. II, p. 202, for example. Howth may have relied more heavily on Arthurian sources than his references suggest. Many of the battle scenes portrayed throughout *The Book of Howth* are highly reminiscent of those in Caxton's edition of Malory. Specific reference is made to Lancelot in Howth's passage on the Battle of Knockdoe (f. 108v).

70 See Malory, vol. I, pp. 44–53. Howth makes a similar reference to this episode on f. 162v.

71 Hadfield, 'Briton and Scythian', p. 395.

72 His battle is also compared to the Siege of Troy, f. A12v. See also the reference to Hector on f. 108v.

73 Howth seems to have had access to Irish sources though I have not been able to identify any versions containing Howth's detail to indicate which served as his source. He cites only 'an old book' (f. A5r), 'another book' (f. A5r), 'the old histories of Ireland' (f. A8r) and 'the Irish chronicles' (f. A10r). See Standish O'Grady, *Silva Gadelica*, 2 vols (London, 1892) and *Transactions of the Ossianic Society*, vols 1 and 4 (Dublin, 1853, 1856). Variants are contained in *The Book of Leinster* and *The Book of Lismore*, among others. See James Carney, 'Literature in Irish, 1169–1534', in *New History of Ireland*, II, esp. pp. 690–3, 701–2; Gerard Murphy, *The Ossianic Lore and Romantic Tales of Medieval Ireland*, reproduced in Eleanor Knott and Gerard Murphy (eds), *Early Irish Literature* (London: Routledge & Kegan Paul, 1966), pp. 145–93; Myles Dillon, *Early Irish Literature* (University of Chicago Press, 1948), pp. 32–50; Cecile O'Rahilly (ed.), *Cath Finntragha* (Dublin Institute for Advanced Studies, 1975).

74 This is the *Agallamh na Senorach*, alternatively referred to as 'The Conversation of Old Men' or 'The Colloquy of the Ancients'. In some versions it is Caoilte who relates the history to St Patrick. See O'Grady, vol. I, pp. 101–265; Murphy,

pp. 55, 161–6; Dillon, pp. 36–40. See also Ann Dooley and Harry Roe (eds/trans), *Tales of the Elders of Ireland: Acallam na Senorach* (Oxford University Press, 1999).

75 The calendar edition here garbles a phrase that had been corrected with inter-lining (p. 10). The copy of *The Book of Howth* in Lambeth Palace Library MS 248 reads correctly: 'and so one after other did come but the giant bound them both and after did agree with them'. See Appendix C. In the pre-Norman period Howth had been the site of numerous battles; see Whitley Stokes, 'The Irish Abridgement of the "Expugnatio Hibernica"', *English Historical Review*, vol. 20 (1905), p. 81 and '*Talland Etair* (*The Siege of Howth*)', *Revue Celtique*, vol. 8 (1887), pp. 47–63; Eugene O'Curry, *Lectures on the Manuscript Materials of Ancient Irish History* (Dublin, 1878). Given the tale Howth records here, he was probably familiar with some of these tales.

76 Walter Stephens, *Giants in those Days* (Lincoln, NE: University of Nebraska Press, 1989), p. 95.

77 Ibid., pp. 67, 70–1.

78 See Kathryn M. Brammall, 'Monstrous Metamorphosis: Nature, Morality, and the Rhetoric of Monstrosity in Tudor England', *Sixteenth Century Journal*, vol. 27 (1996), pp. 3–21 and Norman R. Smith, 'Portentous Births and the Monstrous Imagination in Renaissance Culture', in Timothy S. Jones and David A. Sprunger (eds), *Marvels, Monsters, and Miracles: Studies in the Medieval and Early Modern Imaginations* (Kalamazoo, MI: Medieval Institute Publications, 2002), pp. 267–83.

79 Stephens, p. 91.

80 For other versions of this document, see Lambeth Palace Library MSS 600, 621, 635. For MS 621 see also *Calendar of Carew MSS, 1515–74*, pp. 1–6. See also BL Add. MS 48015 and TCD MS 842.

81 For a similar document, see Trinity College Library MS 581.

82 For a similar document, see Lambeth Palace Library MS 608.

83 For a similar document see TCD MS 581.

84 As it begins on the recto of f. 155 and covers the full recto and verso of ff.155–8, the point of its inclusion cannot be determined by scribal use of blank folio space as elsewhere. Its folios were bound out of order, 156–8 followed by 155, apparently while still in Howth's possession, for he included notes to the foot of ff. 155v and 158v indicating their correct order.

85 Finglas noted that decay began under Edward III. Howth retained this passage in his copy, see f. 150r.

86 Where Howth included that reference on f. 128v he referred to its appearance in 'old books and in the prince's record'. Whether one of those citations referred to this document is unknown.

87 John Lydgate, *Fall of Princes*, Henry Bergin (ed.), 4 vols (Washington, DC: Carnegie Institution of Washington, 1923–7), vol. I, p. x, hereafter referred to as Lydgate. Howth's folio reference for another entry from Lydgate, on Zenobia, indicates that he used the 1527 edition printed by Richard Pynson (Folger Shakespeare Library STC 3176).

88 Lydgate, vol. III, pp. 979–82. This poem is addressed by St John D. Seymour in *Anglo-Irish Literature 1200–1582* (Cambridge University Press, 1929), p. 100. He surmised that it was unlikely to be of Anglo-Irish origin but failed to identify its source as Lydgate.

89   *Statutes at Large, Ireland*, vol. I, pp. 306–12. Their holdings had been dissolved under Henry VIII, restored under Mary, and retaken by the crown in 1560. Howth's inclusion of Kilmainham on the list of lands transferred from the Knights Templar to the Knights Hospitaller is incorrect, though an error frequently reproduced into the early twentieth century; see Colum Kenny, *Kilmainham: the history of a settlement older than Dublin* (Dublin: Four Courts Press, 1995), p. 29.

90   Lydgate, vol. I, p. 324. For the full passage in Lydgate from which this was extracted, see vol. I, pp. 319–24. This passage was often isolated for inclusion in other collections in the late medieval period; see Rossell Hope Robbins, *Secular Lyrics of the XIVth and XVth Centuries* (Oxford: Clarendon Press, 1952), p. 262. The phrase 'guerdon full covenable' is here rendered 'fit reward', capturing the meaning but losing the rhyme.

91   Howth later added a genealogy of Brian Boru to the bottom of the folio and the passage of the Battle of Clontarf was then begun on the verso. Seymour also noted this piece in his address of literature in *The Book of Howth*; as above, he failed to identify its source as Lydgate though here he erroneously asserted its Anglo-Irish origin, p. 99.

92   Lydgate, vol. I, p. 323.

93   Valerie McGowan-Doyle, 'Fall of Princes: Lydgate, Sir Henry Sidney and Tudor Conquest in *The Book of Howth*', in Thomas Herron and Michael Potterton (eds), *Ireland in the Renaissance* (Dublin: Four Courts Press, 2007), pp. 74–87.

94   Nigel Mortimer, *John Lydgate's Fall of Princes: narrative tragedy in its literary and political contexts* (Oxford University Press, 2005), p. 244.

95   'May the writer of the red book be associated with the lot of those on high/ May the robber of the red book be linked with the death of the wicked.' This was entered in the manuscript in the form standard to the genre *Carmen Figuratum*; it is given here in unscrambled form. My thanks to John Barry of University College Cork for translation assistance and identification of its genre. Barry also notes that this is a relatively elementary example of the genre. See also Seymour, p. 101.

96   Compare ff. 60f–61r with TCD MS 581, ff. 70r–72v. It is more likely that Howth copied from that source rather than vice versa. See James Frederick Ferguson (ed.), 'A Calendar of the Contents of the Red Book of the Exchequer', *Proceedings and Transactions of the Kilkenny and Southeast of Ireland Archaeological Society*, vol. 3 (1854–5), pp. 35–66; Newport B. White (ed.), *The Red Book of Ormond* (Dublin: Irish Manuscripts Commission, 1932); 'The Red Book of the Diocese of Ossory', in *Tenth Report of the Royal Commission on Historical Manuscripts* (London: HM Stationery Office, 1885), pp. 219–65; Richard Leighton Greene (ed.), *Lyrics of the Red Book of Ossory* (Oxford: Blackwell, 1974); Gearoid MacNiocaill (ed.), *The Red Book of the Earls of Kildare* (Dublin: Irish Manuscripts Commission, 1964); and BL Add. MS 40674. *The Red Book of the Diocese of Ossory* and *The Red Book of Ormond* have sustained damage and lost folios upon which this couplet possibly once existed.

97   'A man doesn't come well (succeed?)/ Unless he drinks standing at the door.' My thanks to Dr Barry for translation assistance; he was also unable to identify a source for this couplet, but notes it is not classical Latin.

98   For discussions of political prophecy, see Lesley A. Coote, *Prophecy and Public*

Affairs in Later Medieval England (Woodbridge: Boydell & Brewer, 2000); Rupert Taylor, *The Political Prophecy in England* (New York: AMS Press, 1967); Keith Thomas, *Religion and the Decline of Magic* (New York: Macmillan, 1971); and Alistair Fox, 'Prophecies and Politics in the Reign of Henry VIII', in Alistair Fox and John Guy (eds), *Reassessing the Henrician Age* (Oxford: Basil Blackwell, 1986), pp. 77–94. Sharon L. Jansen Jaech also has many works on political prophecy, including *Political Protest and Prophecy under Henry VIII* (Woodbridge: Boydell & Brewer, 1991) and 'British Library MS Sloane 2578 and Popular Unrest in England, 1554–56', *Manuscripta*, vol. 29 (1985), pp. 30–41.

99 For a discussion of the authority and power prophecies were perceived to hold, in particular 'ancient' prophecies such as Merlin's which Howth cites here, see Coote, pp. 41 and 238, and Thomas, p. 396. Finglas referenced these same prophecies in his 'Breviate', though to other ends.

100 The projection that Ireland would be conquered only shortly before Doomsday was contained in *The English Conquest of Ireland. The Book of Howth* included this prophecy on f. 49v. It was one of the prophecies to which Howth referred the reader in his note on f. 176v. For this prophecy in Giraldus Cambrensis see A.B. Scott and F.X. Martin (eds), *Giraldus Cambrensis: Expugnatio Hibernica* (Dublin: Royal Irish Academy, 1978), pp. 232–3.

101 Taylor, p. 106; Jansen Jaech, *Political Protest and Prophecy under Henry VIII*, p. 19; Fox, p. 93. The promulgation of political prophecy was made a felony in 1542, revoked in 1547, reinvoked in 1550, repealed once more in 1553, and reimposed in 1563. The 1563 statute clearly included Ireland. Its text states: 'That if any person and persons after the first day of May next coming do advisedly and directly advance, publish, and set forth by writing, printing, signing or any other open speech or deed, to any person or persons any fond, fantastical or false prophecy, upon or by occasion of any arms, fields, beasts, badges or such like other things accustomed in arms, cognizances or signets or upon or by reason of any time, year or day, name, bloodshed or war to the intent thereby to make any rebellion, insurrection, dissension, loss of life or other disturbance within this realm or other the Queen's dominions . . .' Statute 5 Elizabeth, c. XV as reprinted in Taylor, p. 106. Howth's inclusion of prophecies and his interpretive marginalia on them contravene every element of this statute.

102 Howth may have had access to any number of manuscript collections of prophecies in circulation, but his precise source cannot be identified. See Jansen Jaech, 'British Library Sloane MS 2578 and Popular Unrest in England, 1554–56', p. 30; Coote, p. 6. For a handlist of compilations of prophecies see Coote, pp. 239–80.

103 Coote, pp. 10, 30–7; Thomas, p. 390; Jansen Jaech, *Political Protest and Prophecy under Henry VIII*, p. 15. For example, the prophecy 'At the exaltation of the moon the lion shall be overthrown; then shall the lion be joined with the lioness and their whelps shall have the kingdom' was attached to Norfolk at his treason trial in 1571 where it was understood to mean that Elizabeth (the first lion) would be overthrown when he (the second lion) married Mary Queen of Scots (the lioness) and their children (the whelps) would inherit the throne; Taylor, p. 107.

104 Jansen Jaech discusses extant collections that contain guides to their decipherment; 'British Library Sloane MS 2578 and Popular Unrest in England, 1554–56',

pp. 32–3.

105   Jansen Jaech, *Political Protest and Prophecy under Henry VIII*, p. 20; Fox, p. 77; Thomas, p. 398. See also Carole Levin, '"We shall never have a merry world while the Queene lyveth": Gender, Monarchy, and the Power of Seditious Words', in Julia M. Walker (ed.), *Dissing Elizabeth: Negative Representations of Gloriana* (Durham and London: Duke University Press, 1998), p. 78.

106   Thomas, p. 407; Coote, p. 11.

107   See Levin, p. 78 and Ilona Bell, '"Souereaigne Lord of lordly Lady of this land": Elizabeth, Stubbs, and the *Gaping Gvlf*', in *Dissing Elizabeth: Negative Representations of Gloriana*, pp. 99–117. See also Norman Jones, *The Birth of the Elizabethan Age: England in the 1560s* (Oxford: Blackwell Publishers, 1993), Chapter Seven.

108   Bell, p. 112.

109   The story of MacMurrough and O'Rourke's wife as a factor in the Anglo-Norman invasion was, of course, well known. The additional sexual detail may have been Howth's embellishment. Howth's version suggests familiarity with the *senex amans* theme of fabliaux, particularly as utilised by Chaucer in 'The Miller's Tale'. Howth's O'Rourke is 'an old man' who has been led by his 'foolish fantasy' to follow 'folly' rather than wisdom as 'being in love with a young gentlewoman . . . such old folks' do (f. 9r). O'Rourke's young wife, much like Chaucer's miller's young wife, is described as following her 'natural' inclinations. See Geoffrey Chaucer, 'The Miller's Tale', in M.H. Abrams (ed.), *Norton Anthology of English Literature*, (6th edn, New York and London: W.W. Norton & Company, 1993), vol. I, pp. 101–17. Howth's fabliau-like version of MacMurrough and O'Rourke's wife is given political, rather than moral, didactic or simply humorous currency, as in fabliaux. Tales incorporating the *senex amans* theme were generally at the expense of the lower classes, but here it is at the expense of the Irish; ibid., p. 101, n. 1. On fabliaux, see John Hines, *The Fabliau in English* (New York: Longman, 1993), esp. Chapters One and Four; Helen Phillips, *An Introduction to the Canterbury Tales: Reading, Fiction, Context* (New York: St Martin's Press, 2000), esp. pp. 54–63.

110   Levin, pp. 89, 91; Bell, pp. 100, 102–3, 110, 113. See also Ilona Bell, 'Elizabeth I – Always Her Own Free Woman', in Carole Levin and Patricia A. Sullivan (eds), *Political Rhetoric, Power and Renaissance Women* (Albany, NY: State University of New York Press, 1995), pp. 57–82.

111   Levin, pp. 86–90.

112   Craig M. Rustici, *The Afterlife of Pope Joan: Deploying the Popess Legend in Early Modern England* (Ann Arbor, MI: University of Michigan Press, 2006), pp. 9, 62–84.

113   Bell, 'Elizabeth I – Always Her Own Free Woman', pp. 58–61 *passim*.

114   Bell, '"Souereaigne Lord of lordly Lady of this land"', pp. 99–100, 108, 111.

115   John Guy, *Tudor England* (Oxford University Press, 1988), pp. 282–3.

CHAPTER FOUR: COLONIAL CONFLICT AND POSITIONING

1   Canny, *Elizabethan Conquest*, p. 152 and throughout for Canny's identification of the slightly expanded period of 1565–76 as one of critical importance.

2 Carew to Cecil, 26 Dec. 1568, SP 63/26/59; Lennon, *Sixteenth-Century Ireland*, p. 184; Brady, *Chief Governors*, p. 134; Crawford, pp. 197–8; Victor Treadwell, 'The Irish Parliament of 1569–71', *Proceedings of the Royal Irish Academy*, vol. 65 C (1966), p. 67; Canny, *Elizabethan Conquest*, p. 68.

3 Treadwell, 'Irish Parliament of 1569–71', p. 57. Treadwell notes that Sidney had already undertaken surveys of land in Ulster in preparation for redistribution even before parliament was convened to formally attaint Shane O'Neill. See also Canny, *Elizabethan Conquest*, Chapter Four. On the destabilisation of Ulster and Munster as a result of land transfers, see Lennon, *Sixteenth-Century Ireland*, p. 184 and Edwards, 'The Butler Revolt of 1569', pp. 233, 245–6.

4 Treadwell, 'Irish Parliament of 1569–71', p. 68. Treadwell remains the standard account of this parliament. It is also discussed, though with some inaccuracies, in C.L. Falkiner, 'The Parliament of Ireland under the Tudor Sovereigns', *Proceedings of the Royal Irish Academy*, vol. 25 C (1905), pp. 508–41, 553–66.

5 Treadwell, 'Irish Parliament of 1569–71', p. 67. Treadwell speculates that 'possibly others of the venturesome West of England clique' involved in plantation projects, perhaps including Humphrey Gilbert, had been placed as members.

6 For anticipated opposition from the Old English, see Queen to Sidney, 13 Aug. 1566, Tomas O Laidhin (ed.), *Sidney State Papers 1565–70* (Dublin: Irish Manuscripts Commission, 1962), p. 36; Treadwell, 'Irish Parliament of 1569–71', p. 66. On Sidney's possible role in influencing the return of members, see Treadwell as above. Treadwell is careful to note that as an accurate list of members of this parliament is not extant precise numbers and alliances cannot be determined.

7 Queen to Sidney, 10 Feb. 1569, *Sidney State Papers*, p. 103. See also Canny, *The Formation of the Old English Elite*, p. 23.

8 Treadwell, 'Irish Parliament of 1569–71', p. 68. See also Hooker's account of this in his parliamentary journal, transcribed by C.L. Falkiner, 'The Parliament of Ireland under the Tudor Sovereigns: Supplementary Paper', *Proceedings of the Royal Irish Academy*, vol. 25 C (1905), pp. 563–6, and Hooker's account in his contribution to *Holinshed's Chronicles of England, Scotland and Ireland*, vol. VI, pp. 342–3. This opposition was also recorded by Lord Chancellor Weston; Weston to Cecil, 17 Feb. 1569, SP 63/27/25.

9 G.A. Hayes-McCoy, 'Conciliation, Coercion, and the Protestant Reformation, 1547–71', in *New History of Ireland*, III, p. 92. For the text of these bills see *Statutes at Large, Ireland*, vol. I, pp. 312–90.

10 Treadwell, 'Irish Parliament of 1569–71', p. 67.

11 For earlier indications of this policy, see George Wyse to Cecil, 20 June 1567, SP 63/21/26; Lord Treasurer Winchester to Cecil, 28 June 1567, SP 63/21/33; Lord Chancellor and Privy Council of Ireland to Queen, 28 June 1567, SP 63/21/34; Memorial for Ireland by Cecil, 24 Apr. 1568, SP 63/24/16; Proviso for the Act of Coign and Livery, 1568, SP 63/26/75.

12 Treadwell, 'Irish Parliament of 1569–71', p. 61.

13 Ibid., pp. 71–5. See also Lord Chancellor Weston to Cecil, 17 Feb. 1569, SP 63/27/25 and Campion, pp. 142–51.

14 See Hooker's journal, in Falkiner, pp. 564–6; *Holinshed's Chronicles*, vol. VI, pp. 344–5; Treadwell, 'Irish Parliament of 1569–71', p. 69.

15 Campion, pp. 145–51.

16 Nicholas White to Cecil, 10 Mar. 1569, SP 63/27/44; Treadwell, 'Irish Parliament of 1569–71', p. 72.

17 For a list of this parliament's sessions see D.B. Quinn, 'Parliaments and Great Councils in Ireland, 1461–1586', *Irish Historical Studies*, vol. 3 (1943), pp. 76–7.

18 Treadwell, 'Irish Parliament of 1569–71', p. 67. *Statutes at Large, Ireland*, vol. I, pp. 345–9.

19 *Statutes at Large, Ireland*, vol. I, pp. 358–9; see also, Canny, *Elizabethan Conquest*, p. 69 and *The Formation of the Old English Elite*, p. 19.

20 *Statutes at Large, Ireland*, vol. I, pp. 359–60.

21 Ibid., pp. 322–38.

22 Brady, *Chief Governors*, pp. 130–1; see also Brady, 'The Attainder of Shane O'Neill, , pp. 28–48.

23 Morgan, 'Giraldus Cambrensis and the Tudor conquest of Ireland', pp. 30–1.

24 Nor did it reference Sussex; see Brady, *Chief Governors*, p. 130.

25 Sidney had begun to press an image of economic decay much earlier; see Sidney to Leicester, 1 Mar. 1566, SP 63/16/35; Sidney to Elizabeth, 20 Apr. 1566, SP 63/20/66; Queen to Sidney, 11 June 1567, *Sidney State Papers*, p. 62.

26 For other advertisement of the benefits of abolishing coign and livery see George Wyse to Privy Council, 20 June 1567, SP 63/21/26; Lord Chancellor to Irish Privy Council and to Elizabeth, 28 June 1567, SP 63/21/34.

27 D.R. Woolf, 'Of Danes and Giants: Popular Beliefs about the Past in Early Modern England', *Dalhousie Review*, vol. 71 (1991), pp. 184–5. Campion similarly made reference to giants, see pp. 28–9.

28 Morgan also notes the discrepancy of this reference which placed the conquest in 1165 rather than 1169 and suggests that this dating may have been altered when the statutes were published in 1172; Morgan, 'Giraldus Cambrensis and the Tudor Conquest of Ireland', p. 31.

29 It was not Giraldus who had omitted these episodes, but the abridgement of Giraldus from which Howth worked; see Morgan, 'Giraldus Cambrensis and the Tudor Conquest of Ireland', p. 34.

30 On the attainder's misrepresentation of the roles played by Sidney and Sussex in dealing with O'Neill see Brady, *Chief Governors*, p. 130.

31 John Guy, 'The Rhetoric of Counsel in Early Modern England', in Dale Hoak (ed.), *Tudor Political Culture* (Cambridge University Press, 1995), p. 292. See also F.W. Conrad, 'The Problem of Counsel Reconsidered: the case of Sir Thomas Elyot', in Paul A. Fideler and T.F. Mayer (eds), *Political Thought and the Tudor Commonwealth* (London: Routledge, 1992), pp. 75–107.

32 Book dedicated by Rowland White to Sir William Cecil on the state of Ireland, *c*.1569, SP 63/31/32. Unlike Howth, however, White only offers his counsel as dictated by duty and does not draw attention to the conflicting counsel offered by the two colonial communities; Canny, 'Rowland White's "Discors Touching Ireland"'.

33 Guy, 'The Rhetoric of Counsel', p. 293.

34 Guy, 'The Rhetoric of Counsel', pp. 293–8; there were also, though, gradations in defining counsel and its executors as the concept evolved over the sixteenth and early-seventeenth centuries. See also Norman Jones, 'Parliament and the Political society of Elizabethan England', in *Tudor Political Culture*, pp. 226–37. The debate regarding the nature of wisdom and its role in one's ability to serve

was applied at both the conciliar and parliamentary levels in England. Jones's discussion of its impact on debates in the English parliament regarding residency and membership is profitably read alongside the analogous and nearly contemporaneous debate in the Irish parliament regarding the residency of newly returned members such as Hooker noted above.

35 Guy, 'The Rhetoric of Counsel', pp. 294, 302; Jones, p. 237. On the conflict between duty and royal prerogative see also David Harris Sacks, 'The Countervailing of Benefits: Monopoly, liberty, and benevolences in Elizabethan England', in *Tudor Political Culture*, pp. 272–91.

36 On humanism in Ireland, see Brendan Bradshaw, 'Sword, Word and Strategy in the Reformation in Ireland', *Historical Journal*, vol. 21 (1978), pp. 475–502 and *Irish Constitutional Revolution*, Chapter Four; Canny, *The Formation of the Old English Elite*, pp. 13–24 *passim*; Lennon, *Sixteenth-Century Ireland*, p. 81 and 'The Counter-Reformation in Ireland, 1542–1641', p. 81. On humanism and the nobility in Europe in general, see Asch, *Nobilities in Transition 1550–1700*, p. 2.

37 White, 'Discors Touching Ireland', ff. 100v and 105v; see also Canny's introduction, p. 443. The comment contained elsewhere in Howth's manuscript anticipating the restoration of stability in Munster as a result of Perrot's appointment was contained within a larger passage Howth copied verbatim from Campion and does not necessarily reflect Howth's position, f. A19v; compare to Campion, p. 106.

38 Quinn, 'Parliaments and Great Councils in Ireland', p. 76; Treadwell, 'Irish Parliament of 1569–71', p. 76.

39 Campion, pp. 98–9.

40 For this letter in Campion, see pp. 104–6. Though Campion's use of this letter supported Sidney's claims of long-standing decay in Ireland, Howth emphasised rather the issue of grievances redressed. For a discussion of the manner in which Campion's history served Sidney's political agenda see Lennon, 'Edmund Campion's *Histories of Ireland* and Reform in Tudor Ireland', pp. 67–83.

41 Sidney to Elizabeth, 18 May 1577, SP 63/58/29.

42 See Brady, 'Conservative Subversives' and *Chief Governors*, Chapters Four and Six; Canny, *The Formation of the Old English Elite*.

43 Pale Lords to Elizabeth and Privy Council, 10 Jan. 1577, SP 63/57/1; Pale Lords to Sidney and the Irish Council, 10 Jan. 1577, SP 63/57/1.i; Questions to be resolved, 14 May 1577, SP 63/58/23; Submission statement, 20 June 1577, SP 63/58/53; Thomas, James and Lavalen Nugent to Sidney, July 1577, SP 63/58/63; Delvin to Lord Chancellor, 20 June 1577, SP 63/58/63.iv; Submission statement, 28 June 1578, SP 63/61/12.

44 Sidney to Elizabeth, 18 May 1577, SP 63/58/29.

45 Brady, *Chief Governors*, p. 215. For a discussion of economic conditions in the Pale at this time, see Lennon, *Sixteenth-Century Ireland*, pp. 189–90 and Canny, *Elizabethan Conquest*, Chapter One.

46 Though see Canny's identification of the opposition's response as one that failed to truly comprehend economic forces, thus their failure to adopt a strategy that might have achieved alleviation of their complaint; *The Formation of the Old English Elite*, p. 21.

47 Thomas, James and Lavalen Nugent to Lord Deputy, 6 July 1577, SP 63/58/63; Richard Nugent to his cousin Thomas Nugent, 6 July 1577, SP 63/58/63.ii; Petition of Baron Delvin and others to Lord Chancellor, 6 July 1577, SP 63/58/63.iv.

48 Richard Nugent to his cousin Thomas Nugent, 6 July 1577, SP 63/58/63.ii.

49 Thomas, James and Lavalen Nugent to Lord Deputy, 6 July 1577, SP 63/58/63.

50 On the O'Mores, see Carey, 'John Derricke's *Image of Irelande*'.

51 Removal of oppositional figures following the cess controversy may also account for Howth's arrest in 1579 on charges of domestic abuse and Nicholas Nugent's execution in 1582.

52 'A man doesn't come well (succeed?) / Unless he drinks standing at the door.' See Chapter Three.

53 Canny, *The Formation of the Old English Elite*, p. 17. See also Carey, 'A "dubious loyalty": Richard Stanihurst, the "wizard" earl of Kildare, and English-Irish identity', p. 61.

54 Brady, 'Conservative Subversives', p. 11.

55 See Steven G. Ellis, 'More Irish than the Irish themselves?: the "Anglo-Irish" in Tudor Ireland', *History Ireland*, vol. 7, i (1999), pp. 22–6 and the rebuttal from Kenneth Nicholls, 'Worlds Apart? The Ellis Two-Nation Theory on Late Medieval Ireland', *History Ireland*, vol. 7, ii (1999), pp. 22–6.

56 Bradshaw, 'Sword, Word and Strategy in the Reformation in Ireland', esp. pp. 488–500; Canny, *The Formation of the Old English Elite*, pp. 17–20 and *Elizabethan Conquest*, Chapter Six.

57 *Holinshed's Chronicles*, vol. VI, p. 4. On language in this period see Vincent Carey, '"Neither Good English nor Good Irish": bi-lingualism and identity formation in sixteenth-century Ireland', pp. 45–61.

58 Canny, *The Formation of the Old English Elite*, p. 29. See also Lennon, *Sixteenth-Century Ireland*, p. 193; 'Mass in the Manor House', pp. 112–26; 'Political Thought of Irish Counter-Reformation Churchmen: the testimony of the "Analecta" of Bishop David Rothe', in *Political Ideology in Ireland 1541–1641*, p. 182.

59 For this assertion during the Nine Years War, see *Calendar of State Papers, Ireland, 1600*, p. 236. See also Canny, 'Irish, Scottish and Welsh Responses to Centralisation, *c*.1530–*c*.1640: a comparative perspective', in Alexander Grant and Keith J. Stringer (eds), *Uniting the Kingdom? The Making of British History* (London: Routledge, 1995), p. 153.

60 Compare to Campion's list, pp. 78–81.

61 On the period 1580–1603 as one of crystallising confessionalism, see Ute Lotz-Heumann, 'Confessionalisation in Ireland: Periodisation and Character, 1534–1649', in Alan Ford and John McCafferty (eds), *The Origins of Sectarianism in Early Modern Ireland* (Cambridge University Press, 2005), pp. 42–6.

CHAPTER FIVE: CIRCULATION OF *THE BOOK OF HOWTH* AND ITS USE

1 On the importance of communities of collectors, see Elizabethanne Boran, 'Ussher and the Collection of Manuscripts in Early Modern Europe', in *Making Ireland Roman*, 2009), pp. 176–94. The assertions that both Robert Beale and Edmund Spenser had access to Howth's compilation are probably erroneous. W.L. Renwick stated that Spenser 'had drawn on the Book of Howth' when writing *A View of the Present State of Ireland*; comparison of their texts does not bear this out (Edmund Spenser, *A View of the Present State of Ireland*, ed. W.L. Renwick (Oxford: Clarendon Press, 1970), p. 199; my thanks to Thomas Herron for pointing out this reference). Renwick's further speculation that Spenser may

have gained access to Howth's text in Dublin Castle was based on the calendar editors' erroneous speculation; see Renwick, p. 220 and *Calendar of Carew MSS*, vol. v, p. xi. The editor of Campion's text, A.F. Vossen, also speculated that Beale, secretary to Walsingham and clerk to Elizabeth's privy council, had access to Howth's text in London, again not borne out by evidence; Vossen, p. 103. In addition to collecting copies of state documents (see BL Add. MS 48015), Beale also copied selections from *Pembridge's Annals* as contained in Laurence Nowell's *Chronica Hiberniae* (BL, Cotton MSS, Domitian xviii, ff. 57v–92v). Vossen's suggestion that Beale's reference to 'larrde Noel' be read 'Lord Howth' was repeated in British Library cataloguing where Add. MS 48015 is identified as 'Annals after Howth and Laurence Nowell' and cross-referenced to pp. 121–69 of the calendared edition of Howth. These pages do contain Howth's excerpts of *Pembridge's Annals*, but a comparison of Howth's excerpts with Beale's indicates that Nowell, not Howth, served as Beale's source. Beale retained the original Latin, as did Nowell, and included many items that Howth did not. Nor is there any evidence that Nowell had seen a copy of Howth's work; a comparison of his excerpts from *Pembridge's Annals* (taken *c.*1574 when Howth's work was not yet complete) with Howth's indicates that each made selective and independent use of that source. The only other possible suggestion that Beale had seen Howth is highly speculative and dubious. Each did include a similar entry for 1212 on Henry Londres, Bishop of Dublin; Howth had taken this entry from Campion, and as Beale had a copy of Campion, it is likely that Campion was his source for that item. However, the *Oxford Dictionary of National Biography* dates Nowell's death *c.*1570 and Campion's work was not completed until 1571. For Beale see Gary M. Bell, 'Beale, Robert' (1541–1601), *Oxford Dictionary of National Biography* (Oxford, 2004). For Nowell, see Retha M. Warnicke, 'Nowell, Laurence' (1530–*c.*1570), *Oxford Dictionary of National Biography*.

2 TCD MS 591, f. 33r.

3 T.K. Abbot, *Catalogue of the Manuscripts in the Library of Trinity College, Dublin* (Dublin: Hodges Figgis & Co., 1900), p. 97.

4 Folio 57 is not blank, as stated by Mario Esposito in *Notes and Queries*, vol. 3 (1917), p. 495. Folio 57 contains a copy of Howth's entry comparing the various dates assigned to the Anglo-Norman conquest. The remainder of the folio, however, is blank. This manuscript is also misidentified in Trinity's Abbot catalogue as a copy of Giraldus Cambrensis with a 'supplement out of the Book of Howth, Fabian, etc., and out of a book written by Primate Dowdall in 1551', p. 99. This supplement is entirely taken from *The Book of Howth* which, of course, includes extracts from Fabyan and the version of *The English Conquest of Ireland* erroneously attributed to Dowdall by Carew on a misinterpretation of Howth's marginalia (see Chapter Three above). A later hand appended information taken from Stanihurst and other sources to this copy of Howth's work (see, for example, f. 146). If MSS 583 and 594 were to be recompiled, several sections remain missing, for example some of Howth's other entries taken from Fabyan, the section on giants, and the poem on the Knights Templar. The only significant omission is ff. 1r–32r, the opening section of Howth's version of *The English Conquest of Ireland*, which may have resulted from lost folios in this copy rather than intentional scribal omission. Roughly 20 per cent of Howth's work, or forty-three folios, is not contained within either MS 583 or MS 594.

5 For MS 594, see f. 57 which references Howth's f. 177; for MS 583 see f. 195 which references Howth's f. 103.

6 Carew's hand is evident in both fragments though whether he patronised the copy's production or acquired an existing copy is unknown. The latter seems more likely for, while the scribe is careful, though not entirely consistent, in copying Howth's marginalia and interlining, none of Carew's marginalia or inter-lining later appended to the original is included here. For a recent study of Carew's collection activities, see Dorsett. See also Ute Lotz-Heumann, 'Carew, George, Earl of Totnes' (1555–1629), *Oxford Dictionary of National Biography* (Oxford, 2004).

7 For Ussher's acquisition of Carew's papers, see Dorsett, pp. 159–60. For evidence of Madden's ownership, see his signature on TCD MS 593, f. 79. The Abbott cata-logue states that Madden's papers were transferred to the Bishop of Clogher's office and from there transferred to Trinity College, Dublin; Abbot, p. iii. Madden's collection also passed through the hands of John Stearne, Dean of St Patrick's; see Mihail Dafydd Evans, 'Madden, John' (bap. 1649–d. 1703/4), *Oxford Dictionary of National Biography*, and William O'Sullivan, 'The Eighteenth Century Rebinding of the Manuscripts', *Long Room*, vol. 1 (1970), p. 19.

8 Dorsett, pp. 58–9.

9 William Nicolson, *The English, Scotch and Irish Historical Libraries* (London, 1776), part v, p. 12.

10 Lyon's reputation as one of Dublin's leading antiquaries led to his engagement for this project; O'Sullivan, p. 19. See also A.C. Elias, Jr, 'Lyon, John' (1710–90), *Oxford Dictionary of National Biography*.

11 O'Sullivan, p. 19.

12 Ibid., p. 19.

13 Abbot, pp. 97, 99.

14 There is no entry for this item in M.R. James, *A Descriptive Catalogue of the Manuscripts in the Library of Lambeth Palace* (Cambridge University Press, 1930). It is indexed in Henry J. Todd, *Catalogue of the Archiepiscopal manu-scripts in the Library of Lambeth Palace* (London, 1812), though there it is identified by its contents rather than as *The Book of Howth*. It was first identified as a copy of *The Book of Howth* in Brian Donovan and David Edwards, *British Sources for Irish History 1485–1641* (Dublin: Irish Manuscripts Commission, 1997), p. 164.

15 This is the nearest extant approximation of a complete copy of *The Book of Howth* though its entries are radically disordered. It is missing only two items from Howth's text: the entry on Saints Patrick and Brigid and the entry on the O'Neill kings. There is some duplication of entries, however, probably due to this manuscript's nature as a collation of once-discrete copies, and four of the entries are incomplete – 'The Field of Ard-kaghe', 'The Field of Fentra', 'England's Right to Ireland' and 'Knight's Fees' – some of this probably due to the loss of folios.

16 Several of the hand changes are due to a change in the scribe making the copy, a practice also evident in Howth's original, rather than to the inclusion of a distinct copy, as on f. 125r.

17 Donovan and Edwards, p. 164.

18 Carew may have acquired other papers of Howth's as well. The copy of *Caxton's Chronicles* bound in Carew's arms (Lambeth Palace Library MS 264)

appears to have belonged to Howth; it contains much of his characteristic marginalia. The calendar editors speculated that Carew acquired Howth's manuscript from Dublin Castle (*Calendar of Carew MSS*, vol. v, p. 228) based on Carew's copy of a document recording knights' fees in Ireland in the reign of Edward II for which there is a similar document in *The Book of Howth* (ff. 155–8). Carew's copy (Lambeth MS 608, f. 40r) noted that he had taken this information from records in Dublin Castle. While there are some oddities regarding Howth's copy – it is in a hand that appears nowhere else in his compilation and may represent an older document incorporated into the manuscript rather than copied into it – it is more likely that Carew and Howth both had access to the same document or a copy of it. There are also several points of difference between Howth's copy and Carew's, suggesting further that Carew did not copy from Howth. Carew was generally careful about citing his sources; in every other case he cites Howth as a source but does not for this item. The calendar editors' speculation also raises the question as to how Howth's manuscript came to be in Dublin Castle, for which there is no evidence. It is more likely Carew acquired Howth's work while in Munster (1600–3), as suggested by notes he did take from *The Book of Howth* (now Laud MS 614). Carew's interests at that time focused on genealogy, annalistic information, Ireland's pre-conquest history and land titles, all subjects in *The Book of Howth* to which he appended marginalia. Carew's role in the Nine Years War brought him into close contact with Howth's grandson, Christopher St Lawrence, from whom he could have acquired the manuscript (see *Calendar of Carew MSS, 1601–03*, pp. 160–1; *Calendar of State Papers, Ireland, 1601–03 with Addenda*, pp. 148, 165, 186; McGowan-Doyle, '"Spent blood"'. Circumstantial evidence does not suggest that Carew acquired Howth's work during his later period in Ireland when his collection activities focused on preparation for the upcoming parliamentary session (see Dorsett, pp. 186–94).

19 Among many other works, see Boran, 'Ussher and the Collection of Manuscripts'.

20 For example, during his 1606 trip to England, Ussher met with Camden and provided him with works of Irish history. Davies and Camden similarly shared material, as did Carew and Camden. Carew, for instance, had been given a copy of *Pembridge's Annals* by Camden (now Bodleian Laud MS 526). See Dorsett, p. 170; Wyman H. Herendeen, 'Camden, William' (1551–1623), *Oxford Dictionary of National Biography*; Ute Lotz-Heumann, 'Carew, George, Earl of Totnes' (1555–1629), ibid.; Sean Kelsey, 'Davies, Sir John' (bap. 1569–d. 1626), ibid. Recovering the transmission of Howth's manuscript and its copies between these collectors is precluded by lack of documentation.

21 Meredith Hanmer, *The Chronicle of Ireland*, in James Ware (ed.), *Ancient Irish Histories: The Works of Spenser, Campion, Hanmer, and Marleburrough*, vol. II (New York: Kennikat Press, 1970 reprint). Hanmer's work has been dated 1571 but this is certainly incorrect; Hanmer cites a number of works not yet available by that date, including Camden, Dowling and Stanihurst. Hanmer's work would have been completed by 1604, the year of his death, and it was probably in progress throughout the 1590s. Hanmer does not appear to have drawn either copies or extracts from Howth's compilation for his own extensive collection of manuscript materials; see Meredith Hanmer's Collection of Manuscripts, SP 63/214/1–46.

22   Hanmer went to Ireland following a tumultuous career as a Church of England clergyman, plagued by charges including sodomy, propagating rumours of Elizabeth's illegitimate pregnancy, and melting down pieces of church bronze for personal financial use. Alan Ford, 'Hanmer, Meredith' (1543–1604), *Oxford Dictionary of National Biography*.

23   Hanmer cites *The Book of Howth* as his source on numerous occasions; see, for example, pp. 28, 31, 63, 80, 88, 89, 90, 101, 102, 103, 182, 282, 296, 300, 335, 337, 380 and 401. He also used *The Book of Howth* elsewhere without citing it; see, for example, pp. 52–3 and compare to *The Book of Howth*, ff. A5v–A6v. For one example of later antiquarian use, see J. Huband Smith, *A Day at Howth* (Dublin, 1857), p. 16. Smith recounted Hanmer's account of Tristram Amorey St Lawrence and the Anglo-Norman conquest as taken from Howth's text.

24   For Hanmer's discussion of de Courcey, the St Lawrence family and the Anglo-Norman conquest, see pp. 296–302 and compare to Howth, ff. 34r–36r and 42r–44r. Hanmer did question the veracity of some of Howth's information, see p. 343; on this occasion he questions information regarding William Marshall taken from 'Sir John Plunket his Collection', clearly a reference to *The Book of Howth*, f. 61v. It should be noted that, unlike Carew, Hanmer understood correctly Howth's note that only the information additional to *The English Conquest of Ireland* had been taken from the work purportedly by Dowdall, not the entire history of the conquest.

25   Geoffrey Keating, *Foras Feasa ar Eirinn. History of Ireland*, David Comyn and Patrick S. Dinneen (eds/trans), 4 vols (London: Irish Texts Society, 1902–14), see vol. I, Chapter Five.

26   William Camden, *Britannia*, Richard Gough (ed.), 4 vols (London, 1806 reprint).

27   Ibid., vol. IV, pp. 222, 324.

28   John Davies, *A Discovery of the True Causes why Ireland was Never Entirely Subdued . . .*, James P. Myers (ed.) (Washington, DC: Catholic University of America Press, 1988).

29   Davies, p. 104. For Davies' other references to *The Book of Howth*, see his notes relevant to pp. 101, 103, 105 and 112. For a study of this treatise, see also Hans S. Pawlisch, *Sir John Davies and the Conquest of Ireland* (Cambridge University Press, 1985). Here again there is no documentation confirming how Davies acquired Howth's work and whether he saw the original or a copy. James Myers argued on linguistic evidence that Davies composed the bulk of *A Discovery of the True Causes* in Ireland, only finishing it in England in the spring of 1612 shortly before its publication (Myers, p. 42). As Davies's references to Howth occur midway through the work and the linguistic style of the surrounding passages matches those sections argued by Myers to have been written in Ireland (referring to Ireland as 'this land', 'here', etc., rather than 'that land', 'there', etc. as he did later in the text), it seems likely that Davies used Howth in Ireland. He may have used the copy which came into Ussher's possession and would remain in Ireland. However, it is also possible that Howth's manuscript and/or the copies of Munster provenance were still in Ireland, suggesting that Carew had not yet removed these items to England. On the shared collection activities of Davies and Carew see Dorsett, pp. 186–94; Myers, pp. 29–30.

30   Now bound as TCD MS 664 and BL Add. MS 4791. Ware indicated his notes from *The Book of Howth* were transcribed on 3 February 1652 (TCD MS 664, f. 189).

His careful notation of folios gives further evidence that Howth's f. A23 was even by this late date not yet bound with *The Book of Howth* (see Chapter Three above); Ware noted specifically that refoliation began after f. 22 of Howth's work (see TCD MS 664, f. 192v).

31 See BL Add. MS 4791, ff. 41r–61v for Ware's copy of this passage from Howth.

32 Walter Harris (ed.), De Scriptoribus Hiberniae. *The Whole Works of Sir James Ware*, 2 vols (Dublin, 1764), vol. II, pt. 2, p. 94. For Hanmer's citation, see p. 296 and compare to Howth, f. 59v. Numerous references have been made to this Dowdall text, but none can be traced back further than Howth.

33 James Ware, *Rerum Hibernicarum Annales, Regnantibus Henrico VII, Henrico VIII, Edwardo VI & Maria* (Dublin, 1664), pp. 23, 72. For this work Ware appears to have utilised notes gathered in 1552; see TCD MS 664, ff. 193v–206v.

34 TCD MS 664, f. 189.

35 There is little evidence that Ware's notes from Howth were subsequently used by others with the exception of Dr Richard Pococke, Bishop of Meath. Pococke obtained notes of Ware's now deposited in the British Library as Add. MSS 4821 and 4822 (formerly Clarendon MSS 34 and 35). Pococke copied only one entry from *The Book of Howth* (on the Knights Templar), but it is unclear whether he took this from Ware's notes or whether Ware did have a copy of *The Book of Howth* that passed to Pococke; see BL Add. MS 4813, f. 45v. I have not yet been able to identify Ware's copy of *The Book of Howth* in the British Library if he did, in fact, have one, nor was Thomas Hardy able to locate this copy in 1858 (see *Calendar of Carew MSS*, vol. V, p. xiv).

36 Richard Cox, *Hibernia Anglicana: or, the history of Ireland from the conquest thereof by the English to this present time*, 2 vols (London, 1689–90); S.J. Connolly, 'Cox, Sir Richard, First Baronet' (1650–1733), *Oxford Dictionary of National Biography*.

37 Cox refers to Howth regularly as Lambeth MS P. He must have consulted Carew's catalogue of papers (now Lambeth MS 636) in order to identify *The Book of Howth* where it was listed as MS P.

38 Ibid.; see, for instance, vol. I, pp. 66, 98, 109 and 121.

39 Ibid., pp. 165–6; Howth, f. 174v. Cox, in fact, gave the folio reference to Howth on this occasion. Cox made little interpretive use of Howth elsewhere, though he did incorporate Howth's discussion of Sussex's recall as lord deputy; ibid., p. 317.

40 Ibid., pp. 33, 43. It is unclear why Cox relied on Hanmer for this passage when he had access to Howth's work, though it is further evidence of the continuing role Hanmer would play in later uses of *The Book of Howth*.

41 Thomas Leland, *The History of Ireland from the Invasion of Henry II*, 3 vols (London, 1773); Norman Moore, rev. Alexander Du Toit, 'Leland, Thomas' (1722–85), *Oxford Dictionary of National Biography*.

42 Ibid., vol. I, pp. 117, 134. For Leland's entire passage taken from Hanmer, see vol. I, pp. 114–48. Leland cited Howth's text variously as 'Book of Howth, MS' (see vol. II, pp. 115, 120) and 'Lambeth P', as it had been cited by Cox (see vol. I, pp. 157, 159), though he incorrectly identified 'Lambeth P' as MS 628 rather than 623, and in one case erroneously associated it with Hanmer; see his reference to 'Hanmer MSS Lambeth P', vol. I, p. 157.

43 Thomas Hardy of London's Public Record Office was unable to locate *The Book*

of Howth in 1858; see his letter of 5 April 1858 to the Master of the Rolls reprinted in *Calendar of Carew MSS*, vol. V, p. xiv. Several years later J.T. Gilbert noted that 'for more than a century past [it] was supposed to have been lost', but recently 'discovered' by John O'Donovan among Carew's papers at Lambeth; J.T. Gilbert, 'The Historic Literature of Ireland', in *The Celtic Records and Historic Literature of Ireland* (Dublin, 1861), p. 417.

44 Ibid.

45 Douglas Hyde, *A Literary History of Ireland* (London, 1899), pp. 210–11.

46 Round, 'The Book of Howth: Part I'; 'The Book of Howth: Part II'; 'The Book of Howth: Part III'.

47 J.H. Round, 'The Conquest of Ireland', in *The Commune of London and Other Studies* (London, 1899), pp. 137–70. His entire essay was based on three sources: *The Book of Howth, The Song of Dermot and the Earl* and the *Expugnatio Hibernica*. The only response Round's critical assessment of *The Book of Howth* generated was a brief rejoinder from Mario Esposito in 1917 which referred not to *The Book of Howth* directly, but to Round's comments regarding *The English Conquest of Ireland*; Mario Esposito, 'The English Conquest of Ireland', p. 495.

48 Richard Bagwell, *Ireland under the Tudors*, 3 vols (London: Holland Press, 1963, reprint), vol. I, p. xi.

49 Ibid., p. 122.

50 Ibid. For the Lambert Simnel affair, see pp. 103–8; for the Battle of Knockdoe, see pp. 120–1; for Surrey, Grey and Bellingham, see pp. 139, 240–1, and 344–5 respectively. Bagwell also appears to have consulted Howth for his account of de Courcy's battles in Ulster, though he does not cite Howth there as he does elsewhere; see, for example, his statement that de Courcy was accompanied by Almeric St Lawrence, vol. I, p. 53, though he may have taken this reference from Hanmer.

51 Seymour, p. 142.

52 Ibid., pp. 100, 143 and 101 respectively.

CHAPTER SIX: CONCLUSION: TUDOR IMPERIALISM AND OLD ENGLISH DISPLACEMENT

1 Brady, *Chief Governors*, p. 215.

2 Brady, *Chief Governors*, p. 213. The Old English did continue to dominate municipal governments; see Lennon, *Lords of Dublin*. However, Howth was concerned with the preservation of Old English influence at the vice-regal level.

3 Brady, *Chief Governors*, p. 213; Crawford, p. 101. On new military appointments under Sidney see Canny, *Elizabethan Conquest*, pp. 53–4. The office of viceroy had already been lost to Old English appointment after the Kildare Rebellion.

4 Canny, *Elizabethan Conquest*, p. 55; Crawford, p. 423. Some were able to retain seats on the Irish council, such as Sir Lucas Dillon, described by Crawford as 'one of the most loyal of the Anglo-Irish'; Crawford, p. 450. Nicholas White, another Old Englishman, held a variety of offices over much of the Elizabethan period, including a position on the Irish council. He supported viceroys on some occasions, for example Perrot, and on others the opposition, as he did in the cess controversy of 1577–8, for which he suffered much difficulty; Crawford, pp. 470–1. Nicholas Nugent, another voice of opposition to the cess on the Irish council, was unjustly executed in 1582; Ellis, *Ireland in the Age of the Tudors*, pp. 308, 318.

5 Ellis, *Ireland in the Age of the Tudors*, p. 308.

6 Brady, *Chief Governors*, pp. 117–18.

7 See Canny, *Elizabethan Conquest* and 'Revising the Revisionist'; Brady, *Chief Governors*.

8 Canny, *Elizabethan Conquest*, Chapter Six.

9 Campion, pp. 12–14.

10 Campion, pp. 145–50.

11 Hooker's diary, pp. 564–6; *Holinshed's Chronicles*, vol. VI, pp. 344–5.

12 As cited in Canny, 'Revising the Revisionist', p. 248.

13 Ibid., p. 249. On Campion and Sidney, see Lennon, 'Edmund Campion's *Histories of Ireland* and Reform in Tudor Ireland'.

14 Sidney to Elizabeth, 20 May 1577, SP 63/58/29.

15 Canny, *Elizabethan Conquest*, p. 152.

16 Lawrence Stone, *The Crisis of the Aristocracy 1558–1641* (Oxford: Clarendon Press, 1965). This work generated immediate and extensive criticism; among many other works see G.E. Aylmer's review in *Past and Present*, vol. 32 (1965), pp. 113–25; D.H. Pennington's review in *English Historical Review*, vol. 81 (1966), pp. 562–5; Robert Ashton, 'The Aristocracy in Transition', *Economic History Review*, vol. 22 (1969), pp. 308–22; and Stuart Woolf, 'The Aristocracy in Transition: A Continental Comparison', *Economic History Review*, vol. 23 (1970), pp. 520–31. See also Steven Ellis, 'A Crisis of the Aristocracy? Frontiers and noble power in the early Tudor state', in John Guy (ed.), *The Tudor Monarchy* (London: Arnold, 1997), pp. 330–39 and his extended earlier discussion of this topic in *Tudor Frontiers and Noble Power* (Oxford: Clarendon Press, 1995).

17 G.W. Bernard, *Power and Politics in Tudor England* (Aldershot: Ashgate, 2000), p. 22.

18 Ibid., p. 35.

19 Campion, pp. 148–50.

20 Asch, Chapter Six; Canny, 'Irish, Scottish and Welsh Responses to Centralisation'. For the role that defence considerations played in the formulation of administrative policies and practices relative to centralisation see Morgan, 'British Policies before the British State'.

21 *Letters and Memorials of State*, vol. II, pp. 137–8.

Index